FELDHERRNHALLE: FORGOTTEN ELITE

Panzerkorps Feldherrnhalle and Antecedent Formations, Eastern and Other Fronts, 1939-1945

ALFONSO ESCUADRA SÁNCHEZ

Series Editor: J.G. Lewthwaite M.A. Ph.D. (Cantab.)
Editor: Robert A. Ball B.Sc. (Hons.)

STAHLHELM SERIES 166

Published by SHELF BOOKS
BRADFORD, WEST YORKSHIRE, U.K.

Published in this form by :
SHELF BOOKS Ⓟ 1996
51 Ascot Drive, Horton Bank Top, Bradford,

West Yorks. UK.

Tel. (01274) 575150 - 24 hour answerphone.
Fax.(01274) 522223

ISBN 1 899765 66 2

Printed in the U.K.

The cover art represents a Feldwebel of the Panzer-Grenadier Division Feldherrnhalle on the Russian Front c1943.

Copies of the original artwork by Simon McCouaig may be obtained from him at the following address:
4 Yeomans Close, Stoke Bishop, Bristol. BS9 2DH.   Tel. (0117) 9686358

The section on Insignia and Emblems (Appendix D) and the Tables of Comparative Ranks (Appendix L) were compiled by Robert A Ball BSc (Hons), who may be contacted through SHELF BOOKS.

British Library Cataloging in Publication Data. A catalogue record for this book is available from the British Library.

SHELF BOOKS

Stahlhelm Series: The History of the Armed Forces of the Third Reich

Fifty years after the end of World War II in Europe, it is felt imperative that the English-speaking world comprehend the perspectives of those who fought on the other (losing) side, which to a great extent can only be appreciated by a familiarity with their unique experiences, particularly on the decisive Eastern Front.

Shelf Books therefore initiates The Stahlhelm Series, consisting of translations of primary sources - often eyewitness accounts by participants - and reprints of secondary literature, which have become established as classics in their field.

Neither translations nor reprints have been edited in any way in order to bring the authors' perspectives and values into agreement with contemporary mainstream attitudes i.e. through deletion or euphemism. Each text is treated as an unique historical document redolent of its era. Given the temporal span between this and the date of publication, additional material has been added to assist the reader wherever it is felt necessary in such a way that it cannot be confused with the original text. This additional material will be found both before and after the main text, paginated separately and distinctively with Roman numerals.

READERS GUIDE TO THE ENGLISH EDITION

Wherever possible, Escuadra's original text has been left unaltered and much care has been taken that the translation is as true to the Spanish original as possible. However, some alterations were felt unavoidable and in most cases necessary, and thus changes carried out are as follows:

1. The original text was in some cases ambiguous when referring to specific units. For instance, "13th" for 13th Panzer Division *Feldherrnhalle* and "Regiment of Grenadiers" for Panzer-Grenadier Regiment *Feldherrnhalle*. Although this is common in Spanish writing, it was felt that, in a book with reference to so many units, it made the English version very difficult to read, especially when using the work as a 'look-up' reference. Therefore most references to units have been altered to their full title.

2. The Orders of Battle, which were originally placed at the end of the relevant chapter, have been grouped as Appendix H.

3. Revision of the Eastern European placenames, given the complexity of the linguistic, ethnic and political history of the region, for which the reader is advised to consult Appendix M.

4. Compilation of a Table of Ranks (Appendix L), a Gazetteer of placenames (Appendix R), a Glossary of useful terms and abbreviations (Appendix S) , and an Index. Terms found in the Gazetteer are found in *italics* in the text.

5. The maps have been completely redrawn and put into the English language. They remain, however, true to the original edition.

6. The illustrations have been greatly expanded and grouped into sections.

7. The appendix dealing with Badges and Insignia (Appendix D) has been re-written and expanded by the Editor to include insignia of the SA-Standarte *Feldherrnhalle* and Luftwaffe *Feldherrnhalle* units.

Publishing History

This volume was translated from the Spanish
edition published by:

**GARCIA HISPAN, EDITOR,
APARTADO DE CORREOS 630,
E-03080 ALICANTE, SPAIN.
Tel (96) 52 09 98 45**

which constitutes the first edition (ISBN 84 87690 02 5):
© **Alfonso Escuadra (1991)**

Translated by Roberta Haigh

LA ÉLITE OLVIDADA
*Historia de las unidades FHH
del Ejército alemán*

Alfonso Escuarda

Prólogo de Erich Klein
Presidente de la Asociación Veteranos de las Unidades Feldherrnalle

García Hispán Editor

The translator credited above may be contacted for professional
purposes through **SHELF BOOKS**

Despite the overwhelming bibliography on the Wehrmacht; its Divisions, its Regiments, and even its regular Battalions throughout World War II, it is surprising that there still exists a veil of silence regarding certain elite units of the German Army.

With this erudite contribution, Professor Alfonso Escuadra clarifies any misconceptions regarding the *Feldherrnhalle*, a unit with a magnificent war record, in which he speaks of the great fighting spirit of the men, particularly at a time when the tide of the conflict had clearly turned against Germany.

For the first time in English, the reader will be able to learn at first hand of the origins of this unit, its fortunes during the course of the war and its complex process of transformation and enlargement which is well-documented by an abundant and unedited quantity of literary and graphical material

CONTENTS

PROLOGUE

On behalf of the members of the former Kampfgruppe Eberhardt of *Danzig*, later to become the 60th Motorised Infantry Division and the III Battalion of the 271st Infantry Regiment, later incorporated into the Panzerkorps *Feldherrnhalle*, I should like to thank Professor Alfonso Escuadra for his successful study, the fruit of arduous and meticulous work. We have here the history of some Wehrmacht formations that were amongst the best in the German Army.

In addition to paying tribute to the memory of our fallen and lost comrades, together with the harsh times which we shared, this work demonstrates the validity of the eternal values of the soldier such as camaraderie, loyalty and courage, passing down to the young soldiers of today our personal experiences in times of hardship.

Moreover, this work fills one of the gaps that existed in the specialised bibliography.

Erich Klein
Hauptmann a. D.
Major (Bw) d. Reserve
President of the *Feldherrnhalle* Units Veterans' Association

INTRODUCTION

The Wehrmacht, as a whole, has been considered one of the best military organisations of all time. Amongst other reasons, this was possible since many of the units of which it was composed demonstrated that their performance in battle was superior to that of their opposite numbers from other countries. Amongst these, without any doubt, number those best known by the general public, such as the *Leibstandarte Adolf Hitler*, the *Großdeutschland*, *Hermann Göring*, etc., specific units which supposedly represented the quintessence of the service or collective that they represented.

These elite divisions have given rise to a good number of books and articles which have included everything from their emblems to details of their weapons, without forgetting the bibliographical references of their most notable officers. As a result it is hardly surprising that whilst the specialised bibliography on the Wehrmacht has dedicated ostentatious studies not to these units but rather to simple divisions, regiments and even regular battalions, the combat history of one of these elite units, I refer, of course, to the *Feldherrnhalle*, has remained overshadowed since the conclusion of World War II, resulting in a situation where even the leading role it played in some of the greatest battles of the World War II has actually been attributed to other formations.

The circumstances that worked together to give rise to this situation are somewhat difficult to pinpoint at first glance. Initially it may be thought that the relationship with the SA, which had made it the only Army unit to retain genuine links with a National-Socialist paramilitary organisation, might have played a role in this respect; but units which were much more highly politicised, as is the case with the divisions of the Waffen-SS, have witnessed how their combat actions have been recounted in detail in a multitude of works which state that they were composed of "soldiers like any other".

It is most likely that the mixed character of the *Feldherrnhalle*, demonstrated by the existence at its core of predominantly military elements, with firm traditions, has led to a situation where, ultimately, in a post-war era characterised by de-Nazification and 'payment for blame', these traditions may have prevailed over the reduced importance that its SA component may have had at one time.

Without resorting to the bold approach of the Russians who at one time used the denomination SA-Panzergrenadier *Feldherrnhalle* Division to refer to these divisions, it must, however, be made plain that the role played by the SA in the process of transformation which was to render these units, elite units, is not, by any means, negligible.

The special treatment given these formations by the OKW, placing at their disposition competent command staff, the most sophisticated war matériel or including them in the most advanced re-structuring and equipment programmes was not in vain. As if this was not sufficient, it should be recognised that the notable actions of the volunteers who had been partially trained by the SA, and who congregated in the

Panzergrenadier Regiment *Feldherrnhalle* - which was eventually the most decorated *Feldherrnhalle* unit - would contribute in no small measure to the brilliance of their wartime-history.

Moreover, there are many coincidences between *Feldherrnhalle* and other elite German units during the last war. As occurred with the *Leibstandarte* or the *Großdeutschland*, a series of emblems set the soldiers of the *Feldherrnhalle* apart from the rest of the Army. In addition, its evolution also indicates clear similarities; all had come about from a specific guard and honours unit, first entering combat as a motorised Regiment, later to become a Panzergrenadier Division, later still a Panzer Division and eventually to be converted into a Panzerkorps.

But none of the above would entitle the *Feldherrnhalle* to occupy a position amongst the elite units of the Wehrmacht had it not been for its magnificent conduct in war; pages filled with accounts of heroism which speak of the great fighting spirit of its men.

At this point it must be said that the great *Feldherrnhalle* units were formed when the tide of the war had already clearly turned against Germany; when the stunning offensives were but a memory of the past and the enemy unleashed upon the Third Reich all its human and material superiority. It was during this period when, thanks to its effective counter-attack capabilities, the *Feldherrnhalle* revealed itself to be one of the most hardy formations on the Eastern Front; where it carried out incredible feats and did not hesitate to sacrifice itself to extermination when circumstances demanded.

In the following pages, we shall attempt to sketch out, properly, the controversial links which existed between these units and the SA; equally, we will provide a detailed view of the process of enlargement and transformation of its tactical structure and, of course, we will offer a perspective on the battles waged by the great unknown amongst the elite units of the German Army.

A. Escuadra
La Línea, June 1990

CHAPTER I

Origins of an Elite

SA-Standarte *Feldherrnhalle*

If we take the name as a guide and go further back in time, the origins of the *Feldherrnhalle* units of the Wehrmacht must undoubtedly begin with the SA Guard Regiment, known as SA-Standarte *Feldherrnhalle*, which was established during one of the most critical periods of the history of this organisation.

From the time of the bloody 'Night of the Long Knives'[1], all dreams of power that had taken shape under the cloak of the SA had faded away; among these dreams the one so desperately cherished by its missing leader, who sought to create a new National-Socialist army from the basis of the Brownshirts. The very same shots that had ended the life of Ernst Röhm appeared to have extinguished the last hopes of any practical realisation of the military traditions of the SA[2].

During the following months, the formerly powerful Sturmabteilung, which had contributed more than any other formation of the Party to the acquisition of power by Hitler, contemplated the coincidence of the progressive reduction of its huge membership and the disappearance of its radical character. Meanwhile, the very reason for its existence seemed to be limited to acting as a mere ornament to the new regime.

From what had been its great tragedy emerged new powers, from amongst which its rival, and formerly subordinate organisation, the SS, emerged in an advantageous position; the military authorities having awarded it the privilege of being able to have its own armed units. These units, known as *Verfügungstruppe*, would be the embryo of the future Waffen-SS divisions by means of which, ironically, the old ideal of the political soldier would be re-born.

However, at the same time as the foundations for the future private SS army were being laid, the aspirations of the new *SA-Stabschef*, Viktor Lutze concerning the creation of an armed SA Regiment to take on the guard and honours services, continued to cause considerable envy. He would have to wait until the end of 1935, when the reconciliation between the Party and the SA had been officially stage-managed during

---

[1] Although the 'Night of the Long Knives' is recorded, to a greater or lesser extent, in the majority of the above-mentioned works of this era, among the monographs dedicated to it we should highlight, among others, Heinrich Bennecke <u>Die Reichswehr und der Röhm Putsch</u> (1964) Beiheft 2, Politische Studien, München or the detailed version by Max Gallo <u>Der Schwarze Freitag der S.A. Die Vernichtung des revolutionären Flügels der NSDAP durch Hitler's SS im Juni 1934</u>, Published in Spain as <u>La Noche de los Cuchillos Largos</u> (1976) Bruguera, Barcelona.

2 Although the SA has been portrayed only as a party political organisation, its real character was based on a occasionally irreconcilable symbiosis of those who understood it to be a simple political organisation, and those who believed that it was first and foremost a military formation. This characteristic ambiguity, demonstrated by those who have investigated the origins of the organisation, was to have a decisive effect on its development.

the last Reichsparteitag[3] so that, eventually, a *carte blanche* could be given to their desires. In these circumstances, surrounded by suspicious glances, the SA-Wachstandarte was born.

This Guard Regiment, the only permanent SA formation, billeted and armed, was to take up once again the assignment formerly carried out by the controversial Stabswachen (Guard units of the SA General Staff), now disbanded. It had also been envisaged that the SA-Wachstandarte would become a type of elite corps, through which future leading officers of the organisation would have to pass. Consequently, the choice of its staff was made using exacting criteria.

All candidates had to belong to the collective of SA veterans and have more than one years' service and, in addition to a minimum height and an optimum physical condition, they were required to possess an impeccable racial background.

As in the case of all elite formations, they were equipped with a special uniform and emblem. On the collars of their brown jackets, on a crimson background, was a white or silver 'W' similar to that used by the Army and SS Guard Regiments. Finally, during the eighth Reichsparteitag, to be held in *Nürnberg* during September 1936, Hitler himself officially awarded the unit the name of SA-Standarte *Feldherrnhalle*.

The name made reference to the mythicised 'March on Munich' of 1923; the desperate gesture by which, *in extremis*, Hitler sought to save his failed coup attempt. It was a gesture that had led to a confrontation with the police just at the entrance to the Odeonplatz; there, under the *Feldherrnhalle*, an arch constructed in the mid-nineteenth century to commemorate the military glory of the fallen Bavarian monarchy, had remained the bodies of fourteen National-Socialists. That episode was to become one of the most venerated myths of all the Nazi paraphernalia.

The new name led to a change in the insignia and the introduction of an emblem that would come to transcend the Standarte; I refer to the brown band with the silver inscription "*Feldherrnhalle*" which, from that moment onwards, would adorn the left cuff of the uniforms[4].

To the sound of Steinbeck's *Regimentgruss*, its brilliant silver gorgets would soon become familiar to the Germans. In tightly-formed columns, its men paraded during the main party celebrations and on the anniversary of Hitler's birthday; they paid the essential tributes and flanked the entrances to the principal headquarters of the organisation. Its presence and discipline, as some witnesses recall, was in no way inferior the elite formations of other organisations or branches of the Armed Forces.

Early in 1937 occurred an event that was to prove of particular importance for the future of the soldiers of the *Feldherrnhalle*. On 12th January, as a present for his 44th birthday, *SA-Stabschef* Lutze awarded Hermann Göring the Honorary Leadership of the Regiment. The former pilot, who had been Supreme Head of the SA in 1923, sported the *Feldherrnhalle* armband on his *SA-Obergruppenführer's* uniform with pride.

Under the effective leadership of Lutze's former Adjutant, *SA-Brigadeführer* Erich Reimann, the SA-Standarte *Feldherrnhalle* at that time numbered six Sturmbanne (Battalions) distributed in Berlin, *München*, Hattingen, Krefeld, *Stettin* and Stuttgart; and later, a seventh Sturmbann in Vienna, whose inhabitants had enthusiastically saluted its columns during the achievement of the *Anschluss*.

---

[3] If it were necessary to define, in a single word, the meaning of the Reichsparteitag of 1934 for the SA, it would be 'reconciliation'. This is made obvious enough by a glance at the filmed record of the Reichsparteitag, shot by Leni Reifenstahl 'Triumph des Willens' or the speeches of the members of the higher echelons of the Party during this period. For more information on these celebrations, see R. Nederling <u>Die Reichsparteitage der NSDAP 1923-1939</u> (1981) Druffel Verlag, Landsberg am Lech, Germany.

[4] For more information I refer the reader to Appendix D: Insignia and Emblems.

With an outward-looking Reich, Göring sought to benefit from his Honorary Leadership, incorporating the excellent human resources of the SA-Standarte *Feldherrnhalle*, which had already received military training, into the ranks of his growing Luftwaffe.

Thus, on 21st May 1938, came an official announcement of the start of courses to prepare the Standarte to be mobilised as an Airborne Regiment in the event of war.

It seemed as if the Czech crisis would precipitate its baptism of fire. On 28th June, the *Feldherrnhalle* Luftlande Regiment (Airborne *Feldherrnhalle* Regiment), was put on a state of alert with the 7th Flieger-Division (7th Air Division of *Generalleutnant* Kurt Student); but, as we know, the situation ended with the Munich Agreement, without even a shot having been fired. Alerted again during the spring of 1939, the Regiment participated in the bloodless occupation of Bohemia and Moravia.

Considered more of a Wehrmacht unit, from the 27th of the previous October, any young man between the ages of 18 and 25 could fulfil his military obligations, enrolling himself as a volunteer in the SA-Standarte *Feldherrnhalle*; the training period was thirty-six months long and could be extended on the basis of periods of the same duration.

Nevertheless, on 31st March 1939, Order 1939/S 49 number 131, by means of which the SA-Standarte recovered, to some extent at least, some of its lost independence, was made known publicly. The Order postponed its subordination to the Luftwaffe and at the same time re-affirmed its role as an SA guard and honours unit. Even so, its links with the Luftwaffe had not disappeared, far from it, now that its members were obliged to fulfil their military obligations within its ranks.

For the men who would have been mobilised as part of the *Feldherrnhalle* Luftlande Regiment, the period which ran between the beginning of the first alert and the end of the last, that is, between 20th June 1938 and 31st March 1939, was recognised as a period of active service. Since this period could not be divided up, many of those who formed part of the now disbanded *Feldherrnhalle* Airborne Regiment were obliged to enrol as volunteers in the Luftwaffe.

So it was that in September 1939, the SA-Standarte *Feldherrnhalle* witnessed four fifths of its men marching to war as part of parachute formations or elite units of the Armed Forces[5]. Nevertheless, on 17th September 1939, a small contingent, roughly equal in number to a battalion, was placed at the disposition of the Army. Few of them could guess that they would end up giving rise to one of the most hardened German elite units of World War II.

Infantry Regiment *Feldherrnhalle*

The group of volunteers from the SA-Standarte *Feldherrnhalle* was bound in the first instance for the Army at the Jüterbog Training Ground in Potsdam, Military District III, where they were assigned to the organisational programme of the new 93rd Infantry Division under *Generalleutnant* Otto Tiemann. A few weeks later, having completed their training, these men became the III Battalion of 271st Infantry Regiment, commanded by *Major* Günther Raben.

With a view to the French campaign, it was incorporated together with its Division in the XXX Corps, (*General der Artillerie* Otto Tiemann), of 1st Army

---

[5] The study of Luftwaffe units composed partially or entirely by members of the SA-Standarte *Feldherrnhalle* would be sufficient for another book. As a simple reference, I will here list only the most important.

Luftlande Regiment *Feldherrnhalle*, 7 Fliegerdivision (1938)

Fallschirmjäger Regiment 1, 7 Fliegerdivision (1940)

Regiment General Göring

Fallschirmjäger Regiment 2 (later *Feldherrnhalle*), 2 Fliegerdivision (1944)

(*Generaloberst* Erwin von Witzleben) which formed part of Army Group C (*Generaloberst* Wilhelm von Leeb); remaining deployed opposite the Maginot Line in the Saar region.

During the first phase of the attack, while the *sichelschnitt* did away with the cream of the enemy's ground forces, it remained in its positions, but, by mid-June, it abandoned them to launch an assault on the enemy fortifications situated to the South of Saarbrücken.

On 15th June, as he was leading his men against a line of bunkers, *Major* Günther Raben fell, mortally wounded. A little while later, a former SA Führer, recently decorated with the Knight's Cross, *Major* Herbert Böhme, who until then had been destined for the 8th Infantry Division as Commander of the III/28th Infantry Regiment, took charge of the Battalion. He would not abandon the *Feldherrnhalle* soldiers until his death in Russia three years later.

Once the Maginot Line had been broken, the Feldbataillon continued to advance towards the Southwest with its Regiment and, towards the end of June, it participated in the battle of annihilation that took place short of Moselle. The French capitulation was obtained to the south of Lunéville, more than one hundred kilometres from their starting point.

Aiming to maintain its SA identity, it had been established that replacements for the battalion should come exclusively from the SA-Standarte *Feldherrnhalle* for which the 5th Company of the 203rd Ersatz Battalion[6] was located in the Güterfelde Barracks in Teltow/Berlin, where the I Sturmbann of the SA-Standarte *Feldherrnhalle* had been billeted since its creation[7].

Any German, or *Volksdeutsche*, (foreigner of proven German origin) between 16 and 33 years old was able to enlist to serve in the Feldbataillon. To do so, in the first instance it was necessary to put in an application to serve with the SA-Standarte *Feldherrnhalle*. Those who were chosen received the basic military training prescribed for the members of the SA-Standarte and, once this was over, they could choose to fulfil their military obligations in the Feldbataillon *Feldherrnhalle*. With this goal in mind, they were passed as fit in the quoted 5/Ersatz Rgt.9 where they completed their training in the use of weapons, reaching the required standard to advance to the Front.

Following a long rest period, during the spring of 1941, the Battalion found itself in the East with its 93rd Infantry Division forming part of the deployment of reserve troops for Operation Barbarossa.

A little while after the start of the invasion, Tiemann's division was assigned to Army Group North (*Generalfeldmarschall* Wilhelm von Leeb), also as reserves, this time of the 18th Army (*Generaloberst* Georg von Küchler). After a short period of inactivity, in mid-July they finally went into action with the XXVI Corps (*General der Artillerie* Albert Wodrig), pushing the enemy back in the direction of Lake Peipus.

Early in August, together with the other battalions of the Regiment, they left the division to form the primary column of the Kampfgruppe '*General* Friedrich' which was also composed of various assault cannon, anti-tank and engineering battalions[8].

---

[6] In his article entitled <u>Die soldaten der *Feldherrnhalle*</u>, published years ago in the German magazine <u>Feldgrau</u>, Klaus Woche lists the first replacement unit as the 203rd Infantry Battalion and later as the 9th *Ersatz* Infantry Battalion; the latter concurs with what appears in a list of the Wehrmacht's *Feldherrnhalle* units given to the author by *Oberst* Klaus Voß, former officer of the 106th *Feldherrnhalle* Panzerbrigade. In the great work of Georg Tessin <u>Verbände und Truppen der deutschen Wehrmacht und Waffen-SS 1939-1945</u>, vol 14, page 80, both reserve companies are quoted as belonging to the Inf.Ers.Btl.9.

[7] OSAF.PO 4 Nr.11215 2.Ang. dated 24 October 1941. Document given to the author by Klaus Woche (Berlin).

[8] The Kampfgruppe *Generalmajor* Friedrich was composed of the following units:
    Infanterie Regiment 271
    Radfahrer Bataillon 402
    Panzer Jäger Abteilung 161
    Pionier Bataillon 662

Its new mission was to protect the flank of the German advance in the Peipus area. However, during the first week of August, the Regiment again found itself advancing against enemy positions and within a few days, more than 8,000 prisoners passed through their rearguard.

Re-integrated into the 93rd, they turned to the north, close on the heels of the Soviet 11th Division, which was retreating towards Kunda and, having crossed the Kingisepp, to the north-east of Narva, began to exert pressure from the south-east on enemy units which had been besieged in the Oranienbaum Cauldron.

It was there that the Russian campaign of 1941 ended for the Feldbataillon *Feldherrnhalle*, during which the men had already begun to distinguish themselves. *Leutnant der Reserve* Walter Evers, commander of the 11th Company was decorated with the *Knight's Cross* and *Leutnant* Rudolf Bärthel, of the 10th, was awarded the *German Cross in Gold*. Both officers came from the ranks of the SA-Standarte *Feldherrnhalle* and their decorations were the only two important distinctions received by the Regiment.

Early in 1942, still with the 93rd Infantry Division, they abandoned their positions in Oranienbaum and during the last few weeks of spring they participated in the campaigns of destruction which sealed the fate of the Red Army's 2nd Army in the Volkhov. One of the officers from the 271st Infantry Regiment was cited in the Army's *Roll of Honour*; the man was Wilhelm Maier, a Sturmführer from the SA-Standarte *Feldherrnhalle* who was then serving as a *Leutnant* in the hardened 11th Company of the Feldbataillon *Feldherrnhalle*.

The unit in which the men from the SA served had distinguished itself brilliantly, becoming the most decorated unit of the 271st Infantry Regiment. *SA-Stabschef* Lutze could consider himself proud of the conduct of his men and swiftly began to explore the possibility of widening the 'patronage' of the SA to larger units. His proposals met with success and on 24th April a second replacement company, the 6th Ersatz Company of 9th Ersatz Regiment fixed its base in Güterfelde, forming a new Ersatz Battalion with the 5th. Replacements for a complete regiment were thus guaranteed.

On 9th August 1942, the following Order arrived from the Führer's Headquarters; "In recognition of the actions carried out by the SA for the future of Germany, I award the 271st Infantry Regiment the denomination of Infantry Regiment *Feldherrnhalle*. On the left forearm, the Infantry Regiment *Feldherrnhalle* will wear a brown band with the inscription *Feldherrnhalle* in silver. Additional dispositions for the execution of the order will be established by the Army's Head of Armaments and the Supreme Commander of the Reserve Army"[9]. Several weeks later, on 11th September, the 5th and 6th Companies of the 9th Ersatz Regiment of Potsdam, detached in Güterfelde, became the Ersatz Infantry Battalion *Feldherrnhalle*[10].

Supplying reserves for an entire Regiment was no easy task for the SA-Standarte *Feldherrnhalle*, thus efforts were made to increase the numbers of recruits enlisting, not only of members of the Standarte but also of any other German of service age. Since the previous spring, it had been established that the Germans belonging to the replacements of 1923, 1924 and 1925 which supplied volunteers to carry out military

---

Schwere Artillerie Abteilung 536

Sturmgeschütze Abteilung 185

[9] Order of the Führer reproduced in a Standarte *Feldherrnhalle* propaganda sheet. Document given to the author by Klaus Woche (Berlin). For more information on the emblems, see Appendix D: Insignia and Emblems.

[10] G. Tessin <u>Verbände und Truppen der deutschen Wehrmacht und Waffen-SS 1939-45</u>, (1980) vol.14, page. 80, Biblio Verlag, Osnabrück, Germany.

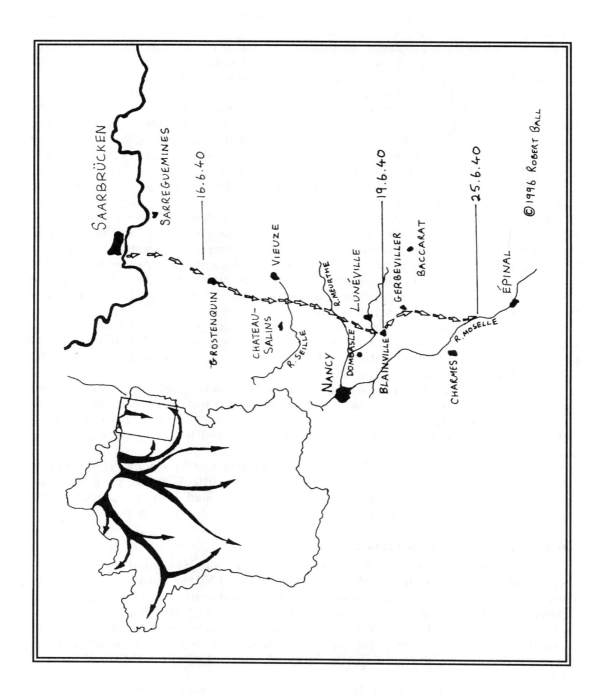

The Feldbataillon *Feldherrnhalle* in France 1940

duties with the *Feldherrnhalle* were exempt from carrying out any obligatory work service[11].

In spite of these problems, the Infantry Regiment *Feldherrnhalle*, "the only unit of the Army exclusively composed of SA volunteers", continued to improve. Now, with the aim of increasing its combat capacity, efforts were made to transform it into a completely motorised formation and the first steps were taken towards this goal.

The Regiment was now authorised to carry a standard similar to that used by the SA-Standarte *Feldherrnhalle* during processions and parades as a regimental ensign, side-by-side with the stipulated black and white flag prescribed for infantry regiments. In this manner, the Infantry Regiment *Feldherrnhalle* also became the only unit in the German Army to swear its oath of loyalty to an Ensign of the Party[12].

Meanwhile, in the East, the *Feldherrnhalle* soldiers had moved south with the rest of the Division; specifically to the Front defended by the XXVIII Corps (*General der Artillerie* Herbert Loch), dependent on the 16th Army (*Generalfeldmarschall* Ernst Busch). In its new location near Lovat, these men continued to distinguish themselves in the battles that were to take place in the area during the autumn of 1942. The fearlessness that was demonstrated at this time by *Major* Herbert-Asmus Winter who commanded the II/Infantry Regiment *Feldherrnhalle* and *Oberfeldwebel der Reserve* Herbert Berger of the 10th Company, received deserved recognition with the award of the *German Cross in Gold* to each of them.

As the Infantry Regiment *Feldherrnhalle* held its ground to the north-east of Loknya, the Battle of Stalingrad raged many kilometres to the south. Its outcome was to have a decisive impact on the future of the unit, since it signified the beginning of the great *Feldherrnhalle* units of the German Army.

Among the twenty large German divisions that were annihilated at Stalingrad was the *Danzig* 60th Infantry Division (mot). Scarcely two weeks after the disaster had occurred, the Infantry Regiment *Feldherrnhalle* was preparing to leave the 93rd Infantry Division and march west, with the aim of helping with the reconstruction of the destroyed Prussian Division.

On 17th February 1943, the veterans of the Infantry Regiment *Feldherrnhalle* mounted trains that were to take them to the peaceable south of France. Their uniforms now shone with valuable decorations and their spirits had been tempered by the experience of more than a year and a half of fighting on the Russian Front.

The 60th Infantry Division (mot)

The establishment of the Panzergrenadier Division *Feldherrnhalle* was to be the first reward to come from the hard work of *SA-Stabschef* Viktor Lutze in his efforts to assimilate the SA into a combat unit; although, unfortunately, a motoring accident prevented him living long enough to enjoy it. The 60th Infantry Division (mot) had been chosen as the basis for the new division which was to continue the representation of the SA on the Front line. As one might expect, the choice was by no means accidental, for this was a division which from its early days had been linked to the Brown Militias of *Danzig*.

From the end of World War I, the 'Free City' was a bastion of German nationalism in the East and the organisations of this persuasion had discovered fertile ground amongst the inhabitants. During the 1920s, the *Stahlhelm*, the paramilitary organisation linked to the *Deutsch-Nationale Volkspartei* (*DNVP*), had established numerous units there which competed with the minority Sturmabteilung of the Nazi

---

[11] OSAF. FO.4Nr. 11215, 3.Ang. "Ersatzgestellung für die SA- Standarte *Feldherrnhalle*', dated 18.2.42.

[12] For more information see Appendix D: Insignia and Emblems.

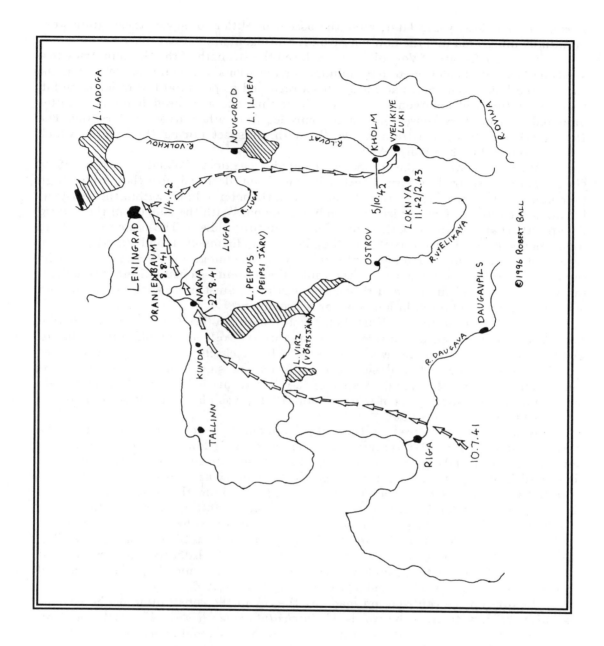

The 271st Infantry Regiment Feldherrnhalle in Russia, 1941-1943

Party. Nevertheless, years later, after the ascent of Hitler to power, these units were eventually integrated into the now massive SA contingents.

Since the Treaty of Versailles had reduced the strength of the German Army to a symbolic force of 100,000 men, paramilitary organisations, especially in 'danger areas' such as the Polish Corridor, had always been regarded as potential future forces to fall back on in times of emergency. As a result of this, the SA based here were better prepared in a military sense than their comrades from other areas of Germany. The *Danzig* SA was to demonstrate its worth in this respect during the months which preceded the outbreak of World War II.

With a view to the proposed campaign against Poland, in May 1939, *Generalmajor* Friedrich Georg Eberhardt had been destined for the Army High Command in the 'Free City' so that, by mobilising the men to hand within the territory, he might organise an force which was ready for combat. With the support of the *Danzig* Senate, Eberhardt began to gather together his future soldiers. These men came from some regiments of Territorial Police, (Landespolizei Regiment 1 and 2), which were organised in an *ad hoc* fashion and into which were also integrated *Danzig* citizens who served as volunteers, the majority of the rank of non-commissioned officers, throughout the Wehrmacht. And finally, and this is the part of greatest interest to us, there were also a good number of SA militiamen under his command.

The then *Hauptmann* Kurt Fett, who, as first officer (Ia) of *Generalmajor* Eberhardt's staff played a key role in the organisation of the Kampfgruppe, tells us: "Another source of personnel was the 'Technische Hochschule Danzig'. The SA also provided some of our technical men, especially for the signals units[13]". It should be pointed out here that the signals branch of the SA (Nachrichten SA), whose men were thoroughly trained in all types of telecommunications, was placed at the disposal of the Wehrmacht when war broke out.

However, these were not the only SA men that were to form part of the embryonic unit of the 60th Infantry Division (mot). In addition to those previously mentioned, the members of the VGAD, the *Verstärkter-Grenz-Aufsichts-Dienst*, or Reinforced Frontier Vigilance Service, organised by the *Danzig* authorities on 1st July 1939 and whose ranks had been constituted with men from the SA-Standarte 5 and 128[14], also came under Eberhardt's orders. *Hauptmann* Fett continues on this point; "The *VGAD*, which drew together almost 1,000 men, had also been organised from the SA. The VGAD was subordinated to the Gruppe Eberhardt until the start of the War. Once the War was underway, it was distributed between the Infantry regiments (on 1st September 1939 Regiments 1 and 2 of the Landespolizei would drop this name and become, respectively, the 243rd and 244th Infantry Regiments)".[15]

To sum up the contribution made by the SA in the constitution of the Gruppe Eberhardt we may turn to the words of *Oberleutnant der Reserve* Heinrich Albrecht, veteran of the 60th Infantry Division (mot) who, in his unedited memoirs, refers to the origins of his Division in the following terms; "We should not overlook the fact that from the SA formations would come a large number of the staff for the units organised in *Danzig* in July 1939"[16].

---

[13] *Oberst i.G.* Kurt Fett <u>Die Aufstellung der Gruppe Eberhardt</u>, page 1 given to the author by the Kameradschaft der Angehörigen der ehemaligen 60 ID (mot) and deren *Feldherrnhalle* Nachfolgeverbände.

[14] For more information on this unit's insignia, I refer the reader to the work of Lt Col John R. Angolia <u>Cloth Insignia of the NSDAP and SA</u>, Roger James Bender Publishing, San Jose, California, USA, page 315.

[15] *Oberst i.G.* Kurt Fett, op. cit., <u>Anlage 1</u>, page 8.

[16] *Oberleutnant der Reserve* Heinrich Albrecht <u>Erinnerungen an die Aufstellung und den Einsatz der II/A.R.160 im Verband der Brigade Eberhardt. 1 Juli bis zum 19 September 1939</u>, original in the possession of *Hauptmann a.D.* and *Major d.Res.d.Bw.* Erich Klein.

From 1st September, the Kampfgruppe Eberhardt distinguished itself on missions such as the famous capture of the Polish Post Office in *Danzig* or the assault of some redoubts defended by the Poles along the Baltic coast. In the wake of the Polish campaign, the Kampfgruppe became the 60th Infantry Division and as such took part in the French campaign, operating close to where the SA of the III/Inf.Rgt.271 was located. At the end of the campaign, on 17th July 1940, it became the 60th Infantry Division (mot) which, in spring 1941, took part in the campaign in the Balkans and then, as part of the manpower for Barbarossa, entered the Soviet Union, becoming besieged with the 6th Army of *Generalmajor* Paulus in Stalingrad[17].

Although with the advent of the definitive plan for replacements for the Wehrmacht, the old ties that existed between the *Danzig* Division and the SA were eventually forgotten, at the end of 1942 there was to occur an event which would highlight that they were still borne in mind by the Brownshirts. When its leaders learned of the huge losses incurred by the unit in the Battle of Stalingrad, they did not hesitate to send, in reserve, a full battalion of volunteers from the SA-Standarte *Feldherrnhalle*. These soldiers served to wipe out the losses suffered by the 120th Infantry Regiment (the new denomination of the 244th Infantry Regiment), which from that moment onwards would be known as the 120th Infantry Regiment *Feldherrnhalle*[18].

Together with the former 271st Infantry Regiment, this was the second regiment that Lutze managed to 'assimilate' to the SA, albeit rather fleetingly, for the 120th Infantry Regiment *Feldherrnhalle* was to succumb, together with the Division, whilst defending the northern zone of the siege. Nevertheless, from Lutze's point of view, its sacrifice had not been in vain, for an initial sounding had been successfully launched; the process for the constitution of a *Feldherrnhalle* division by means of replacement units for the 60th Infantry Division (mot), with its survivors used as a basis, had remained on the table and was to be carried out in the South of France the following spring.

---

[17] Précis of the combat history of Kampfgruppe Eberhardt, later the 60th Infantry Division (mot).

Polish Campaign (1939)

Between 1st and 19th September, battles in *Danzig, Oxhöft* and *Hela*. Then began the transformation to the 60th Inf Div which would culminate in *Groß Born* on 26 January 1940.

French Campaign (1940)

At the end of January, deployed on the western Front, in the Saarbrücken area. In mid-June, assault on the Maginot Line to the south of the city and then participated in the battle of annihilation on the Moselle. Towards the end of July, remained in France as an occupation force. On 17th July 1940, it was refitted as 60th Inf Div (mot).

Balkan Campaign (1941)

Following training early in the year in Romania and Bulgaria, in April 1941, penetration of Yugoslavia with the Pz. Gruppe Kleist. Fighting in Kruševac, Kragujevac, Pristina and Mitrovica. Security force in the Belgrade region. Part of the Division present until May, fighting in Greece with the 5th Pz.Div. Finally, in June, transferred to Silesia as reserve for the Army Group South.

Russian Campaign (1941/43)

At the end of July, march through *Cracow-Lviv-Mariampol*. Participated in the Battle of *Berdychiv*, near *Bila Tserkva* and in the siege of Uman. In September 1941, combat in the *Dnyepr*, at the *Dnipropetrovsk* bridgehead. In October, advance south in the battle of the Azov Sea. Then transferred to *Mariupol-Taganrog*. Between November and December participated in the battle of Rostov on the Don. In the wake of the fall of the city, retired to the Mius sector, proceeding to defend it from the north of Tangarog. Between January and April 1942, dedicated to the defence of the Mius sector, and later of the *Donyets* in a zone situated to the south of *Izium*. In May, counter-attack together with the 1 Panzer Army in *Kharkiv*. Early in the summer, breakthrough across the *Donyets* as far as the Don in Kalach. In August, attacked Stalingrad, with Paulus' 6th Army. In November defends the northern sector and is encircled by the end of the month, being progressively destroyed. Remnant forces capitulate early in February 1943.

[18] Rolf O.G. Stoves Die Gepanzerten und Motorisierten Deutschen Großverbände 1935-45 (1986) Podzun-Pallas-Verlag, Friedberg, Germany, page 187.

The Feldherrnhalle in Munich

Göring during a collection surrounded by senior Luftwaffe and SA officers. On the left sleeve of his uniform is the brown cuff-title of the *Feldherrnhalle*.

Sentry of the *Feldherrnhalle* in 1938. On the helmet can be seen the Luftwaffe eagle.

Feldwebel Josef Gollas, who won his Knight's Cross as a Platoon Leader (Zugführer) of the 6/Inf.Rgt.106 (15th Inf.Div.). He is seen here as an SA-Sturmführer leading a section of the SA-Standarte *Feldherrnhalle*.

Arcade of the *Feldherrnhalle* in Munich. A plaque and a Guard of Honour permanently marked the spot where, during the 1923 *Putsch*, the first fourteen martyrs of the Nazi movement died.

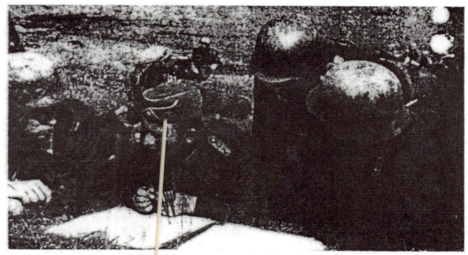

Officers of the Feldbataillon *Feldherrnhalle* go over the last details before the attack on the Maginot Line fortifications. Mid-June 1940.

(Left) Major Günther Raben, *SA-Standartenführer* and commander of the Feldbataillon *Feldherrnhalle*, killed 15.6.40 whilst leading his men against the Maginot Line.

(Below) Visit of SA-Stabschef Viktor Lutze to the wounded of the Feldbataillon *Feldherrnhalle* after the first battles in France.

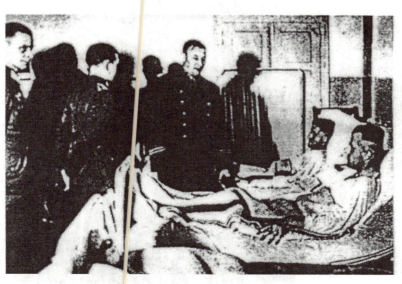

Parade of the
Feldbataillon
Feldherrnhalle in
Güterfelde after the
conclusion of the
Western Campaign. At
the front the SA-
Feldzeichen.

Escorted by two officers, the standard of the SA-Standarte
Feldherrnhalle is photographed in Güterfelde. This standard would be
converted into the ensign of the Feldbataillon *Feldherrnhalle*.

The Palace at Güterfelde, where the Feldbataillon
were quartered.

Visit of *SA-Stabschef* Viktor Lutze to the
Feldbataillon during the `sitzkrieg`.

The Feldzeichen of the *Feldherrnhalle* at
the front of a column being paraded
between the barrack huts at Güterfelde.

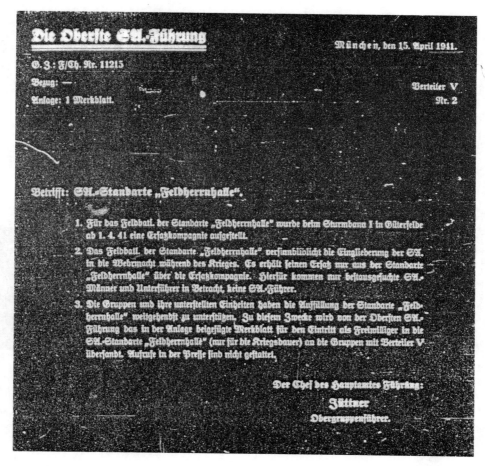

The Supreme SA Command
Ref: F/Ch. nr 11215
re: -

enclosed: 1 information sheet

Munich, 15 April 1941

distribution key V
nr 2

Regarding: SA-Standarte 'Feldherrnhalle'

1. For the Feldbatl. of the Standarte 'Feldherrnhalle' a replacement company had been raised from the 1.4.41 at the Sturmbann I in Güterfelde.

2. The Feldbatl. of the Standarte 'Feldherrnhalle' symbolises the integration of the SA into the Wehrmacht during the war. It receives its replacements from the Standarte 'Feldherrnhalle' only through the replacement company. For this only SA men and Unterführers of the best quality will be considered, no SA-Führers.

3. The groups and their subordinated units have to support the replenishment of the Standarte 'Feldherrnhalle' as far as possible. For this purpose the Supreme SA Command distributes to the groups with distribution key V the enclosed information sheet for the joining of volunteers of the SA-Standarte 'Feldherrnhalle' (only for the duration of the war). Appeals in the press are not allowed.

The Chief of the Hauptamt Führung
Jüttner
Obergruppenführer

The III FHH/Inf.Rgt.271 forming part of the 93rd Infantry Division on the Eastern Front. Images of the first battles of the soldiers of the *Feldherrnhalle* in northern Russia, mid-July 1941.

Soldiers of the *Feldherrnhalle* get ready to cross the Kingisepp River, north-east of Narva.

Major (later *Oberst*) Herbert Böhme, a former leader in the SA who had won the Knight's Cross with the 8th Infantry Division. Commanded the Feldbataillon *Feldherrnhalle* after the death of Raben.

Positions of the 271st Infantry Regiment on the Volkhov.

Shock troop of the *Feldherrnhalle*, Winter 1941/42.

Leutnant der Reserve Walter Evers, head of the 11th Company of the *Feldherrnhalle*, who won the Knight's Cross at the beginning of December 1941.

Feldherrnhalle soldiers during the Russian Campaign of 1942.

Another image of the Russian Campaign, 1942.

Men of the Grenadier Regiment (mot) *Feldherrnhalle*. Winter 1942.

(Left) A former SA man, now an NCO of the *Feldherrnhalle* on the Eastern Front.

(Above) *Oberst* Herbert Böhme, commander of III/Inf.Rgt.271 and later of the Gren.Rgt.(mot) FHH. Böhme won his Knight's Cross in 1940 and received the oakleaves on the 27th December 1943.

(Left) *Oberfeldwebel* Herbert Berger, platoon leader of the 10/Gren.Rgt.(mot) FHH

CHAPTER II

The Panzergrenadier Division *Feldherrnhalle*

Organisation

The reconstruction of the new Division from the remains of the destroyed 60th Infantry Division (mot) took place in Nîmes (France) during the spring and early summer of 1943. The process of reconstruction was carried out in accordance with the outlines laid down for the new Panzergrenadier divisions, now dependent on the Inspectorate of Panzer Troops (Insp.d.Panzer Waffe), from 1st March 1943, under *Generaloberst* Heinz Guderian. Initially, these units were not intended to contain armoured elements although the Army Command had envisaged two exceptions; firstly with its most exclusive unit, the Panzergrenadier Division *Großdeutschland* and secondly, in fact, with the new Panzergrenadier Division *Feldherrnhalle*. Eventually, the original objective was achieved; now the SA 'sponsored' a division for which there was a multitude of reasons for it to be considered an elite unit.

Towards the end of March, the survivors of the destroyed 60th Infantry Division (mot) reached the south of France and a short while later the first recruits from its reserve units were incorporated. On 15th April 1943, the bases of the Division's Füsilier Regiment were established. This grouped together the remains of the two Infantry Regiments of the 60th Infantry Division (mot). This was duly completed with young recruits. The 92nd Infantry Regiment (mot) provided, in addition to the Staff of the Regiment, the III Battalion and the 13th Company; while with the men from the 120th Infantry Regiment (mot) *Feldherrnhalle*, the I Battalion and 14th Company were formed. On 20th June, they officially became the Füsilier Regiment (mot) *Feldherrnhalle* headed by *Oberst* von Hagen.

The very same day, the former Infantry Regiment (mot) *Feldherrnhalle*, which had been in Nîmes since the end of May under the command of Herbert Böhme, from then on an *Oberst*, was officially integrated into the new Division as Grenadier Regiment (mot) *Feldherrnhalle*.

The new Panzer Artillery Regiment *Feldherrnhalle* was formed from the remains of the 160th Artillery Regiment (mot), and the survivors of the 891st Panzergrenadier Regiment, which had also been destroyed. The reconstituted artillery formation of the division was to be under the orders of *Oberst* Walter Kaegler.

Equally, the rest of the former 160th Panzer Abteilung. was to be strengthened, allowing the existence of an exceptional armoured battalion which, equipped with assault cannon (*Sturmgeschütze* III and IV) would operate under the orders of *Hauptmann* Erich Oberwöhrmann, a veteran officer of the tanks of the 1st Panzer Regiment.

The Division was completed by the Reconnaissance Battalion (Panzer Aufklärungs Abteilung *Feldherrnhalle*)) whose men arrived at the end of March from the Krampnitz Academy for Panzer Troops II (Panzer Truppenschule-II); the Signals Battalion (Nachrichten Abteilung (mot) *Feldherrnhalle*) of *Hauptmann* Hans Schulte, the Engineer Battalion (Pionier Bataillon (mot) *Feldherrnhalle*), the Anti-Aircraft Battalion, (Heeres Flak Abteilung *Feldherrnhalle*), the new denomination of the Army's 282nd Anti-Aircraft Battalion, and the rearguard services.

In this way, on 22nd June 1943, the Panzergrenadier Division *Feldherrnhalle* was born. At its head from mid-May had been *Generalmajor* Otto Kohlermann[19], a forty-six year old under whom served the Head of Operations, *Oberstleutnant* Felsch. By now all the members of the Division wore on their cuffs the characteristic brown band that had previously been prescribed as an emblem of the *Feldherrnhalle* Regiment[20]. At the same time, the former divisional insignia that reproduced the red shield with two white crosses of the city of *Danzig* was exchanged for a black insignia which depicted in the centre the esoteric rune of the wolf (Wolf-rune)[21].

The Division's reserve units also adopted the new emblems and changed their denomination for that of Ersatz Brigade *Feldherrnhalle*. At the head of this Brigade was the former Wehrmacht delegate to the Stabschef of the SA, *Generalmajor* Froemert[22], who had as his Adjutant the young *Oberleutnant* Peters.

Except for the Grenadier Ersatz Bataillon *Feldherrnhalle* (*Feldherrnhalle* Training and Reserve Battalion)[23], stationed in Güterfelde, Berlin, all the replacement units for the new *Feldherrnhalle* division were to be found around *Danzig*. Thus, whilst the former was answerable to the III Military District (Wehrkreis Berlin-Brandenburg), the rest came under the Military Districts of Prussia, (Wehrkreis I East Prussia and XX West Prussia) and were co-ordinated via a Liaison Department named Wehrmeldeamt *Feldherrnhalle*, located in Potsdam.

It was obvious from the very beginning that the recruits which the SA-Standarte *Feldherrnhalle* was able to provide would scarcely be able to fulfil the personnel requirements of an entire regiment and that, consequently, to hope that from its ranks would emerge sufficient troops to supply a whole division was pure fantasy[24]. For this reason only a small proportion of the men of the Panzergrenadier Division *Feldherrnhalle* would come from the ranks of the SA; the majority would come from the drafts mobilised within the corresponding military districts.

Similarly, neither did the immense majority of the officers come from the SA, and as a result, taking the division as a whole, the aim of "representing the SA on the Front line" was more symbolic than real.

---

[19] For more information, see Appendix E: *Feldherrnhalle* Generals.

[20] John R. Angolia and Adolf Schlicht Uniforms and Traditions of the German Army (1986) James Bender Publishing, San José, California, USA, vol.2, p.97. However, the division is still identified as the 60th Infantry Division (mot), in common with other works where this reference appears.

[21] For more information, see Appendix D: Insignia and Emblems.

[22] For more information, see Appendix E: *Feldherrnhalle* Generals.

[23] According to K. Woche, on 8 April 1943, there was a reorganisation within the Wehkreis III reserve regiment, which was divided into the Gren.Ausb.Btl.*Feldherrnhalle* which remained in Güterfelde, and the Gren.Ersatz Btl. (mot.) *Feldherrnhalle* which was billeted in Arnswalde (Pomerania). However, in the detailed work of Georg Tessin Verbände und Truppen der deutschen Wehrmacht und Waffen-SS 1939-45 (1980) Biblio Verlag, Osnabrück, vol.XIV, p.80, undertaken with the collaboration of the Bundesarchiv-Militärarchiv in Freiburg, is it noted that this Regiment, previously known as the Ersatz Infantry Regiment *Feldherrnhalle*, was divided on 23 September of the previous year and remained the Ausb.Btl. in Arnswalde.

[24] To resolve the reserve problems of the *Feldherrnhalle* Regiment alone, the OSAF had requested that each SA-Standarte (except those of the Marine SA), should supply volunteers for the regiment between 1 May and 1 September 1943. Klaus Woche, op. cit. pp.77-102.

Thus it should be noted that when some veterans now repeat their belief that the only thing which linked them to the SA was the name and use of the flag[25], we should point out that in certain units, such as the Grenadier Regiment (mot) *Feldherrnhalle*, the presence of SA volunteers was fairly numerous and that, in more or less significant quantities, they were also present throughout the Panzergrenadier Division *Feldherrnhalle*.

If we go more deeply into the participation of the SA in the establishment and training of the men of the Panzergrenadier Division *Feldherrnhalle*, it could be said, as a general rule, that the path followed by the SA volunteers as we have already mentioned, began with their entry to the SA-Standarte *Feldherrnhalle* from where they were immediately sent to Training Battalions which were answerable to the SA-Standarte *Feldherrnhalle* (Ausbildungsbataillone), in which they received a course of basic military training over a period of between six and eight weeks.

Among the testimonials that the author has been able to gather together from the veterans of the *Feldherrnhalle* there are several references to training. One of the veterans commented that "in 1943...the reserves for the (*Feldherrnhalle*) units were trained by the SA-Standarten (sic) 1-8 and during this training period the soldiers wore the brown uniforms of the SA"[26]. Another put it in these terms; "Enlisting in the SA was never a condition for being a member of the *Feldherrnhalle* units. Only the youngest recruits were summoned to one of the 12 Sturmbanne which were distributed throughout the Reich, to receive a training programme some six weeks long. However, they were not members of the SA either".[27]

Some clarification is called for on this point. Despite the fact that in principle membership of the SA or the Hitler Youth was obligatory, from February 1942 recruits coming from the mobilised drafts could enlist with the SA-Standarte and be immediately enrolled with the *Feldherrnhalle* reserve units[28] which explains the fact that they were not members of the Sturmabteilung.

Members of the SA or not, what is certain is that a good number of soldiers from the Panzergrenadier Division *Feldherrnhalle* and subsequent *Feldherrnhalle* formations received an initial stage of military training in the training battalions of the SA-Standarte *Feldherrnhalle*.

The number of Ausbildungsbataillone varied between seven and twelve according to the supply of recruits. We have ventured to offer a list of the location of some of their barracks, showing the Sturmbann of the SA-Standarte *Feldherrnhalle* located there and to whom they were answerable. They are, in order:

Barracks	**Sturmbann**
Güterfelde	I Sturmbann
Arnswalde	II Sturmbann[29]
Grossglockersdorf	III Sturmbann
Hemer	IV Sturmbann
Vienna	VII Sturmbann
Konin	IX Sturmbann
Warsaw	X Sturmbann

---

[25] Erich Klein, *Hauptmann a.D. und Major d.Res.d.BW* in a letter to the author (24.04.1989).

[26] Klaus Voß, *Oberst d.Res.d.BW* in a letter to the author (27.04.1989).

[27] Friedrich Bruns, ex-*Gefreiter und Fahnenjunker-Unteroffizier*, author of the book <u>Die Panzerbrigade *Feldherrnhalle*</u> in a letter to the author (07.08.1989).

[28] OSAF F.O.4 Nr 11215 dated 18.02.1942.

[29] The Grenadier Ersatz Battalion (mot.) *Feldherrnhalle*, previously in Berlin as part of the Ersatz Infantry Regiment *Feldherrnhalle* was billeted there from 23 September 1942.

The officer entrusted by the Oberst SA Führung (SA Supreme Command) with the supervision of these training battalions was the commander of the I/SA-Standarte *Feldherrnhalle* in Berlin, *SA-Brigadeführer* Kübler; something which should not surprise us since we know that the SA reserve services for the Army had been centralised there from the outset.

Thanks to his work, many of the recruits to the *Feldherrnhalle* divisions wore a field-grey uniform for the first time and received a basic military training that would later be reinforced and completed by the training staff in the reserve units. The result of this work did not cease to have a profound impact on the exceptional performance of these formations on the battle field.

Security Missions in the West

From the moment of its constitution, the new Panzergrenadier Division *Feldherrnhalle* remained on exercises in the Nîmes-Montpellier area until, on 1st August, it received an order to transfer to the Italian frontier, specifically to the Nice-Cap Ferrat sector, its mission to protect the line of the Var River.

On 8th September, the capitulation of Fascist Italy had shattered the Axis. Immediately, the division was sent to the Monaco-Menton-Ventimiglia zone where it was involved in disarming the units of the Italian 8th Army. A short while later, it was entrusted with the task of protecting the roads which ran the length of the French Riviera and along the Mediterranean coast; roads which had acquired particular importance for it was along this route that German divisions were to carry out the planned march on Italy.

During this time, the division was subordinated to *General der Infanterie* Baptist Kniess within the 19th Army of Army Group D (later OB West), commanded by *Generalfeldmarschall* Gerd von Rundstedt.

At the end of October, the *Feldherrnhalle* began its transfer by rail towards the north of France, specifically the Arras-Doullens sector where it was to remain at the disposal of the 15th Army of *Generaloberst* Hans von Salmuth.

There they carried out a tactical exercise as a division, which, among others, was to count on the presence of *Generaloberst* Heinz Guderian in his capacity as Inspector General of Armoured Weapons (Gen.Insp.d.Pz.Waffe), the man who was ultimately responsible for the new Panzergrenadier divisions, and that of the *General der Panzertruppen* Leo Geyr von Schweppenburg, the new Commander-in-Chief of *Panzer Group West*. After these manoeuvres, the leaders completed their war training with an intensive three-week course.

However, more men were urgently needed in the East and at the beginning of December, the soldiers of the Panzergrenadier Division *Feldherrnhalle*, their training completed, (although there were still problems of cohesion), left the relative tranquillity of occupied France to climb aboard the trains which would take them to the Central Sector of the Russian Front.

Combat in Vitsyebsk

Virtually since the suspension of Operation Zitadelle, the Wehrmacht had lost the initiative on the Eastern Front. The German Armies had suffered such heavy casualties that the new contingents were scarcely able to make up for a third of the losses. Added to this was the huge loss of equipment; in this respect all the units were functioning below par.

They faced a Red Army which was a great deal different to that which they had encountered at the beginning of Operation Barbarossa. To their traditional numerical superiority, the Russians had now added an abundance of materiél in the front line and, what was more important still, officers who had gained experience in the instructive previous years of the war. After the German failure in the offensive mounted on the Kursk salient, the Eastern Front had buckled under the thrust of Soviet offensive power. The Wehrmacht had been obliged to retreat in many places, the Siege of Leningrad had (deteriorated?) at the start of the year, the vast areas conquered in the offensive of 1942 had been lost and the soldiers from Army Group South (*Generalfeldmarschall* Erich von Manstein) had retreated, relentlessly pursued by the threat of a siege of strategic proportions.

Army Group Centre (*Generalfeldmarschall* Günther von Kluge), had also be subjected to a severe test. His men had been forced to retreat, leaving behind in Russian hands the important enclaves of Orel, Smolyensk or Bryansk, in order to take refuge behind a defensive line, constructed along a series of 'fortress cities' which, until that point, had served to contain the enemy advance.

To illustrate the state of anxiety which reigned amongst the troops on the Eastern Front, I turn to the words of Alan Clark, author of <u>Barbarossa. The Russian-German Conflict 1941-45</u>: "As the winter of 1943 approached, a feeling of gloom and despair permeated the German Army...They were still deep inside Russia,...they found themselves slowly retreating across a bleak and hostile landscape, always outnumbered, perpetually short of fuel and ammunition, constantly having to exert themselves and their machinery beyond the danger point. And behind them lay bitter memories of what midwinter was like"[30].

The men and vehicles of the Panzergrenadier Division *Feldherrnhalle* began to arrive in the sector of Army Group Centre during the second half of December 1943. However, despite the fact that there had already been sizeable battles, they were not to be sent to the zone of combat straight away, but were to remain as reserves for the Army Group in the rearguard; a set of circumstances which was exploited by Kohlermann to finalise the assembly of all tactical elements.

The sector covered by Army Group Centre, barely two months under the command of *Generalfeldmarschall* Ernst Busch, painted a picture of a dangerous salient around the 'fortress city' of Vitsyebsk. Nobody doubted that the enemy's first efforts would be directed there.

This zone was defended by the 3rd Panzer Army, commanded by *Generaloberst* Georg Hans Reinhardt who had repeatedly and unsuccessfully proposed to the head of the Army Group, as well as the OKH, that they should carry out a correction of lines with a view to adopting a more favourable deployment. His reports always met with the same response; "Each soldier must fight where he is, not even one foot back." As a result, his three Corps had prepared themselves as follows: the IX Corps, with their new commander, *Generalleutnant* Rolf Wuthman, covered the sector situated to the north of Vitsyebsk; the LIII Corps, under the command of the recently-appointed *General der Infanterie* Friedrich Gollwitzer were concentrated on the outskirts of the city, and the VI Corps, of *General der Infanterie* Hans Jordan defended the southern flank.

In November, these troops had had an opportunity to appreciate the strength of the new Red Army. Tanks followed by masses of infantry had managed to open a breach five kilometres wide in their lines of defence. On that occasion, only an unexpected thaw allowed the Germans to exploit the situation when the mobility of the enemy had become bogged down in the sticky Russian mud. Nevertheless, what would happen when the frozen ground provided a perfect surface for Soviet tanks?

---

[30] Alan Clark <u>Barbarossa. The Russian-German Conflict 1941-45</u> (1967) Orion, London, p 369

Such conditions had already materialised by mid-December, and there was a great fear that the Russians would once again go on the offensive, again breaking through the front, this time along the line of contact between the IX and LIII Corps, which had allowed them to introduce a key offensive position to the north of Vitsyebsk.

Conscious of the seriousness of the situation, the Army Group mobilised its reserves. Before long, *Generalleutnant* Otto Kohlermann received the order to move.

However, even before the Division reached its new destination in the 3rd Panzer Army, twelve Russian Divisions, supported by six armoured brigades, again broke through the front to the south of Vitsyebsk, between the VI and the LIII Corps. Once the advances were reflected on the maps, different General Staffs could see that the Russians were not intending to nibble at the bait so as to compromise the bulk of their divisions in a direct assault on the 'fortress city' as the OKH had hoped, but realised that their offensive positions went further than the 'stumbling block'. They had overrun the German defensive mechanism on both sides and had subsequently closed in on the Vitsyebsk rearguard and thus sealed the fate of Gollwitzer's troops. This was effectively a repetition of what the Wehrmacht had done for the first time in Czechoslovakia four years earlier.

Despite tenacious resistance, the Russians succeeded, by means of a southern route, in reaching the Leningrad-Kiev highway. It was here, on 23rd December, that they launched into battle with the men of the Panzergrenadier Division *Feldherrnhalle*.

With great speed, various elements such as the reconnaissance units and the engineers, supported by artillery and assault cannon, formed a Kampfgruppe under the name of *Sperrverband/Pz.AOK3*. They were forced, as quickly as possible and at any price, to shore up the zones that had come under threat. Later, the Division would be incorporated into the VI Corps under *General der Infanterie* Hans Jordan.

The Panzergrenadier Division *Feldherrnhalle* immediately prepared to launch a desperate counter-attack using the armoured vehicles of the Panzer Abteilung *Feldherrnhalle* as attack forces. Even so, this action had been organised by side-stepping an important tactical principle; the *Feldherrnhalle* was to advance on unknown territory. On the one hand this was due to an adverse weather report which prevented any airborne reconnaissance missions and, on the other, by a lack of time to obtain this information by means of patrols. Thus, in its first offensive action since Stalingrad, the Division was to fight blind.

So it was that just before dawn broke on Christmas Eve, 1943, the assault groups and tanks of the Division threw themselves upon the Russian positions. Initially all seemed to be progressing well but the tank commanders from the Panzer Abteilung *Feldherrnhalle* realised that it would be impossible to exploit their initial success since the terrain had thrown up unforeseen difficulties which impeded their advance. A few hours later many vehicles were totally immobilised, becoming perfect sitting ducks for the anti-tank fire and Russian artillery shells. There was no alternative but to retreat. However, although it was impossible for Kohlermann to continue the counter-attack to the bitter end, his action eventually denoted the point of inflexion of the Soviet penetration in that sector.

By now the soldiers of the Panzergrenadier Division *Feldherrnhalle*, together with their comrades of the VI Corps, from the 246th Infantry Division (*Generalmajor* Falley) and the 256th Infantry Division (*Generalmajor* Albrecht Wüstenhagen), and the 14th Infantry Division (mot) (*Generalleutnant* Hermann Flörke) which had been severely punished, of the LIII Corps, went to the defence of their positions. These forces were faced with fearsome Soviet attacks in a bloody battle that lasted throughout January 1944. Even so, the defence of their positions was not all that was demanded of Kohlermann's men.

On 11th January, *Oberst* Herbert Böhme received the order to occupy a hill to the south of Vitsyebsk with his grenadiers. Eight tanks and six assault cannon, under the command of the recently-arrived *Oberleutnant* Erich Oberwöhrmann would support the assault. Advancing from the left, the armoured vehicles managed to rout the strong enemy positions and reach their objective, a settlement situated on a nearby hill. From there, Oberwöhrmann could see the difficulties with which the grenadiers were having to deal.

The Russians had concentrated their artillery on the assault groups of the Panzergrenadier Division *Feldherrnhalle* and, from hidden positions in the woods, they were subjecting them to fierce punishment. Despite the fact that his orders went no further than the taking and defence of the hill, *Oberleutnant* Oberwöhrmann could not remain impassive, watching as his comrades were killed.

Without any hesitation he took up the sword and, although unable to rely on any sort of cover, he gave the order to attack to his armoured vehicles. The *Feldherrnhalle* panzers were taken by surprise, sowing confusion in the face of the solid anti-tank front organised by the enemy. After a short and bloody battle, the Russians retreated in a disorderly fashion, leaving many casualties behind. A total of seven heavy tanks, twenty-six cannon and a great quantity of arms fell into German hands.

Back at home, the press described the event as follows: "Thanks to the audacity, determination, and personal courage shown by *Oberleutnant* Erich Oberwöhrmann, at the head of his Panzer Abteilung *Feldherrnhalle*, the operations carried out to the south of Vitsyebsk met with success; this important attack, launched against numerically superior enemy forces, led to Oberwöhrmann being awarded the Knight's Cross[31].

As an indication of the harshness of the combat sustained by the Panzergrenadier Division *Feldherrnhalle* during January 1944, we could turn to the high levels of casualties registered; one of the worst-hit units was, unsurprisingly, the Grenadier Regiment (mot) *Feldherrnhalle*. The casualties suffered by the officers of the Division were particularly high. In addition to *Oberst* Herbert Böhme, who was killed on the 27th, four Battalion commanders fell whilst leading their men, among them *Ritterkreuzträger* Walter Evers who, following his promotion to *Hauptmann*, commanded the unit with the greatest SA tradition within the Division, the III/Grenadier Regiment (mot) *Feldherrnhalle*. Nevertheless, at the end of the month, and largely thanks to their sacrifice, the defensive battle to the south-west of Vitsyebsk was listed amongst the Wehrmacht's victories.[32]

In general terms, it was obvious that the Panzergrenadier Division *Feldherrnhalle* had dealt well with its bloody baptism of fire and, as one of its officers was later to write, had provided "a superb example of inter-unit co-operation"[33]. The artillery had been employed magnificently, paralysing the enemy with heavy fire and preparing the ground for the advance of their comrades. For their part, the exceptional performance of the infantry and the tanks had obtained important decorations for their officers, among them two Knight's Crosses; one, as we know, was to adorn the black uniform of the head of the Panzer Abteilung *Feldherrnhalle* and the other graced the field-grey jacket of the commander of the I/Füsilier Regiment (mot) *Feldherrnhalle*, *Major* Georg Wilhelm Schöning.

---

[31] The reconstruction of this action has been taken from information supplied to the author by *Hauptmann a.D.* Erich Oberwöhrmann.

[32] There are a large number of works which describe the fighting around Vitsyebsk during winter 1943. In particular, considering the perspective from which we view it, the most valid is undoubtedly that of Werner Haupt <u>Die Schlachen der Heeresgruppe Mitte 1941-1944 Aus der Sicht der Divisionen</u> (1983) Podzun-Pallas-Verlag, Freidberg, Germany, pp.242-265.

[33] E. Klein <u>Artillerie Regiment 9 (mot) 160/Pz.Art.Rgt.*Feldherrnhalle*</u>, p.32. An unedited work, placed at my disposal by the author.

However, valiant men of the *Feldherrnhalle* could not have imagined just how short-lived their well-deserved rest would be. Even as fighting continued in the sector, the Russians had unleashed their winter offensive against the Army Group North. The evolution of this offensive necessitated that all their efforts be channelled in that direction and soon the Panzergrenadier Division *Feldherrnhalle* received the order to march. On 24th March, several trains crammed with the first contingents from the Division headed north.

The embarkation arrangements were not themselves without incident. For example, while the men of the Stabsbatterie (Staff Battery) of the II/Panzer Artillery Regiment *Feldherrnhalle* (*Major* Froese) proceeded to deposit their equipment on the platforms, there was a huge partisan attack including mortar blasts which left several men dead, among them their commander, *Oberleutnant* Henke. At the end of January, due to the great need for reinforcements, the units of the division which remained in the Vitsyebsk region were rapidly transported to the north by aircraft.

Feldherrnhalle in the Battle of Narva

The situation which *Generalleutnant* Kohlermann discovered upon his arrival on the Northern Front was roughly similar to that which had accompanied his entry into the hostilities with the Division a few weeks previously. Army Group North, under the command of *Generaloberst* (soon to be *Generalfeldmarschall*) Walter Mödel from 9th January, had been forced to retreat its divisions to the so-called 'Panther' position which extended from the Gulf of Finland as far as the 'fortress-city' of Pskov, to the south of the Lake of the same name.

The Siege of Leningrad had been over for some time, but with the movement of retreat to the new line, whose defence before Hitler had cost the previous Commander-in-Chief of the Army Group (*Generalfeldmarschall* Küchler) his job, the Germans had been able to improve their tactical machinery so much that, thanks to the fact that three-quarters of the new front was occupied by the Peipus and Pskov Lakes, a great number of troops had been 'liberated', which was necessary for the reinforcement of other sectors.

The defence of the zone enclosed by the northern shores of the Peipus and the Gulf of Finland was entrusted to a new formation created specially for the task: the *Armee Abteilung Narva* or Narva Army Detachment. This mixed Army/Waffen-SS unit was led from 22nd February by *General der Infanterie* Johannes Frießner and was composed of the III (Germanische) SS-Panzerkorps under the command of the legendary *SS-Obergruppenführer und General der Waffen-SS* Felix Steiner on the left and the German Army's XXVI Corps, under the orders of the future *Armee Abteilung Narva* commander, *Generalleutnant* Anton Grasser.

At the start of February, the Russians had launched a strong offensive in this sector, with the aim of opening up the routes for the invasion of Estonia. The German defences situated to the south of Narva, on the river of the same name in the Kriivasoo region, were overrun by the force of the Soviet divisions, whose vanguards managed to reach the Vaivara sector.

After a brief period during which the division was assigned to the LIV Army Corps (*General der Infanterie* Otto Sponheimer) of the 18th Army (*Generaloberst* Georg Lindemann)[34], and with scarcely sufficient time to get a measure of the new front, the soldiers   of   the   Panzergrenadier   Division   *Feldherrnhalle*

---

[34] Georg Tessin op.cit. p.76.

The Advance Towards Minsk-Narva

were again sent into combat as a *Sperrverband,* on this occasion under the orders of the *Armee Abteilung Narva.*

In this manner, whilst in Narva the Russian assaults crashed against the solid barrier of the Waffen-SS, to the south-west of the city, they were largely contained by the resolute defence of the *Feldherrnhalle.* In a similar way to what had happened in Vitsyebsk, its entrance in combat was to mark the end of enemy penetration on its front.

From 13th February, *Generalleutnant* Otto Kohlermann temporarily passed the command of the division to an *Oberst,* and was never to return to his former unit. His competence as an artillery expert had won him the title of *Höhere Küsten Artillerie Kommandeur West* or Supreme Head of Artillery on the Western Coast. His substitute was to be *Oberst* Albert Henze, a Prussian from the south of Brandenburg, who would later become a *Generalleutnant* and would be awarded the *Knight's Cross with Oakleaves* and the *German Cross in Gold.* This able officer was to head the division during the defensive operations of the next two months. Initially, thanks to those reinforcements, the German troops had succeeded in containing the Soviet assault. They were immediately ordered to protect the weakened front.

Although the Red Army had halted in its advance, it continued to exert great pressure. When the zone protected by the Panzergrenadier Division *Feldherrnhalle* was in the process of thawing, meteorological conditions prevented the tank advance and the Russian infantry, with solid support from their artillery and air force, launched furious waves of attacks on their positions. Many of the casualties registered during that period would be caused by the bloody hand-to-hand fighting into which many of the incursions degenerated. The artillery duels were equally harsh, and the *Feldherrnhalle* artillery did not cease to suffer from the effects, as *Hauptmann* Erich Klein recounts: "Due to the impact of an enemy artillery shell in the area of the I/Panzer Artillery Regiment *Feldherrnhalle* command post, its commander, *Major* Schulte, was badly wounded and had to be immediately transported to the Field Hospital in Tartu in a Fieseler Storch, but he did not survive. The head of the 1st Battery, *Oberleutnant* von der Heydt and the head of the 3rd Battery, *Leutnant* Seher were also killed. As a result, the command of the I/Panzer Artillery Regiment *Feldherrnhalle* fell to *Oberleutnant* Klein, (the only surviving Head of Battery in the battalion), whose work during these battles would be awarded with the *German Cross in Gold*[35].

Once the power of the Russian offensive had been absorbed, the bridgehead obtained by them to the west of Narva was divided into two sectors, called "Ostsack" and "Westsack", both of which extended across the railway line on both sides of Vaivara. The main priority of the *Armee Abteilung Narva* was now to eliminate this bridgehead. For this, the Panzerkampfgruppe Strachwitz was organised, thus named in honour of its commander, the *Generalmajor* with an interminable name: Hyazinth Graf Strachwitz von Gross-Zauche und Camminetz, who, at the end of March, managed to dislodge the Russians from the "Westsack".

In order to destroy the "Ostsack", some Panzer units and Grenadiers operating in the sector, among them those belonging to the Panzergrenadier Division *Feldherrnhalle,* were put at the disposal of the Strachwitz. This time, its objective was the definitive expulsion of the Soviet troops from the western bank of the Narva.

The Panzergrenadier Division *Feldherrnhalle* was to fight in this special operation under the command of its new commander who had arrived to replace Henze. He was also a forty-eight year old *Oberst,* a former *Ulan* officer, who had started the war as Adjutant to the XV Panzerkorps and had obtained experience in the 7th Panzer Division, firstly at the command of the *Kradschützen* Battalion, and later the Grenadier

---

[35] Erich Klein op.cit. p.33.

Regiment; units with which he had been awarded the *Knight's Cross* and the *German Cross in Gold*. His name was Friedrich Carl von Steinkeller. On 3rd March, recently arrived from the short course for Divisional Commanders, he was placed, for the first time, at the front of a unit of this magnitude.[36]

Five days later he took over as commander of the Panzergrenadier Division *Feldherrnhalle*, which together with the 502nd Panzer Abteilung (*Major* Wilhelm Jähde), was deployed as the spearhead for the Panzerkampfgruppe Strachwitz. The 61st Infantry Division (under the command of the former German Military Attaché in Madrid, *Generalleutnant* Günther Krappe), the 122nd Jäger Division (commanded by *Oberst* Hero Breusing), and the 170th Infantry Division (under *Oberst* Sigfried Hass) - both of whom found themselves in a position similar to von Steinkeller, that is, *Obersten* with command of a Division - also formed a part of the deployment.

The offensive was to get underway in terrible weather conditions. Spring had been late, prolonging the thaw. The rivers and lakes had overflowed, submerging large zones of the combat area, and so control of the few routes which were still passable by vehicles became an objective of critical importance.

At 0435 hrs on the rainy morning of 19th April, the *Feldherrnhalle* Grenadiers, their sights set on these routes, launched themselves against the vanguard positions of the "Ostsack". While this was occurring, in the rearguard, Oberwöhrmann's tanks waited to join the attack. After a terrible battle, the division's assault groups succeeded in conquering and defending a route of penetration for the tanks. Later on, it would be discovered that they had been the only ones to do so; the rest of the regiments had been bled white in front of enemy positions. During these days, the courage of *Oberfeldwebel* Herbert Berger of the 10/Gren.Rgt.(mot.) *Feldherrnhalle*, one of the veterans who had distinguished himself fighting in the same area with the Feldbataillon *Feldherrnhalle* in 1941, was rewarded with the Knight's Cross.

Thanks to this victory by the *Feldherrnhalle* infantry, the armoured vehicles of the Panzerkampfgruppe Strachwitz were able to advance. As they crossed the sector, the tank drivers could see for themselves how the craters made by the shells, now filled with water, had been transformed into death traps for many of their injured comrades.

On its advancing front, the enemy began to be repelled, but soon all hopes of winning a definitive victory were to be frustrated by Soviet artillery. The Russians concentrated their fire on the German columns and the tanks were forced to retreat. Many of them became stuck in the mire and were blown up by their own men. Later attempts did not succeed in changing the situation. On 24th April, the command of the *Armee Abteilung Narva* ordered the suspension of operations[37].

In the end, the enormous sacrifice made by the *Feldherrnhalle*, amongst others, with its terrible toll of men and machinery, had not be recompensed by the expulsion of the enemy to the other side of Narva[38]. Even so, they had managed to stabilise the situation, the Russian winter offensive had been stopped and the Kriivasoo bridgehead reduced. In its northern adventure, the *Feldherrnhalle* had made a significant contribution to the development of containment and counter-attack operations and von Steinkeller could thus honourably turn his first page as commander of the division.

At the end of April, the *Feldherrnhalle* would again be on the move. However, it would need to replace the men and equipment that it had lost. For this purpose, part of the men, the bulk of the Panzer Abteilung *Feldherrnhalle*, the I (self-propelled)/Panzer Artillery Regiment *Feldherrnhalle* and the I/Grenadier Regiment (mot) *Feldherrnhalle*

---

[36] For more information, see Appendix E: *Feldherrnhalle* Generals.

[37] A detailed study of the operation in the Narva region during spring 1944 may be found in the work of Werner Haupt <u>Die Heeresgruppe Nord</u> (1966) Podzun Pallas Verlag, Friedberg, Germany.

[38] Erich Klein, op.cit. p.34.

marched to *Arys* and *Elbing* where they could rest and complete their ranks with new recruits from the Ersatz Brigade *Feldherrnhalle* as well as collect new materiél, among which were to be found brand-new armoured vehicles and self-propelled artillery.

While the men of the *Feldherrnhalle* rested and recuperated from the losses they had suffered in Narva, dark clouds gathered over the Army Group led by *Generalfeldmarschall* Busch. It was enough to glance at the map to realise that they found themselves in a dangerous situation following the retreat of the distinguished German Armies from the south of Russia. Their right flank was virtually suspended in the vacuum created by an enormous pocket that extended for some 400 kms, to the east. In the highest military circles, all seemed to be in agreement that the Red Army would, over the course of the next few months, try to mount a destructive manoeuvre. The question was how the Soviet strategists would plan it.

Little by little the hypothesis had been adopted that the Russians would mount a great offensive from the north of the Ukraine, their primary objective being to reach the Baltic coast so as to isolate, in one single movement, the combined forces of Army Groups North and Centre. Convinced that this would be the case, the German command had decided that the strong point of the defence should be located in the south, and channelled all the available reserves in that direction, among them the Panzergrenadier Divisions.

If events were to unfold as the Germans predicted, the remainder of the front could only expect attack of secondary importance. They put their trust in the system of 'fortress cities' to counter them.

However, it has already been demonstrated that this system had its Achilles Heel and that, in addition to condemning, tactically, the garrisons, the strategy was based on debatable predictions regarding the behaviour of the enemy. If, as the Germans themselves had taught the world during the initial phases of their Blitzkrieg, these strongpoints were overrun by the attacker and the entire system collapsed, the troops manning these 'fortresses' would be wiped out and the whole defence would be weakened by the *a priori* immobility of these men. The Russians had already given dangerous signs of this during their attack on Vitsyebsk a few months previously.

The errors accumulated, the great offensive from the south failed to materialise, and the assault which the Russians were preparing in the central sector of the Front was not a diversionary attack but the greatest offensive ever launched by the Red Army in its entire history. More than 2,200,000 men, grouped in 166 divisions, backed up by 31,000 cannon, 6,000 aircraft and 5,200 tanks launched a frontal attack on 440,000 poorly-armed Germans, spread along more than 1,000 kilometres, in 30 divisions, of which a large number were not even in optimum combat condition.

The Panzergrenadier Division *Feldherrnhalle* was one of the few units possessing armoured elements present in this sector of the Front. As a reserve for the OKH, it was situated in the rearguard of the 4th Army that was led by *General der Infanterie* Kurt von Tippelskirch. This Army, composed from left to right of the XXVII Corps (*General der Infanterie* Paul Völkers), XXXIX Panzerkorps (*General der Artillerie* Robert Martinek) and XII Corps (*Generalleutnant* Vincenz Müller), were located in the centre of the front of the Army Group, occupying forward positions with the 'fortress cities' of Orsha and Mahilyov as bastions to the east of the Dnyepr.

In particular, the elements of the *Feldherrnhalle* were situated to the south-west of Mahilyov, behind the positions of the XXXIX Panzerkorps. Early in June, the division was still not complete; part of the artillery regiment and the tank battalion were still being transferred from Germany where they were being re-equipped. They had to wait until 14th June for the train carrying the remains of the division to arrive at their rearguard. Even so, there were still gaps to be filled.

The new recruits were startled for the first time during the dawn of 20th June when a series of explosions shook the German rearguard transforming it into absolute chaos. In a massive action, which was perfectly co-ordinated, almost all the 100,000 partisans who operated behind the lines of the Army Group blew up railway tracks, bridges, roads, warehouses, military installations etc.; the German military intelligence services could hardly have had any doubts that something on a very large scale was hatching on the other side. Two days later, on the third anniversary of the beginning of Operation Barbarossa, 22nd June 1944, the Red Army unleashed its great offensive of destruction against Army Group Centre.

Tragedy in Minsk-Mahilyov

Ten thousand cannon launched a cascade of fire on the sector of the 3rd Army which, throughout the day, had been able to see the Russian tanks, followed by masses of mobile infantry, break through the front in deep incursions. On the following day, they also broke through the 4th and 9th Armies.

Straight away, von Steinkeller, who had ascended to *Generalmajor* just three weeks previously, received an order to put himself at the disposal of *General der Infanterie* von Tippelskirch, Commander-in-Chief of the 4th Army. A few hours later, the Division was incorporated into the XXXIX Panzerkorps, marching towards Mahilyov with the order to "stem the enemy breach which has opened in the east of the city."

When von Steinkeller informed the Headquarters of the XXXIX Panzerkorps, its commander, *General der Artillerie* Robert Martinek, evidently opposed to the way his superiors were responding to the crisis, answered; "Come to stem a breach? Exactly which breach are you referring to? There are breaches everywhere here! Your true position should be behind us, on the Byerazina, so that then at least we would have a line of containment for when we cannot hold on any longer on the Dnyepr. And it won't be long before that happens!..."[39]

During a meeting with *Oberstleutnant* Waldemar Ratzel, Commander-in-Chief of the Panzer Artillery Regiment *Feldherrnhalle*, located in the same battle-field, *Generalmajor* Herbert Michaelis, commander of the 95th Infantry Division, showed himself to be of the same opinion; "What the devil are you doing here at this bridgehead? You'd be more use if you deployed your excellent equipment behind the Byerazina.[40]

It slowly became clear just how erroneous the senior commanders' appreciation of the Russian offensive had been. The majority of the Division's senior officers seemed to be clear that fighting for the Dnyepr bridgehead would be futile and that their men would probably be sacrificed for the sake of an inaccurate approach. In spite of everything, just as they had been ordered, the *Feldherrnhalle* entered into action 100 kms to the east of the Byerazina; there, before the Dnyepr, they were forced to fight alone in a hopeless battle to salvage that which had already been lost. After a few hours of fierce fighting, the XXXIX Panzerkorps was on the edge of collapse and von Steinkeller, whose men fought along the railway line, which disappeared off in the direction of Chavusy was obliged to begin the retreat.

The retreat towards Mahilyov was orderly and well-managed. The rearguard was covered by the 18 self-propelled *Wespe* cannon of the I/Panzer Artillery Regiment *Feldherrnhalle* which, under the orders of *Oberleutnant* Erich Klein, managed to completely mislead the Russians with a few quick changes of position, remaining until the last *Feldherrnhalle* unit had abandoned the bridgehead.

---

[39] Paul Carell Hitler's War on Russia, Vol. II Scorched Earth (1970) Corgi Books, Transworld Publishers Ltd. London, p. 540.
[40] E. Klein op.cit. p.35.

However, von Steinkeller's report to the Headquarters of the XXXIX Panzerkorps left no doubts as to who commanded on the battlefield; "The success with which I was able to carry out my retreat to Mahilyov owes more to my good luck than to my ability to command."[41]

The following day, while *Generalfeldmarschall* Busch continued to discuss the abandonment of the Dnyepr bridgehead with Hitler, all the XXXIX Panzerkorps was withdrawn towards the west. Elements of the *Feldherrnhalle*, backed up by the guns of the II/Pz.Art.Rgt.*FHH* Battalion, confronted the Russian armoured forces which pressed on from the north-west where they had hemmed in their comrades from the 12th Division with the order to defend the 'fortress city' down to the last man.

The combat undertaken by the Division to the east of the Dnyepr merits the following comments made by one of the officers; "In the sector of the Front affected by the Soviet offensive, twenty (sic) experienced German divisions were deployed and virtually all of them were sent east. Within a time-span of forty-eight hours, the 200,000 men had been defeated as a result of the ineptitude demonstrated by the highest level of command. The action which occurred 30 kms to the east of the Dnyepr by the Panzergrenadier Division *Feldherrnhalle* served no useful purpose and constituted unnecessary waste for our units."[42]

On 27th June, on his own initiative, *General* von Tippelskirch, ordered the retreat of the whole Army towards Barysav, with the intention of crossing the Byerazina. To defend a retreat that was already a reality, *Generalfeldmarschall* Busch ceased to command the Army Group and was replaced by *Generalfeldmarschall* Walter Mödel, who was to authorise all troop movements undertaken by von Tippelskirch's men, including the evacuation of Barysav where the far-sighted *General* Martinek was to meet his death.

The XXXIX Panzerkorps existed only on paper; the remains of its divisions now tried to reach the Byerazina. The marshy area in which they found themselves limited their escape route to only one pass which extended between Moscow and Minsk; like a funnel through which poured a whole Army in retreat. This appeared to give new validity to the yellowed pictures with which the Count of Segar had illustrated his writings on the tragedy suffered, in those same regions, by Napoleon's Grande Armée.

The Division retreated in order, covering its flanks and rearguard until it reached the mentioned passage. The Soviet air force, undisputed master of the skies, discharged its fury on the defeated column. According to one of the officers from the *Feldherrnhalle*; "It happened that the road, without any protection whatsoever, was strafed by low-flying enemy aircraft. There amounted an impressive number of destroyed tanks and vehicles of all kinds, paralysing the advance...[when it came to crossing the river] the worst of it was that the small passes and bridges were rotten and caved-in under the weight of overloaded vehicles. The disaster followed its course...The only route of withdrawal between Mahilyov and the Byerazina turned into a traffic jam"[43].

On 30th June, von Steinkeller's men had broken down into a multitude of *Kampfgruppen* which advanced, fighting, towards the Byerazina. Supplies were simply non-existent; munitions, fuel, and food-supplies had been exhausted. They reached the river at the beginning of July. Fortunately they were able to find a bridge that appeared to be in good shape and the remnants of the *Feldherrnhalle* crossed the Byerazina by means of the bridge. On the eastern bank, were many abandoned vehicles with neither

---

[41] Paul Carell op.cit. p.540.
[42] E. Klein op.cit. p.36.
[43] E. Klein op.cit. p.37.

fuel nor munitions; the tanks and assault cannon were blown up so as to avoid their capture by the enemy. It was a desolate spectacle. Thus, on 2nd July, the Panzergrenadier Division *Feldherrnhalle* , already stripped of most of its heavy weaponry, contemplated from the western bank, how their engineers had blown up the bridge.

However, worse was still to come. A few hours later, the two great pincer formations mounted by the Red Army closed in on the Minsk sector, on the rearguard of the 4th Army. Together with several tens of thousands of their comrades, the men of the *Feldherrnhalle* had been encircled. After a meeting held in the pocket by the commanders of the surviving Corps and Divisions, it was decided to try to escape. The majority were to manage it by moving towards the west and; for his part, von Steinkeller decided to try his luck by concentrating his efforts in the south.

The decimated *Kampfgruppen* of the Division, pursued relentlessly by the enemy air force, through an area infested with partisans, played their last card by trying to make a last ditch attempt to reach German lines. For most this attempt ended tragically. Thus, on 9th July, *Generalmajor* von Steinkeller's Group, in which the commander of the Panzer Artillery Regiment *Feldherrnhalle, Oberstleutnant* Ratzel Waldemar was also to be found, was surrounded and captured after a brief fight.

The same fate awaited the group led by the Divisional Head of Operations, *Oberstleutnant* Felsch, who fell whilst fighting with his comrades. The same was to occur with the soldiers following *Oberleutnant* Bellin, whose men were decimated during the course of their unsuccessful attempt to break the enemy lines. Only one small formation, led by *Hauptmann* Adolf Lepach managed to open a way through and, continually fighting, reached *Ebenrode* through East Prussia. A few hundred grenadiers, six tanks, 16 armoured vehicles and a dozen vehicles full of wounded men, was all that remained of the Panzergrenadier Division *Feldherrnhalle*. The rest lay along the length of the Russian Front, particularly in the area around the Dnyepr and the Byerazina or were painfully making their way in the direction of Soviet concentration camps.

A few days later, integrated into a column of more than 50,000 prisoners, at the head of which were to be found a score of Generals, the soldiers captured from the Panzergrenadier Division *Feldherrnhalle* went through the humiliating experience of a five hour march through the main streets of Moscow.

Parade of the new Panzergrenadier Division *Feldherrnhalle*
in Nîmes (France), 20th June 1943.

Flag of the SA-Standarte *Feldherrnhalle* in front of the
Tribunal of Honour during the parade in Nîmes.

Generalleutnant Otto
Kohlermann, C-in-C of the
Panzergrenadier Division
Feldherrnhalle and SA-
Obergruppenführer
Jüttner preside over the
parade at Nîmes.

Generalleutnant Kohlermann talks with his men.

Obergefreiter of the *Feldherrnhalle*, on whose tunic can be seen the SA-Wehrabzeichen, so common amongst the SA veterans who fought with this unit.

(Left) According to the SA-Standarte *Feldherrnhalle* news-sheet, this Oberfeldwebel of the Panzergrenadier Division *Feldherrnhalle* distinguished by single-handedly destroying a Russian tank, Winter 1943.

The standard of the SA adopted by the *Feldherrnhalle* units would appear during the Nîmes parade escorted by two *Ritterkreuzträger* belonging to the two elite units of the German Army: the *Großdeutschland* (right) and the *Feldherrnhalle* (left).

A group of veterans of the Panzer-Grenadier Division *Feldherrnhalle*. Few of these men would survive the disaster of the collapse of Army Group Centre during the Summer of 1944.

Images of the Panzer-Grenadier Division *Feldherrnhalle* on the Eastern Front in 1944. Soldiers of the *Feldherrnhalle* marching towards their positions on the central sector of the Eastern Front.

A group of highly-decorated veterans of the *Feldherrnhalle* are
received by Goebbels. Among them are Major Wilhelm Schöning (first
left) and Oberleutnant Herbert Berger (sixth left).

Generalmajor Werner Fromert, commander of the Ersatz und
Ausbildungs Brigade *Feldherrnhalle*, with (on his left) his Adjutant,
Oberleutnant Peters

Generalmajor Hyazinth Graf
Strachwitz von Gross-Zauche und
Camminetz, under whose command
the soldiers of the *Feldherrnhalle*
served during the Battle of Narva.

Gefreiter Reinhold Neumann. On this
excellent study can be seen all the
'distinctions' of the *Feldherrnhalle* units.

This photograph was taken during the official reception offered to the directors of the Foreign Student Association and Cultural Attachés of the various embassies by the Humboldt Klub, the Students Association of the Humboldt University of Berlin, which took place in the club's rooms on 19th November 1943.
In it we can see Dr Gmelin (right), Honourary President of the Humboldt Klub since may 1943, in conversation with the head of the Spanish students. Despite the fact that he was a *Bereichleiter* of the Party (Chief of a Gau department) he wears the field grey Army uniform of a *Stabsgefreiter*. Above the left pocket can be seen the ribbons of the War Merit Cross 2nd Class, Eastern Campaign Medal and one other not identified. On the pocket he wears the badge of the *Altherrenbund der Deutschen Studenten* (German University Alumni Association) and the War Merit Cross 1st Class. On the cuff is the distinctive *Feldherrnhalle* cuff-title. Considering the date, Dr Gmelin must served in the Panzer-Grenadier Division *Feldherrnhalle*.

Sturmgeschütz of the
Panzergrenadier Division
Feldherrnhalle.

Prisoners are brought in, including
women.

The section commander of a
Schützenpanzerwagen (APC).

Panzergrenadiers move forwards for the attack under the protection
of a StuG

In the turret of a *Panzerspähwagen* (Armoured Scout Car).

Panzergrenadiers move out from the jump-off point to the attack.

A section 'bails out' and goes over to the fighting on foot.

Speed and superiority of fire-power made the Panzergrenadier an enemy to be feared.

The Panzergrenadier fought with the most modern weapons of war.

The Cannon-armed Panzerspähwagen. Speed, manoeuvrability and heavy firepower were its hallmarks.

Oberst Albert Henze, (here in General's uniform) commander of the Panzergrenadier Division *Feldherrnhalle* between 13th February 1944 and 13th April 1945.

Hauptmann Erich Oberwöhrmann, one of the most experienced commanders of the *Feldherrnhalle* Panzer units. He won his Knight's Cross on 7th February 1944, for his audacity leading the Panzer batallion of the Panzergrenadier Division *Feldherrnhalle.*

Major Wilhelm Schöning, one of the most charismatic leaders of the *Feldherrnhalle.* As a reward for his heroic performance during the battles which occurred during the siege of Budapest, he received the Oak Leaves to his Knight's Cross.

CHAPTER III

The New *Feldherrnhalle* Panzer Formations

The SS-Panzergrenadier Division *Feldherrnhalle*

During the second half of July 1944, the survivors of the destroyed Panzergrenadier Division *Feldherrnhalle* began to be withdrawn from the Russian Front. For some of these men, evacuated from Stalingrad by some miracle during the previous winter, this was no more than macabre repeat of the disaster suffered by the then 60th Infantry Division (mot). Few of these weary survivors would have been able to hazard a guess at the ambitious plans for the reconstruction of the lost unit which were circulating in the offices of one of the most powerful organisations in the Third Reich, Himmler SS.

In 1943, its reconstituted had been verified, albeit in a rather particular way, so as to accentuate the presence, at its core, of the SA within the framework of the Army. This time, as the *Reichsführer*'s military specialists had planned, things were going to be different. They argued that it was the Waffen-SS, as the true representation of the 'New National-Socialist Ideological Army' that should be responsible for the task of reconstructing the *Feldherrnhalle* Division[44]. Still plagued by lack of manpower, the Waffen-SS had already tried to enlist young SA recruits to its ranks; it had even created a special emblem for them, a black rhombus with the SA symbol in silver, which was hardly used due to the lack of enthusiasm with which the Brownshirts greeted these plans[45].

Now, however, with the official sanction that the Führer himself had given to their aspirations, the Waffen-SS officers hoped, with one last triumph, to make up for the disappointments suffered so far in this area. Letting its own imagination run away with it, they even planned the creation of an entirely new Corps, where SA volunteers would fight under the flags of the *siegrunen*, organised in two new divisions: the SS-Freiwillige Panzergrenadier Division *Feldherrnhalle* and the SS-Freiwillige Panzergrenadier Division *Horst Wessel*.[46]

However, despite the time which had elapsed since the last confrontation, and the large numbers of deserters, above all from the SA-Führers who had left the organisation in search of better opportunities wearing the black uniform, of the many

---

[44] Werbschrift für die *Feldherrnhalle*, p 27, copy in the possession of the author.

[45] R J. Bender and Hugh Page Taylor Uniforms, Organisations and History of the Waffen-SS Bender Publications, San José, California, USA. Vol. I p.101, and Rudolf Kahl Uniforms and Badges of the III Reich Military Collectors Service, Holland, Vol. II pp.88-89.

[46] Résumé of the meeting held between Hitler and the Reichsführer-SS on 16 June 1944. Dr. Klietman. Other references to the plans for the constitution of the SS-Freiwilligen Division *Feldherrnhalle* can be found in the article by Richard Landwehr, Waffen-SS divisions that never were! Siegrunen, Vol 5 No 1 (25) p 7, Glendale, Oregon, USA, March 1981

campaigns which had been orchestrated since 1934 to encourage camaraderie between the SA and SS, the old grudges and rivalries persisted and the bulk of the SA, from where the recruits for these new formations should have come, failed to demonstrate the slightest interest in enlisting. It was again shown that, for the most part, they still preferred to fulfil their military obligations as simple soldiers in the Wehrmacht.

Moreover, if what was really expected was that the survivors of the Panzergrenadier Division *Feldherrnhalle* be incorporated into the new SS formations, there can be no doubt that the plan would have met with the opposition of the veterans, especially those belonging to the officer corps, who felt better able to identify with the military traditions of their former *Danzig* unit than with the paramilitary militias of the Nazi regime[47]. Nevertheless, the lack of SA volunteers and the subsequent abandonment of the plan by Himmler reduces all this to mere speculation.

Thus, the SS-Freiwillige Panzergrenadier Division *Feldherrnhalle* was only to exist on paper and although the SS-Freiwillige Panzergrenadier Division *Horst Wessel* would operate as such, despite possessing the name of one of the martyrs most venerated by the SA, it had, for the most part, to fill its ranks from among the Hungarian *Volksdeutsches*[48]. The mission to reorganise and equip the new *Feldherrnhalle* division was to continue to be the absolute responsibility of the Army. For its part, the OKH also appeared to be attracted by the idea of exploiting the reorganisation to increase its size, putting down the bases of a future Panzerkorps *Feldherrnhalle*.

At that point in time, the Wehrmacht was trying to rebuild its armoured forces by means of the organisation of the Panzerbrigades. These were formed from the basis of the Panzer Abteilung and a battalion of Panzergrenadiers. These Brigades would then be assimilated by the remainder of those Divisions which had been destroyed or weakened to generate new Panzer Divisions. Finally, these divisions unified their administrative and support services within the framework of a Corps. It was in line with this outline that the question of a new elite *Feldherrnhalle* unit was to be posed[49].

Phoenix I. Autumn 1944

However, all the plans previously mentioned went unnoticed by the group of survivors, in whose minds the harsh images of death and destruction which they had witnessed during Army Group Centre's great disaster were still fresh. The majority of them were taken to the Warthelager Training Ground, in Posnania, situated in *Wehrkreis* XX, while the rest, some 400, remained in the *Mielau* camp, in Western Prussia, in *Wehrkreis* I. Both groups were to form the embryos of the new *Feldherrnhalle* units.

In Warthelager, the veterans remained under the orders of *Oberst* Günther Pape, a competent officer whose conduct with the 3rd Panzer Division now permitted him to wear the *Knights Cross* with Oak leaves with pride before the new soldiers. His

---

[47] The only work dedicated to a *Feldherrnhalle* formation, <u>Die Panzerbrigade 106 *Feldherrnhalle*</u>, written by Fredrich Bruns, states, in the first pages, that these were soldiers like any others. This is also the position which is maintained by the present Kamaradeschaften, of the 106 *Feldherrnhalle* and the *Feldherrnhalle* Division. Moreover, the detailed correspondence which the author had kept up with veterans of these units also confirms the desire of these veterans to restate that they were of a strictly military nature. Although these statements are necessarily partial and although, as Klaus Woche assures me with regard to the relationship between the SA and the division, the veterans avoid certain realities regarding their unit, it remains true that the majority of these units, headed by their officers, did to a certain extent, identify themselves with the Nazi paramilitary formations, to the point where they renounced their status as regular soldiers in the Army.

[48] It had been planned that all the insignias, collar patch emblems and vehicle signs of the 'Horst Wessel' would incorporate the SA insignia, but in fact none of them did eventually use it.

[49] For more information on these plans, I refer the reader to the work of Albert Seaton <u>German Army 1939-45</u> (1985) Meridian Book, New York, pp.242 and 264-267.

injuries had kept him away from the Front for a long period and following his graduation from the Divisional Commander's course, he had been sent to Warthelager[50]. His mission there was not an easy one. He had to blend the long-awaited mass of recruits with the handful of survivors until he was able to structure them into new combat units. Nevertheless, it is also true that, in addition to the preferential treatment which the OKH gave the *Feldherrnhalle* in terms of armaments and reserves[51], and the enormous war experience accumulated by these men, it was also able to draw on the invaluable competence of *Oberstleutnant* Hans Schöneich, who occupied the post of Chief-of-Staff.

In principle, the weary survivors were grouped according to their weapons in cadre battalions. Thus, in *Arys*, the I (self-propelled) Battalion of the Artillery Regiment (mot) *Feldherrnhalle* (I(Sfl)/Art.Rgt.(mot)*FHH*) was formed from the artillerymen; the infantry was concentrated in the I (armoured) Battalion/Panzergrenadier Regiment *Feldherrnhalle* (I(gp)/Pz.Gren.Rgt.*FHH*) and those belonging to the Panzertruppen formed a reduced Panzer Abteilung *Feldherrnhalle* (Pz.Abt.*FHH*). Very soon, the reserve units for the Division began to send personnel; the vast majority coming from the regions where the division usually recruited, although it should be said that a certain number of them had been through the SA training battalions. Together with them returned groups of convalescents and men on leave, such that within a few days, the veterans of these three battalions were already spread out among the new regiments, their own experience making up for their comrades' rawness.

The reborn *Feldherrnhalle* Grenadier Regiment, partly thanks to the inclusion of a complete battalion of Jägers that, under the denomination of Jäger Battalion *Feldherrnhalle* had been organised in Dresden within Wehrkreis IV (Saxony), was again composed of three battalions. Apart from this regiment, a fourth battalion that was destined to serve as a back-up force in one of the mentioned Panzerbrigades was also established under the name of Panzergrenadier Bataillon (gepanzerte) 2110 *Feldherrnhalle*.

The Artillery Regiment also made up its numbers. Its preparation was due, in large part, to the good work of *Hauptmann* Adolf Lepach, who in the process demonstrated organisational capabilities that were just as outstanding as his conduct in battle. His efficiency, however, would separate him from his old unit since the High Command took him up again in Warthelager, giving him the opportunity to make a career as an officer on the General Staff.

The majority of the veterans of the Panzertruppe, together with the reserves that they had received from the 10th and 18th Reserve Battalions (10th and 18th *Ersatz Abteilungen*) were grouped in the new Panzer Abteilung 2110 *Feldherrnhalle*, while the rest were destined for a battalion of assault cannon known as the Panzerjäger/Sturmgeschütz Abteilung *Feldherrnhalle*[52].

Within the OKH plans for the constitution of a Panzerkorps *Feldherrnhalle*, and with a view to the divisions of which it was composed having real links with the former Panzergrenadier Division, the assembly of the units established in Warthelager was carried out following two different tactical structures.

---

[50] For more information on his biography, see Appendix E: *Feldherrnhalle* Generals.

[51] The fact that this division enjoyed privileges with respect to the distribution of arms and personnel appears to be demonstrated by the speed with which its reorganisations were carried out and is due both to the special attention which was given it for political reasons, as well as its inclusion of the most favourable plans of the OKH. This point was also personally confirmed to the author by *Major* d.R.d.Bw. and *Hauptmann* a.D.u.Kdr.d.I/Pz.Art.Rgt.*FHH*, Erich Kelin.

[52] The technical details of the reorganisation of the division have been taken from the work of Rolf Stoves Die gepanzerten und motorisierten deutschen Grossverbände 1935-1945 (1986) Podzun-Pallas-Verlag, Bad-Nauheim, Germany, p. 247

Thus, the Grenadier Regiment, the Artillery Regiment and the Battalion of Assault Cannon, together with other lesser formations, were grouped under the orders of *Oberst* Pape in one unit which was obviously not of sufficient size to be termed a division and which, when it was mobilised, would be known as the Kampfgruppe Panzergrenadier Division *Feldherrnhalle*. On the other hand, the Panzer Abteilung and the Grenadiers of the 2110 formation formed the bulk of the 110th Panzerbrigade *Feldherrnhalle*, whose command would be entrusted to one of the most highly-decorated officers from the former division, *Oberstleutnant* Georg Wilhelm Schöning.

As we can see, at first glance the two units seemed to complement each other and together they would have amounted to an entire division, but, in accordance with OKH directives, they were to be completed by the assimilation of other men with whom the two *Feldherrnhalle* divisions, which were destined to operate together, would conform. They were divisions with new structures whose origins were thus located directly in the Panzergrenadier Division *Feldherrnhalle*. Nevertheless, the development of events would impose its own pace upon the establishment of the Panzerkorps *Feldherrnhalle*.

As the new *Feldherrnhalle* formations were being prepared at the end of the summer of 1944, the Wehrmacht was on the retreat on virtually all fronts. In the west, the Allied forces were closing in on the frontiers of the Reich with great strides; most of Italy had been lost and Finland had had to be evacuated. On the Eastern Front, following the collapse of Army Group Centre, the Russians had advanced as far as the gates of *Warsaw* itself and, having cornered a large number of troops in Courland, were now posing a direct threat to German territory in East Prussia.

In the Balkans, Germany had seen how her former allies, Romania and Bulgaria, had turned their weapons against her; the south-eastern front, protected by a weak line of weary units, was also on the point of collapse. It was the precariousness of the situation that motivated the mobilisation and transfer of the *Feldherrnhalle* units, still in the process of re-organisation, to Hungary, where they were to continue their preparations. In this manner, by mid-August, (barely a month after the tragedy in Russia), the first trains, overcrowded with the soldiers from Schöning, left Pomerania and headed south.

By travelling through allied Slovakia, the men of the 110th Panzerbrigade *Feldherrnhalle* reached their new encampments at the Training Ground at Örkény, situated 35 kms to the south of Budapest, within a few hours. There they received 100 or so armoured vehicles and, most importantly, 36 *Panther* tanks which were to form the basis of their fire-power.

Following in their footsteps, at the beginning of September, the Kampfgruppe Panzergrenadier Division *Feldherrnhalle* was established in Miskolc, in the north of the country where, having received the rest of its equipment, it turned to completing its training by means of a series of courses in combat and tactical exercises.

On 14th September, whilst their comrades of the 110th Panzerbrigade *Feldherrnhalle* were already working on security missions in the outskirts of the politically-unstable Magyar capital, *Oberst* Günther Pape was officially appointed as Führer, or interim Commander, of the Kampfgruppe Panzergrenadier Division *Feldherrnhalle*.

The 13th Panzer Division *Feldherrnhalle*

At the end of September, the Örkény Training Ground began to record an unusual amount of activity caused by the arrival of the remaining veterans of the 13th

Panzer Division[53]. Having suffered great losses during the last battles fought in Russia and Romania, this unit had been able, albeit only partially, to reform some of its tactical elements, thanks in particular to the OKH having sent several *Feldersatz Marschkompanie* from Wehrkreis XI (Central Germany - from where the division originated), Wehrkreis XX (West Prussia) and Wehrkreis XVII (Northern Austria).

A group of soldiers from the *Feldherrnhalle* reserve battalions had already served in the 13th Panzer Division. A few months earlier in fact, on 31st May 1944, a Grenadier Regiment known as the 1030th Panzergrenadier Regiment *Feldherrnhalle* had been incorporated into the division to complete the 93rd Panzergrenadier Regiment that had been greatly weakened by the huge losses incurred on the Dnyestr. Although these forces had been all but destroyed in August 1944, they would bring with them some consequences which would culminate, as we will see, in the following autumn when, at the end of September, *Oberst* Gerhard Schmidhuber (who had scarcely taken on the leadership of the 13th)[54] was to receive an order to join the remains of this unit with the 110th Panzerbrigade *Feldherrnhalle*. From this union would come another of the Panzer Divisions planned by the OKH, whose command, moreover, was to fall to the mentioned *Oberst*. With amazing speed and the co-operation of the *Feldherrnhalle* officers, the assembly operation was mounted such that, by early October, the OKH orders had already become a reality.

Thus, the former Commander of the disbanded 110th Panzerbrigade *Feldherrnhalle*, *Oberstleutnant* Georg Wilhelm Schöning, remained as commander of the new 66th Panzergrenadier Regiment; in which two battalions were now grouped together, the first composed of the men from the former 2110 Panzergrenadier Battalion (gp) 2110 *Feldherrnhalle*, of that Brigade, and the second, composed of the reinforced remains of the old 66th Panzergrenadier Regiment of the 13th Panzer Division.

In the same way, the Panzer Abteilung 2110 *Feldherrnhalle* was united with the Panzer Abteilung of the 13th which breathed new life into the decimated 4th Panzer Regiment, while the lesser units of the Brigade were distributed throughout the new nucleus of Divisional Troops. Equally, we should highlight the fact that in order to compensate for the many casualties, several *Feldherrnhalle* officers were transferred to other units within the new division.

In this way, on 1st October 1944, deploying four regiments, two of infantry, one of artillery and one of Panzers, in addition to other lesser units, the new 13th Panzer Division *Feldherrnhalle* was born[55]. The same day that he took command, Schmidhuber was promoted to *Generalmajor* and *Oberstleutnant* i.G. Arthur von Ekesparre, who

---

[53] Upon his arrival at the Örkény Training Ground, the 13th Panzer Division had an infantry regiment, a tank battalion, two artillery battalions, one signals battalion, and another of engineers.

[54] For more details on his biography, see Appendix E: *Feldherrnhalle* Generals.

[55] There is some controversy as to the true denomination adopted by the new division. It appears that the name which, from then on, identified the unit formed from the unification of the 13th Pz.Div. and the Pz.Brig.110 *Feldherrnhalle* was the 13th Panzer Division *Feldherrnhalle*. The first reference that the author could find of the existence of this denomination appeared in the memoirs and documents provided by the Kameradschaft der Angehörigen der ehermaligen 60 ID (mot) und deren *FHH*-Nachfolgerverbände, the association of veterans of the *Feldherrnhalle* Division; a denomination which, moreover, appears more in line with the new reality of the division. Veterans of the 13th Panzer Division confirmed to the author the incorporation of the term *Feldherrnhalle* at the same time as the mentioned unification (K.Bentin *Oberleutnant* in the 13th *Feldherrnhalle* Panzer Division, them *Major* of the Bundeswehr. Latter to the author, dated 22.11.1989.).

However, the 13th Pz.Div/Tradtitionsverband does not recognise the adoption of the name *Feldherrnhalle* by its unit in February 1945 when, from the remains of the 13th *Feldherrnhalle* Panzer division, the 2nd *Feldherrnhalle* Panzer Division was organised. It must be said, however that this is backed-up by the notes belonging to *Generalmajor* Franz Bäke's, (last commander of the division who was not to take command until 9 March 1945). On the other hand, the objective of the plans of the OKH with respect to the *Feldherrnhalle* Panzerkorps, was to organise the divisions, as they were later to be organised, as the 1st and 2nd *Feldherrnhalle* Panzer Divisions, so that the previous situation had to be joined with the provisional nature which the denomination employed was to have, more than anything for propaganda motives, but which, in honour of the truth, is a better reflection of the division than any other.

before long would adorn his uniform with the *Knights Cross*, was to serve in the post of Head of Operations with its Staff.

Counter-attack Force in Hungary

Early in October 1944, the disaster suffered by the Germans on the southern flank of the Eastern Front had cost Army Group South more than 100,000 men. So as to avoid complete annihilation, its Commander-in-Chief, *Generaloberst* Johannes Frießner, under whose orders the *Feldherrnhalle* had already fought to the north of the Peipus, had been forced to retreat with its two armies, the 16th - commanded by *General der Artillerie* Maximilian Fretter-Pico - and the 8th - under *General der Infanterie* Otto Wöhler - behind the Hungarian border where in difficult conditions it tried to construct a new defensive Front.

Due to this enforced movement, the German troops in Greece and Yugoslavia launched a mad dash to avoid becoming besieged; but what was most important was that the Ploeşti oil fields, which for the last few years had been breathing life into the German war machine, had been lost forever.

On the 6th October, whilst virtually the entire length of the Eastern Front was relatively calm, the Russian armies unleashed the so-called Operation *Debrecen* from the south-east, the objective of which was the conquest of the rest of Transylvania and western Hungary; a manoeuvre which would also permit them to prevent the retreat of the entire 8th Army and establish the necessary bases for the future assault on Budapest. Operating with powerful armoured formations, the Soviets broke through to the north, concentrating their efforts on the cities of Arad and Salonta. The Hungarian troops were crushed by the first onslaught and the Russian tanks swiftly began to open large breaches in the defence mechanism mounted by the eroded units of the 6th Army.

A few hours after the attack, in the Headquarters of the 13th Panzer Division *Feldherrnhalle*, Schmidhuber received his first order to go to war as a *Generalmajor*. The division, now assigned to the III Panzerkorps of *General der Panzertruppen* Hermann Breith, was to go swiftly into combat, following the Szolnok-Debrecen axis to cut off the spearhead of the enemy attack by the flank and link up, in the Püspökladany region, with the 1st Panzer Division of *Oberst* Eberhardt Thunert. This would allow them to re-establish the continuity of the Front.

As quickly as possible, a rapid intervention group was organised whose combat force was composed of *Major* Bernhard Gehring's *Panthers* and the first battalion of Grenadiers from the 66th Panzergrenadier Regiment which was highly mobile thanks to their supply of armoured vehicles. The Austrians of the Reconnaissance Battalion (Pz.Aufkl.Abt.13) who were at its head had already departed.

On the cuffs of many tank drivers and grenadiers could be seen the brown cuff-titles which reflected their links with the old *Feldherrnhalle*. In this way, since the soldiers serving under Pape were still in Miskolc, it was their comrades of the 13th Panzer Division *Feldherrnhalle* to whom should be attributed the honour of marking the return of the *Feldherrnhalle* to the War in the East.

Nevertheless, this advance was not going to be easy for, just a few hours after it started, Gehrings' vanguards were shattered in Karcag against solid anti-tank positions with which the enemy flanks were equipped. This contingency gave Schöning the opportunity to discover what his men were made of.

With the precision and agility which they had obtained over the course of their intensive training, and under the expert direction of their veterans, the soldiers of the 66th Panzergrenadier Regiment launched an assault on the Russian positions. Within

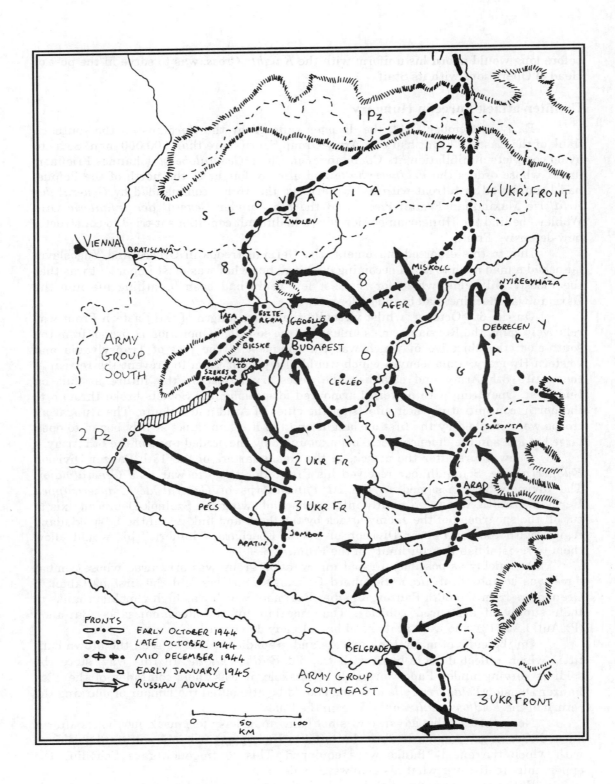

Operations of the *Feldherrnhalle* Divisions in Hungary. Evolution of the Front Lines of the Army Groups to Late 1944

a few hours, following a violent confrontation, they succeed in expelling the enemy from their trenches and parapets and forced them to retreat to the south. Again the creaking sound of the heavy *Panther* tracks could be heard and the advance route was unobstructed.

The speed with which the action had been achieved allowed Gehring's tank drivers to surprise the armoured Russian forces which were concentrated on the outskirts of Püspökladany, crushing them before they had time to react. By the afternoon, the grenadiers occupied the city and by the following morning, Schmidhuber could know with satisfaction that they had managed to establish contact with the 1st Panzer Division to the south-east of the city. A little while later, while the I/93rd Panzergrenadier Regiment and II/66th Panzergrenadier Regiment battalions were entrusted with the task of combing the terrain, the artillery, with the rest of the 13th Panzer Division *Feldherrnhalle*, prepared itself for defence.

The coup carried out by the 13th Panzer Division *Feldherrnhalle* temporarily halted the progress of Operation *Debrecen* in that sector, for the breach through which the key manoeuvre by the Russians was to have come, had been closed and had consequently isolated their vanguard forces. From then onwards, the main objective of the Russians was to break through the reconstituted front of the German III Corps at any price.

Schmidhuber was conscious of what was to come upon them. His radio-operators had managed to intercept a series of enemy messages which left no room for doubt regarding their intentions. Thus far, the expertise and fearlessness of his men had achieved his first triumphs, but what would happen when the Russians pitted the enormous numbers of men and machines opposite them, upon the Division?

On the 9th, their positions, which extended the length of the access route to Debrecen, suffered all the intensity of the offensive power of the Red Army. The clash was brutal. In Karcag, enemy pressure was soon unbearable and they only managed to bear it in Püspökladany at the cost of great losses. The harshly-punished zone of contact with the 1st Panzer Division was scarcely maintained by a single company of Füsiliers. The tanks of the 4th Panzer Regiment tried to reach the most threatened areas and only the rapid deployment of the Grenadiers of the I/66th Panzergrenadier Regiment would save the link with the 1st Panzer Division that maintained, albeit only for a few hours, the continuity of the Front.

However, neither the great fighting spirit of these units nor the personal heroism of soldiers such as *Leutnant* Fix who, within the space of a few minutes managed to destroy six enemy tanks, would be sufficient to make amends for the obvious inequality of the fight. Schmidhuber's men had held their ground and, paying the price of great losses, had borne the Russian assault, but as time went by, the danger of disintegration steadily increased. With the aim of avoiding the complete destruction of the unit, they began to retreat to the north, to a more favourable line of defence that was to be established to the south-west of Nádudvar. However, the movement itself conceded the loss of the link with the 1st Panzer Division. The Front had fallen again.

Both the Russians and the Germans had accurately gauged the consequences of this break. If the Soviets managed to send in all their armoured vehicles, all the 8th Army, which was retreating from the Carpathian Mountains, towards the Tisza, would find itself hopelessly besieged. For this reason, the primary concern of the Germans was to now halt this penetration, at least for as long as was necessary to allow the retreat of Wöhler's Divisions.

Under pressure from the lack of reserves, Army Group South decided to mobilise what they had at hand. Among the available troops was the Kampfgruppe Panzergrenadier Division *Feldherrnhalle* that awaited the arrival of the 109th

Panzerbrigade in Miskolc which it was to join to form the planned Panzer Division *Feldherrnhalle*. However, both units were to be alerted and, if they were to fight in the same sector, it would be as independent formation within the 6th Army.

Without even having completed the organisation process, Pape's soldiers received the order to repel the Russian tanks and re-establish the link that had been lost with the III Panzerkorps to which they were now subordinated. It was an order that appeared ask a great deal more than they were capable of, but it was no more than a consequence of the lack of reserves suffered by Frießner.

They were once again launched into battle in the sector most fraught with conflict, among exhausted units, against an enemy that was greatly superior both in terms of men and weaponry. In spite of it all, on 11th October the men of the Kampfgruppe Panzergrenadier Division *Feldherrnhalle*, fighting side-by-side with their comrades from the 109th Panzerbrigade and the 13th Panzer Division *Feldherrnhalle*, succeeded, after an enormous effort which appeared *a priori* impossible, in stemming the breaches which had opened between the 1st Panzer Division and the 13th Panzer Division *Feldherrnhalle*.

The crisis once again seemed to be under control. Now, the main concern was to contain the Russians long enough to allow the retreat of their comrades behind the Tisza. To this end, the *Feldherrnhalle* units mounted a series of fierce local attacks to the west and north-west of Debrecen which would serve to minimise the progress of the enemy. During this fighting, all the units planned by the OKH for the future Panzerkorps *Feldherrnhalle*, had operated together for the first time.

By the middle of the month, both the 13th Panzer Division *Feldherrnhalle* and the Kampfgruppe Panzergrenadier Division *Feldherrnhalle* received an order to retreat to the north to reinforce the defensive mechanism mounted in front of the Tisza, a mechanism that was to protect the escape routes for the 8th Army. Thus, the 13th Panzer Division *Feldherrnhalle* remained deployed in the Hortobagy-Puszta zone whilst, further to the north, the Kampfgruppe Panzergrenadier Division *Feldherrnhalle* took charge, from the 21st, of protecting the Hajduböszörmeny and from that date onwards, the defence of the Tisza crossings in Polgar.

The transfer of these units coincided with the re-starting of the Russian advance to such an extent that, within a few hours, their armoured vanguards could be seen from Pape's new positions. The cavalcade of Russian tanks had even impressed the Germans. However, in their desire to reach Wöhler's rearguard, progress had been made in parallel with the German deployment, dangerously exposing their left flank to the Divisions of the 6th Army. This flank, moreover, was particularly poorly protected due to the problems which the Soviet infantry had encountered in following the pace of their armoured forces. Stalin's Generals were aware of the risk that this might entail, but decided to ignore it in the belief that the Germans were too weakened to mount a counter-attack.

But, just as the Allies were surprised in the Ardennes, the God of War had kept back a surprise for the Russians concerning the amazing recovery capabilities of the German units. For the Commander of Army Group South, the time had come to make them pay dearly for their oversight. Without a moment's hesitation, on 23rd October 1944, Frießner launched one of his units perpendicular to the Russian flank, while the Divisions of the 8th Army supported the action from the east.

The Kampfgruppe Panzergrenadier Division *Feldherrnhalle*, the 109th Panzerbrigade, recently arrived from Debrecen, and the rest of the units of the III Panzerkorps jumped from their positions and, via Nyíregyháza, launched themselves on the Soviet positions. In front of the Tisza, the Russians would still have an opportunity to feel the power of attack of these formations.

Supported by their artillery, the *Panthers* marched in the vanguard, followed by the armoured vehicles carrying grenadiers. *Major* Gehring, Commander of the I/Pz.Rgt.4, described these actions in the following words; "The men of my Kampfgruppe were composed, in addition to my Panzer Abteilung, of II/66 and part of the 13th Panzer Artillery Regiment. At 10.00 we began the attack. We pounded the Russian flank, capturing the pieces of an entire artillery battalion, and even lorries of American origin loaded to the brim. Under cover of our tank fire, the grenadiers cleaned out the Russian positions. All that we did not need was destroyed instantly. *Oberleutnant* Erdmann (*Oberleutnant* Otto Erdmann, commander of the 2/Pz.Gren.Rgt.66), received the *Knights Cross* for this action (9.12.44)"[56].

All in all, according to an OKH communiqué, Frießner's counter-attack had cost the Russians about 20,000 men, (be they dead or taken prisoner), 900 cannon and 1,000 tanks. The Russian offensive was halted early enough to allow the retreat over the Tisza of the troops of the 6th Army; a movement that some would class as being just as important as that achieved in Russia in 1943.

Following the Divisions of the 8th Army, the rest of the German troops abandoned the eastern shores of the river. The 13th Panzer Division *Feldherrnhalle* would march within the III Corps as far as the zone to the south-east of Budapest; whilst the Kampfgruppe Panzergrenadier Division *Feldherrnhalle* established itself to the east of Hatvan, some 50 kms from the Hungarian capital where, finally, it appeared that the prescribed union with the 109th Panzerbrigade would take place.

In conclusion, we should say that the role played by the *Feldherrnhalle* units in conjunction with the operations carried out on the right-hand bank of the Tisza, was of fundamental importance[57]. Its men had repeatedly been used as combat forces, in the most threatened sectors on several occasions and had succeeded in containing and repelling enemy forces of far greater superior, saving the continuity of the Front. Eventually, the weight of the energetic counter-attacks which had permitted Wöhler's forces to escape had again fallen upon them. Actions such as these provide all the justification needed for the inclusion of the *Feldherrnhalle* formations amongst the most noteworthy elite formations of the German Army.

The Panzer Division *Feldherrnhalle*

As we noted earlier, at the end of October 1944, the Kampfgruppe Panzergrenadier Division *Feldherrnhalle* and the 109th Panzerbrigade, a formation that, in its final stages, had been under the command of the experienced *Feldherrnhalle* Grenadier *Oberstleutnant* Joachim Helmuth Wolff, joined together to the east of Hatvan[58]. The reorganisation of the men took place with the same speed and, broadly speaking, followed the same lines as in the case of the 13th Panzer Division *Feldherrnhalle*. Thus, the Panzergrenadier Regiment *Feldherrnhalle* of the Kampfgruppe Panzergrenadier Division *Feldherrnhalle* was stripped of its III Battalion so as to constitute, using the men from the 2109th Grenadier Regiment and the former staff of the Brigade, a new regiment which was to go under the name of Panzer Füsilier Regiment *Feldherrnhalle*.

Similarly, from the basis of Pape's Panzerjäger Abteilung *Feldherrnhalle* and the 2109th Panzer Abteilung, were respectively organised as the II and the I Abteilung of a

---

[56] Arbeitsgruppe 13 Pz.Div., Der Schicksalsweg der 13 Panzerdivision 1939-1945 (1986) Podzun-Pallas-Verlag, Freidberg, Germany, p205

[57] One of the best studies of the operations undertaken by the Tisza is the work of H Kissel Die Pz.Schlachten in der Puzsta im Oktober 1944 (1960) Neckargemünd, Germany.

[58] For more information, see Appendix C: 109th Panzerbrigade *Feldherrnhalle*

new Panzer Regiment *Feldherrnhalle* for the Division. The rest of the units of the Brigade - medical, Flak, maintenance personnel, supplies etc., were unified with their opposite numbers from the Kampfgruppe.

In this way, on 1st November 1944, the Panzer Division *Feldherrnhalle* was formed. Scarcely a week later, the former commander of the Kampfgruppe, still an *Oberst*, would be placed at its head, whilst *Oberstleutnant* Wolff, in much the same way as Schöning with the 13th Panzer Division *Feldherrnhalle*, came to lead the Panzergrenadier Regiment *Feldherrnhalle*.

Combat Beyond the Tisza

However, the defensive success of the Germans to the east of the Tisza had been achieved at a cost of great sacrifice. The human casualties had been high, but the losses incurred in terms of tanks and assault cannon were well above what the Wehrmacht could afford at that time. The hardy soldiers of the *Feldherrnhalle* divisions were confident that, after the last combats, the Russians would have no alternative than to halt so as to make up for their losses, thus enjoying a period of relative calm. Nevertheless, only a few hours had gone by since the last of their units had crossed the Tisza, when the Red Army again went on the offensive in the direction of Budapest.

From their bases in Kecskemét, a powerful offensive formation approached the capital, reaching the city of Cegléd situated 50 kms to the south-east. At the same time, from the Baja sector, just in the zone of contact between Frießner's troops and Army Group F, a dangerous pincer formation was taking shape that threatened to cut off the German supply routes, isolating Budapest from the west.

As a result, the *Feldherrnhalle* Divisions were not able to enjoy their well-deserved rest. The renewed attack was not only to keep these units on alert, but, moreover, was to make them aware that the weight of the counter-attack that the Germans were preparing, was going to fall, to a great extent, upon them. Schmidhuber received the order to mount a counter-attack under his own steam in the city of Ócsa, whilst Pape's men, together with the men from the Waffen-SS would do the same further to the north, in the Vecsés sector.

After their retreat from the Tisza, the 13th Panzer Division *Feldherrnhalle* had moved directly towards the south-east of Budapest, where it had barely had time to draw breath before, on 2nd November, the Division again got underway. Within a few hours, *Generalmajor* Schmidhuber received the first reports from his reconnaissance unit. According to this, the positions where they had envisaged organising their defence, had already been overrun by the enemy; the troops which had been garrisoned in that sector of the front had simply disappeared. As *Oberstleutnant* Schöning could see from the news, the town of Ócsa, in which his grenadiers were to be deployed, was already in Russian hands.

Further to the north, the troops of the recently-constituted Panzer Division *Feldherrnhalle* marched from the Hatvan zone. The outlook of its Commander was hardly any more favourable. An enemy formation, even more numerous than that which opposed their comrades, had taken Vecsés in the wake of irresistible advance. In spite of it all, the confidence that the command had placed in them was not to be proven misplaced, and having assessed the seriousness of the situation, the *Feldherrnhalle* soldiers reacted swiftly. *Oberstleutnant* Wilhelm Schöning, availing himself of only his staff and a squad of explorers, stood firm on the ground before Ócsa. Straight away, *Major* Gehring was deployed to head a Kampfgruppe again composed from the I/Pz.Rgt.4 and the I/Pz.Gren.Rgt.66, and, under orders to repel them, he launched himself upon the Soviet armoured columns. Similarly, the arrival of reinforcements enabled them to wipe

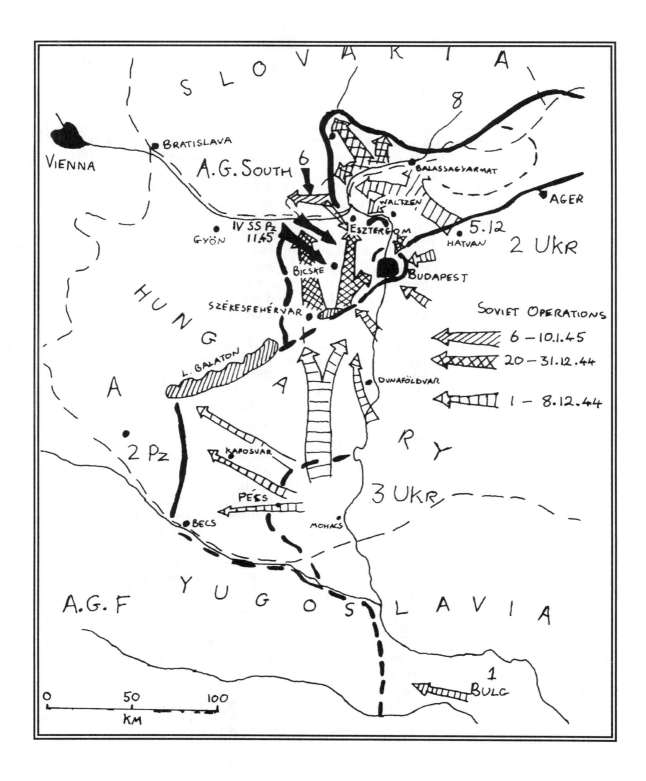

**Operations of the *Feldherrnhalle* Divisions in Hungary. Soviet
Movements Late 1944 - Early 1945**

out the penetration that the enemy had managed to achieve to the north of Ócsa and the city once again fell into German hands.

Further to the north, Pape's men operated with the 8th SS-Kavallerie Division *Florian Geyer* and some elements of the 13th Panzer Division *Feldherrnhalle*, which had arrived from the south and succeeded in containing the advance, expelling the Russians from Vecsés. The counter-attack was even to extend a few kilometres further to the east, as far as the city of Üllő, whose defensive positions initially contained his men. But Wolff's Grenadiers proved that they were as able as their comrades of the 13th Panzer Division *Feldherrnhalle* and, following some very violent fighting, the German flag was once again flying over the roofs of the city by dusk on 3rd November. A few hours later, these troops were on the defensive.

The Panzer Division *Feldherrnhalle* was entrusted with defending the sector situated to the south-east of Monor and to the north of Vecsés. This city, entrusted to the Waffen-SS, was lost once again within the space of a few hours and it was again the tanks and assault cannon of the *Feldherrnhalle* that constituted the spearhead of the operation organised to retake the city; which occurred, in fact, after a bloody street battle on 5th November 1944. It was to be more than a month before the Russians would again enter the city.

To sum up, the entry into combat of the *Feldherrnhalle* divisions had, as usual, proved to be decisive. The Russian offensive to the south-east of Budapest had been halted and its vanguards had been forced to retreat, allowing the Germans to recover the territory that they had lost. The intervention of the 13th Panzer Division *Feldherrnhalle*, mounting a counter-attack in the Ócsa sector and the decisive contribution of its men in the success of the operations undertaken further north, would merit recognition from Frießner himself, who was later to write that the paralysing of the Soviet advance which threatened Budapest from the south-east had been a direct consequence of the intervention of the 13th Panzer Division *Feldherrnhalle*[59].

Army Group South, for its part, reported that; "The enemy formations which advanced from Kecskemét were quickly repelled. Now they are in the Bugyi-Alsónémedi-Ócsa sector where they have been blocked by the 13th Panzer Division *Feldherrnhalle*. The success achieved by the enemy in its penetration of the bridgehead has been fleeting."

Following the counter-attack, both divisions were regrouped and assigned to the defence of new sectors. The 13th Panzer Division *Feldherrnhalle* momentarily left the Panzerkorps, for on the 5th it was subordinated to the LVII Panzerkorps, commanded by *General der Panzertruppen* Friedrich Kirchner. Under his orders, they would be involved in local actions aimed at "relieving the pressure" on the Budapest Front only to once again come under the orders of Breith (III Panzerkorps/Panzergruppe Breith) by the middle of the month, fixing positions to the north-east of the Hungarian capital. The Panzer Division *Feldherrnhalle*, which was now entrusted with covering the Gödöllő-Vác line, had been deployed just to its left for a few days.

According to the veterans, during this period, the 13th *Feldherrnhalle* would be profoundly tested in a defensive battle that would cost it dearly. Its artillery would have an opportunity to demonstrate that it was a key element in the system of containment and, on more than one occasion, its grenadiers would give proof of unparalleled fearlessness, re-conquering, albeit only briefly, the village of Vasad. But the greatest

---

[59] Johannes Frießner <u>Verratene Schlachten, Die Tragödie der deutschen Wehrmacht in Rumänien und Ungarn</u> (1956) Holsten-Verlag, Hamburg, Germany.

sacrifice made, (although it would not be translated into spectacular tactical consequences), may be perfectly grasped from the terrible increase in casualties[60].

By mid-December, the 66th and 93rd Panzergrenadier Regiments were decimated and the 4th Panzer Regiment could hardly count on a few tanks. Moreover, the losses had been particularly numerous among the command. There were units that had lost 50% of their officers. Some battalions were entrusted to *Leutnante*, and men of the stature of *Major* Gehring, to whom until that point the most important divisional counter-attack missions had been entrusted, had also been lost.

During those days, the Panzer Division *Feldherrnhalle* was also subjected to a harsh punishment, for during the 12th-14th, whilst other sectors were relatively calm, the Russians concentrated their attacks on the Division, launching its battalions continually in frenetic assaults; assaults which, one after another, were finally to be dashed on the defensive positions organised by Pape.

During the last fortnight of November, the north-eastern flank came under fierce pressure from the Russian forces who attempted to isolate Budapest from the north. The *Feldherrnhalle* soldiers not only held their positions, but also, when the situation demanded, handed over some of their men to help defend other threatened sectors. Thus it was on 23rd November, the day on which Pape had been forced to sent part of his Panzergrenadier Regiment *Feldherrnhalle* and *Hauptmann* Klein's assault cannon to the Csepel sector which was in the same suburbs of the capital, with the aim of containing the surprise attack which the Russians had unleashed in the sector. After several days of combat, these men, together with elements of the Waffen-SS, managed to halt enemy penetration and organise a defensive position.

This success of this action, which had been led by the Commander of the Grenadiers of the Panzer Division *Feldherrnhalle*, *Oberstleutnant* Joachim Hellmuth Wolff, hovered in the air during the celebration of the festival of its Patron, an event to which, in addition to the Commander of the Division, would also been invited several of the participating officers. That was to be the last relaxed occasion which Pape would be able to share with many of those men.

On 5th December, the Russians launched a fierce attack on the positions defended by the *Feldherrnhalle* Divisions to the north-east of the bridgehead in Budapest. For several hours, thanks primarily to the artillery, they managed to hold off the enemy's armoured columns. Finally, however, exploiting the Hungarian units' lack of anti-tank capacity, the Soviet armoured vehicles succeeded in infiltrating the flanks of the German units. Their reaction was to avoid a general collapse of the sector, but they were unable to prevent the enemy tanks from reaching the Danube in Vác, to the north of Budapest. Once the front had been broken, the situation was untenable and Pape and Schmidhuber soon received orders to retreat to a new defensive line which was practically on the outskirts of Hungarian capital.

In this way, the Panzer Division *Feldherrnhalle* retreated to the Dunakeszi-Alag-Kisalag-Fót line, while the 13th Panzer Division *Feldherrnhalle* retreated to between Fót and Rakospalota. After this retreat, the fate of both divisions, as well as the rest of the German troops in the bridgehead, was unmistakably decided.

During the last week of December, while pressure continued to be applied from the north, east and south, the Soviet division that advanced from the south-west managed to break through the German supply lines and link up on the Danube, with the units coming from the Vác. Destiny was thus to condemn the soldiers of the *Feldherrnhalle* to the desperate experience of a siege.

---

[60] <u>Arbeitsgruppe 13 Pz.Div</u> op.cit. pp 207-208

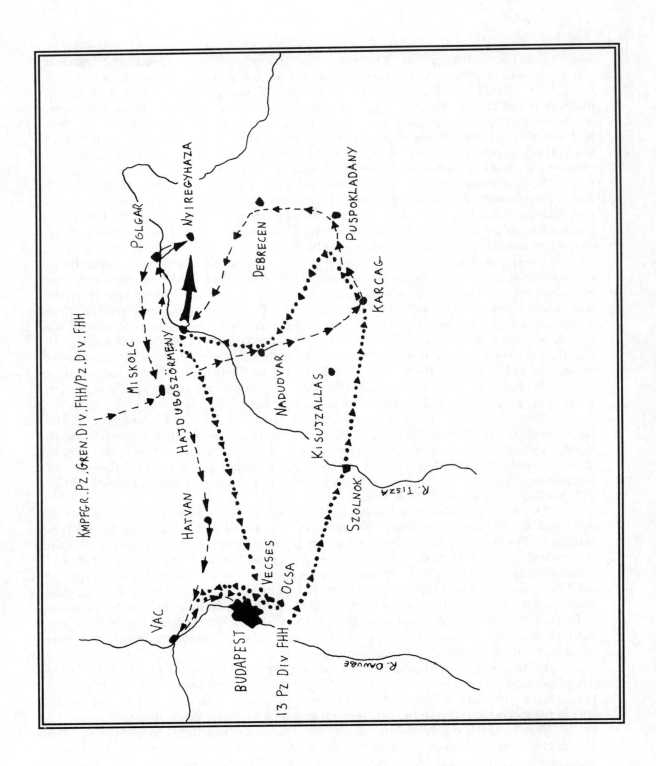

The *Feldherrnhalle* Divisions in Hungary

CHAPTER IV

Glory and Death in Budapest

Besieged!

In addition to the *Feldherrnhalle* Divisions, two Waffen-SS divisions, the remains of a few Hungarian divisions and a number of police, anti-aircraft and engineering units had also been trapped by the tenacious Soviet pincers[61]. In total, there were about 70,000 men, confronting whom were deployed more than twenty enemy divisions and brigades[62].

The Soviet Generals believed, and with good reason, that the conquest of Budapest would be over in two to three days. Obviously they failed to take into account the great fighting spirit of the men of the besieged units. From 25th December, they would remain under the command of *SS-Obergruppenführer und General der Polizei und der Waffen-SS* Karl von Pfeffer-Wildenbruch, as Commander-in-Chief of "Fortress Budapest"[63]. However, there were elements of the *Feldherrnhalle* divisions which were not besieged. These were part of the 13th Panzer Division *Feldherrnhalle*, its field hospital, part of the Pz.Nach.Abt.13 and some men from the maintenance units.

Nevertheless, the fortunate circumstances which applied to the Panzer Division *Feldherrnhalle* were not to prove as accidental as that of its comrades. As the Commander of the I/Pz.Art.Rgt.*Feldherrnhalle, Hauptmann* Erich Klein recounts, on 21st December, several days before the siege was consolidated, *Generalmajor* Pape had appeared in person in the Battalion's Command Post and, using the red combat

---

[61] In addition to the Panzer Division *Feldherrnhalle* and the 13th Panzer Division *Feldherrnhalle*, the units besieged in Budapest were broken down according to the Order of Battle of the Garrison of 'Fortress Budapest' at the end of December 1944. Source: Georg Maier <u>Drama zwischen Budapest und Wien. Der Endkampf der 6 Panzerarmee 1945</u> (1985) Munin Verlag, Osnabrück, p. 490.

GERMANS UNDER THE COMMAND OF IX SS-GEBIRGSKORPS
8th SS-Kavallerie Division *Florian Geyer*, 22nd SS-Kavallerie Division *Maria Theresia*, Kampfgruppe Kündiger, 6th SS-Polizei Regiment, 12th Flak Regiment, 751st Army Engineer Battalion, 4th Alarmbataillon; in total, including the *Feldherrnhalle* divisions, 33,000 men.

HUNGARIANS UNDER THE COMMAND OF I HUNGARIAN CORPS
10th and 12th Hungarian Infantry Divisions, the remains of the 1st Hungarian Armoured Division and the 1st Hungarian Cavalry Division, the Group Veresváry, the Anti-Aircraft Regiment *Budapest*, a self-propelled artillery Group (battalion), five Police battalions, three battalions of army engineers and two infantry battalions; in total, 37,000 men.

[62] In addition to two air fleets, the men of the Red Army deployed in Budapest at the end of December amounted to: 17 Infantry Divisions (two of them Romanian), two Mechanised Brigades, one Armoured and a Romanian Cavalry Division. Moreover, we should add the numerous armoured units and artillery assigned independently to the Army and Russian Army Group.

[63] Once the position was considered a 'Fortress' it relied on the OKW and all troops within it were grouped as a 'Garrison' under a single command.

telephone, had ordered that the Divisional Staff prepare to march to the Balaton where it should take charge of a Kampfgruppe. In this way, neither the General nor his Staff would be with the Division during the fateful days that were drawing near; according to R. Stoves, there was also a battalion of grenadiers marching with them, another of artillery, an anti-aircraft company, and one of engineers[64]. From then on, the command of the Division would be assumed by the Commander of the Panzergrenadier Regiment *Feldherrnhalle*, *Oberstleutnant* Joachim Helmuth Wolff[65].

Proposals to carry out an escape attempt to the west had been rejected by the OKH; the garrison in Budapest had to hold out at all costs, until they were liberated by a rescue operation mounted from the outside. The High Command endeavoured to make the enemy commit a large number of troops to the conquest of the city, which would have enabled the Wehrmacht to reconstruct the disjointed front. In view of this, there was no other option for those who found themselves besieged than to prepare to fight the defensive war that drew near.

For many of them, this was to be their sixth Christmas at war; a Christmas which brought to mind the Christmas that some of the *Feldherrnhalle* veterans had spent in the siege of Stalingrad two years ago. The same circumstances and the same obsessions had repeated themselves. Would their rescuers manage to reach them? Would it be possible for them to contain the Russians until then? But, above all, the greatest question was, would they be fortunate enough to return to Germany?

Christmas in the "Kessel"

The two *Feldherrnhalle* divisions were deployed to the east of the Danube. The Panzer Division *Feldherrnhalle* defended the northern zone, opposite the Ujpest district, whilst the positions of the 13th Panzer Division *Feldherrnhalle* extended from Fót as far as the district of Rakospalota, to the east and north-east of the capital. However, elements of the *Feldherrnhalle* divisions also fought, grouped into other formations, to the west of the Danube.

Even before the siege was completely closed, the command had decided to group together the remains of the tank regiments from both divisions and the self-propelled *Hummel* cannon from their artillery regiments into a rapid intervention force which was highly mobile and could call on significant firepower. Thus, on the night of 23rd-24th December, these elements had abandoned the sectors which were defended by their respective divisions and, under the denomination of Panzergruppe *Feldherrnhalle*, crossed the Danube making their way to the south-east of the city, where the principal assault forces of the enemy were concentrated at that time. While their comrades celebrated Christmas Eve 1944 in the austerity of their trenches to the east of the Danube, the soldiers of the Panzergruppe would be enveloped in an inferno to the west of this river. Thanks to the notes of the Commander of the *Hummel* Battalion of the Panzer Division *Feldherrnhalle*, were are able to reconstruct in some detail that tragic Christmas Eve.

During the course of its progression from the southern suburbs of Buda, the Panzergruppe reached Törökbálint, where it came across Russian positions which it destroyed without too much difficulty. During the afternoon, the primary encounters occurred in the hills to the north of Budaörs. Here, the entry into action of the

---

[64] Erich Klein, op.cit. p.42.
[65] The Commander of the Panzer Division *Feldherrnhalle*, together with his HQ (Stab/Pz.Div.*Feldherrnhalle*) headed a Kampfgruppe composed from the remains of the 11th Panzer Regiment and, as a part of the IV Panzerkorps, would participate in the rescue operations. In spite of the fact that contact, according to the veterans, was maintained between Wolff and Pape, the latter did not intervene directly in the conduct of the battle carried out by the Panzer Division *Feldherrnhalle* within the siege.

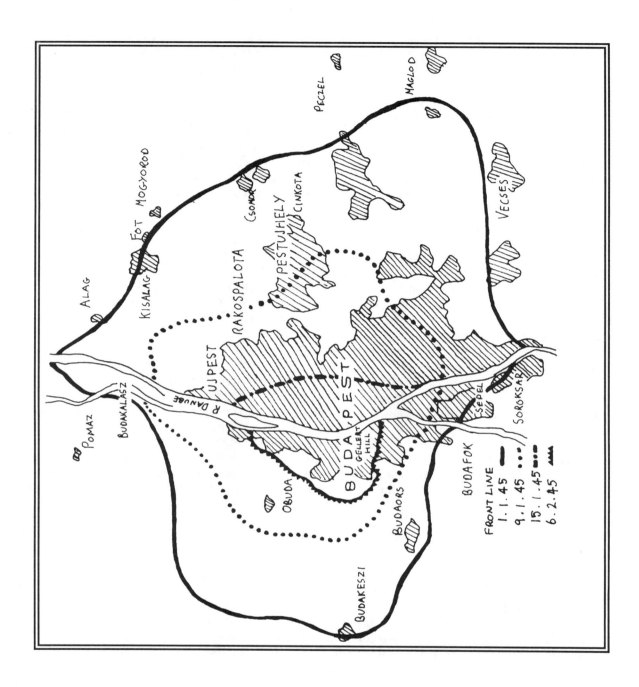

The Battle of Budapest

Feldherrnhalle armoured units allowed them to confront a large enemy attack. After a few hours, the Russians retreated, leaving on the battlefield a score of tanks and almost a thousand men. Thanks to this local success, the Germans were able to organised the defence of the sector as they wished.

Very soon, the solidity of the new positions would be tested. During Christmas Eve, the Russians again went on to a general attack; the Germans trenches were once again the scene of terrible hand-to-hand fighting. In spite of all this, the enemy was forced to retrace his steps without having achieved his goal. Nevertheless, the feeling of victory did not last long, for on Christmas morning, the Soviet artillery concentrated its attack on the tenacious soldiers of the Panzergruppe; those who had once thought of stopping the completion of the siege of Budapest with their few weapons now witnessed the enormous superiority of the Red Army reaffirming the unreality of their fleeting hopes.

The action unleashed by the Soviet artillery on that day had not only affected the sector defended by the *Feldherrnhalle* Panzergruppe, but had extended, with greater or lesser intensity, to the whole area under siege. Thus, the contingents of the *Feldherrnhalle* divisions which found themselves on the other side of the Danube would spend that Christmas subjected to one of the fiercest bombardments of its history. For the oldest amongst them, there was no room for doubts; the Russians were preparing the final assault on the Hungarian capital.

Once enemy efforts at penetration to the west had been halted, it turned to the zones in the east, north and south of the basin. On the 26th, whilst the Panzer Division *Feldherrnhalle* remained firm in its sector, the front defended by Schmidhuber's division was perforated to the south of Mogyoród. After almost two days of fighting, the enemy advance could be contained, albeit only momentarily, for on 29th December, supported by tanks and aircraft, the Russian infantry exploited the Hungarian units' little remaining combat capacity and succeeded in breaking through the lines of defence in the Csömör, from where they dominated one of the main access routes into Budapest. For a few hours at least, this incursion was contained by means of a counter-attack, but in the longer term, it was eventually to force the Germans to alter their positions by means of a retreat of the defensive perimeter.

Combat at the Eastern Bridgehead

Albeit at great cost, the Budapest garrison had succeeded, by means of a high number of casualties, in burdening the few advances made by the enemy until that point; as a veteran of the 13th Panzer Division *Feldherrnhalle* would recall, there was a certain frustration at the thought that the Russians could always replace their great numbers of men and machinery that were lost, whilst for them this was obviously impossible. In his own words, this soldier had hit the nail on the head, and as a result, it is not surprising that the greatest worry of the Commander-in-Chief of Budapest, rather than pressure from the enemy, was, at that time, the organisation of airborne supplies. If this was not carried out immediately, the Budapest garrison would not even be able to resist for another week.

During the night of the 29th-30th, the 'planes of the Luftwaffe brought in the first supplies, taking advantage of the return journey to evacuate two hundred and sixty eight of the several thousand of those who were injured and who, in inhuman conditions, quivered in the basements and refuges of the city. Almost a quarter of a million well-supplied Russian soldiers were deployed around the Budapest garrison, which was composed of tens of thousands of German and Hungarian soldiers - exhausted, bereft of heavy weaponry and permanently lacking in munitions and equipment. Ironically, the nearer the OKH got to attaining its objective, the worse the situation got for those who were besieged. On the last night of 1944, a concentrated force of 10,000 cannon unleashed a tempest of fire on the defenders' positions.

However, if 1944 had ended in brutal fashion, the first day of 1945 was to re-awaken the hopes of the garrison when the following message from the vanguard of the rescue forces sent by the High Command reached them; "We are on our way; hold out!"[66].

At the beginning of January, the airborne supply route had managed to alleviate, albeit rather precariously, the crisis of food and munitions. The command of the fortress concentrated the fire of the anti-aircraft pieces which they were able to gather together, so as to cover the vital routes and locations for the aeroplanes. At the same time, in an effort to replace the high numbers of casualties suffered, the rearguard services were sent to the front, where they mixed with the panzer and artillery soldiers who, following the destruction of their heavy weapons, were used as infantry.

Within a week, this scenario changed radically. The Russian artillery had destroyed the only aerodrome available which, moreover, in addition to rendering the evacuation of wounded men from then on impossible, also meant that airborne supplies would have to be brought in exclusively by air-drop, whose cargoes would not always end up in sectors dominated by the Germans. And as if this was not enough, during the second week of January there would be a worsening of the meteorological conditions which would completely rule out any aircraft taking to the air. The supply crisis reached incredible levels. To add insult to injury, the first rescue operation had to be suspended since it was impossible to break deeply enough into Russian positions. A second attempt also had to be cancelled a few days later[67].

All of this coincided with the unleashing of a powerful Russian offensive that was concentrated above all on the eastern sector of the pocket; a sector in which four-fifths of the *Feldherrnhalle* divisions found themselves garrisoned[68]. On 7th January, the Red Army broke through the Front at Kispest. Two days later, from the Csömör-Cinkota sector, deep enemy penetration advanced, irresistible, towards the Danube. As a result, the Panzer Division *Feldherrnhalle* was exposed in its sector and had to retreat, abandoning the district of Ujpest, whilst the 13th Panzer Division *Feldherrnhalle*, a great deal more affected by the attack, retreated to Rakospalota and Pestujhely. In the face of this enemy avalanche, Schmidhuber and Wolff were only able to field the daring of their men. Without the support of their heavy weapons, silenced by a lack of munitions, the infantry of the *Feldherrnhalle* divisions launched a desperate attempt to contain the Russians, an attempt that would end in terrible butchery. There was wild street fighting throughout the basin during that period.

One of the *Feldherrnhalle* veterans recalls; "With all hope of help from outside lost, the battle inside the siege continued, cruelly, in each and every house and street, every flat and basement; which demonstrates the great spirit of sacrifice of our soldiers"[69]. A journalist from a neutral country, a witness to the exceptional battle wrote; "It is a terrible battle, we have not seen anything like this since Stalingrad...Streets, and

---

[66] This was the message sent out by *SS-Obergruppenführer* Herbert Otto Gille, Commander-in-Chief of the IV SS-Panzerkorps and the person who, for those besieged, represented the last hope of getting out alive.

[67] The first two rescue operations sent to Budapest were 'Konrad 1' which was launched by the IV SS-Panzerkorps to the north-west of the capital between 1-8th January 1945, and 'Konrad 2' launched from the south-west by the III Pz.Korps between the 9th and the 12th January. For more detailed information, with plentiful cartographic illustrations of these operations, I refer the reader to the work of Georg Maier Drama Zwischen Budapest und Wien (1985) Chapter 2, "Das ringen um Budapest", pp. 21-92, Munin Verlag, Osnabrück.

[68] The German forces in the eastern bridgehead were composed, apart from the *Feldherrnhalle* divisions, of a Flak unit and a battalion of police.

[69] Arbeitsgruppe 13 Pz.Div op.cit. p 210

courtyards are filled with corpses and the whole city is enveloped in a cloak of dust and smoke"[70].

The command posts had been buried under the debris and the front, rather than existing, had to be guessed at, by joining together the pockets of resistance which, here and there, marked out the mountains of rubble and destroyed buildings. Within a few hours, the total number of casualties suffered by these units increased by several hundred. The fact that one of its largest units, the 93rd Panzergrenadier Regiment had to be disbanded and its men sent as reserves to the 66th Panzergrenadier Regiment, which was also decimated, serves as a simple indicator of the blood spilled by the *Feldherrnhalle* Divisions. On 14th January, the Supreme Commander of Budapest noted; "In the midst of artillery, aircraft and tank actions, new waves of attackers are continuously launched against the eastern bridgehead. The enemy only manages to take piece after piece of the defensive ring, thanks to the relentless pursuit by its artillery and aircraft..."[71].

The battle that the troops deployed to the east of the Danube were mounting became pure folly in all respects. Nobody in Budapest doubted that the eastern zone would fall; however, even when the bridges which joined the two sectors of the capital, the only escape routes, were initially affected by enemy actions, the High Command refused to allow the evacuation. Before long, as some units had feared, there would be no more units to evacuate.

At 1900 hrs, on 17th January, the communication which gave a *carte blanche* to the Commander-in-Chief of the Fortress finally arrived. At 2200 hrs the first contingents of the Pest garrison crossed the Danube. Under cover of darkness, the transfer of troops, materiél and the many injured men was carried out in a systematic and extremely orderly fashion, bearing in mind the circumstances in which it took place. At seven o'clock on the morning of the 18th, the engineers blew up the last bridges over the Danube. The evacuation had been satisfactorily completed. It is hardly necessary to say that the troops that had undertaken to protect the rearguard during this manoeuvre and were, of course, the last to leave the eastern bank of the great river belonged to the *Feldherrnhalle* divisions[72].

A little while later, the heroic behaviour of these units was publicly acknowledged. The Commander-in-Chief of the 13th Panzer Division *Feldherrnhalle*, *Generalmajor* Gerhard Schmidhuber was decorated with the "Oak Leaves", as was *Major* Wilhelm Schöning, Commander of the Panzergrenadier regiment *Feldherrnhalle*. These men would later become the only Army officers to obtain the prized decoration whilst fighting in a *Feldherrnhalle* unit. In addition, four Knight's Crosses were awarded, one to the interim commander of the Panzer Division *Feldherrnhalle*, *Oberstleutnant* Wolff; six soldiers of the *Feldherrnhalle*, three in each division, had also been decorated with the *German Cross in Gold* from the outset of the battle[73].

Consequently, it should not be surprising that in the message dated 21st January, sent by the Führer to the garrison in Budapest, praising the fearlessness shown during the latest combats, preferential mention was made of the men of the

---

[70] Ibid.

[71] Précis of the official communiqué from von Pfeffer-Wildenbruch (13.1.1945), reproduced by G.Maier, op.cit. p.61.

[72] Artbeitsgruppe 13th Panzer Division, op.cit. p. 210 makes the following reference; "The eastern bridgehead was evacuated on the night of 17th-18th January 1945. Eventually only Schmidhuber's Group defended it, composed of the remains of the 13th Panzer Division and part of the Panzer Division *Feldherrnhalle*. This might suggest some subordination of Wolff to Schmidhuber as his hierarchical superior, bearing in mind that, due to the tremendous punishment they received, the divisions might very well have joined their remaining men together".

[73] For more information, see Appendix G entitled 'Heroes of the '*Feldherrnhalle*' units of the German Army'

Feldherrnhalle divisions whose behaviour during this fight was exalted as an example to be copied by the rest of the Wehrmacht formations.

Combat in the Western Bridgehead

Under the denomination of 'Konrad 3', without the perspectives opened by the start of a new rescue operation, the evacuation of the eastern bridgehead had been reduced to a flight towards no particular destination. The move had also benefited the Russians, allowing them, on the one hand, to withdraw troops from that sector so as to reinforce their mechanism in the west and, on the other, so as to concentrate the firepower of their arms on an ever smaller area.

Having abandoned the eastern bank of the Danube, the soldiers of the *Feldherrnhalle* divisions made their way south to take charge of the defence of the southern zone of Buda. Virtually all the German and Hungarian artillery was gathered up and put under a single command. In the words of *Hauptmann* Klein; "Three quarters of the defence of the pocket was entrusted to the *Feldherrnhalle* divisions...Due to the terrible munitions shortages, the direction of fire had to be undertaken by a single Artillery Command...[consequently] All the heavy weapons from their respective sectors were subordinated to their artillery. Thus, for example, in the I/Panzer Artillery Regiment *Feldherrnhalle*'s zone, 72 cannon were rounded up, amongst which were some belonging to the Hungarian units, one SS Cavalry Division and some from Flak"[74].

At that time, the Russians were trying to fragment the pocket, opening up a route from the north. The Germans had been forced to retreat from Margitsziget, while all the north and north-western zones had been involved in violent combats. Initially, the troops deployed there had managed to contain the enemy at the cost of severe losses but a few days later the front had broken into pieces.

The Commander of Budapest had to lend a hand to what he termed his "last men", who were none other than the armoured *Feldherrnhalle* divisions. Thanks to the expertise of the technical services, these forces still possessed tanks and assault cannon and were immediately sent north where they took part in many local skirmishes. During these actions, tank and artillery men again demonstrated that in spite of the losses suffered, and the punishment and privations to which they had been subjected, they still retained some of the counter-attack force which had characterised their war record on the Eastern Front since the end of 1943.

The official communiqué from the IX SS-Gebirgskorps only mentions the despatch of men belonging to the 13th Panzer Division *Feldherrnhalle* but there is evidence that Wolff's men also participated in these counter-attacks[75]. The Commander of the *Hummel* Abteilung, of his Artillery Regiment states; "The Russians had occupied a hill situated to the north of the city and a counter-attack was organised which was to be supported by the 2/Panzer Artillery Regiment *Feldherrnhalle*. The head of this Battery, *Oberleutnant* Machemer, together with a handful of his valiant artillerymen, placed himself in the vanguard of the attack, and succeeded in recovering the hill having repelled the enemy. The plunder of machine guns and mortars was enormous. The battery returned to the Battalion straight away. They were mentioned in the Corps' Order of the Day for this action[76].

On 27th December, thanks to the *Feldherrnhalle* armoured units, the Waffen-SS was able to contain the Russians and organise, albeit rather precariously, a slim line of resistance. Nevertheless, the defenders of Budapest had their sights set on the south

---

[74] E. Klein op.cit. p.43.
[75] E. Klein op.cit. p.43.
[76] E. Klein op.cit. p.43.

rather than the development of this battle, and within a few hours the rescue troops under *Obergruppenführer* Otto Gille were only 18 kms, away. Dr. Hübner, of the medical services of the Panzer Division *Feldherrnhalle*, wrote; "Each hour there are new rumours regarding the location of *Obergruppenführer* Gille. We have received a telegram from the Führer and even a message from Himmler. But as far as we are concerned, we can only holdout for another few days, perhaps only a few hours"[77].

For *Generalmajor* Schmidhuber, this was an opportunity not to be overlooked. Gille's weary forces had become bogged down in the enemy's defence mechanism. Consequently, if they wanted to break out of the siege, the assault would have to come from within. For this they would have to leave the tremendous battle of destruction in which they had been involved until then, so as to concentrate the rest of their flagging energy on the launch of a rupture attack that would allow them to link up with the vanguards of 'Konrad 3'. For the decorated *General*, it was simply a case of 'now or never.'

For several days, the Staff of the 13th Panzer Division *Feldherrnhalle* had planned to break the siege from within, but this was never carried out because the High Command did not put its trust in such a mission. From that moment on, the battle of Budapest would become a hopeless fight. The air supplies improved somewhat at the end of the month only to be reduced to practically nothing at the beginning of February. The soldiers knew that soon their arms would fail to fire through a lack of ammunition. The daily rations had dropped to a bread roll, a sliver of meat and five grams of butter; in short, tiredness and poor nutrition also began to take its toll.

A worse tragedy than at the Front was occurring in the city's basements and refuges, if that was possible. During these days, almost 11,000 wounded German men were crowded together in desperate conditions among the ruins of Budapest. On a daily basis, the report from the Commander of the Fortress described his situation using adjectives which contrast with the coldness of the earlier language of the staff. With shortages of medicines and first aid services, poorly fed and subject to temperatures that dropped below zero, the majority of them would die in the following days.

In the midst of this depressing situation, the first aid services of the *Feldherrnhalle* divisions in Budapest gave true lessons of camaraderie and loyalty, earning the eternal thanks and admiration of their comrades. In this respect, the Chief Medical Officer of the Panzer Division *Feldherrnhalle*, *Oberfeldarzt* Dr. Bulle, who was mortally wounded whilst he was attending the worst cases in the same sector, should be singled out. Equally, Doctor Hübner, Bulle's replacement, and Doctor Osten, who preferred to march to captivity under the Russians than abandon their injured men deserve a mention. There is also Dr. Seeger, Chief Medical Officer of the 13th Panzer Division *Feldherrnhalle* who, among others, saved the life of the Commander of the 66th Panzergrenadier Regiment, and the brave *Oberarzt* Dr. Knappe of the Panzer Artillery Regiment *Feldherrnhalle* and a large etcetera, in which we should include, over and above the German personnel, the handful of courageous Hungarian nurses to whom many of the seriously wounded men from both divisions owe their last treatment.

The veterans of the 13th Panzer Division *Feldherrnhalle* would, at some later date, write of these first aid units; "We should offer our thanks and personal consideration for the sacrifice and selflessness displayed by the medical services of the division...[which] especially during the siege of Budapest, working in unimaginable conditions, in an ever decreasing area, always lacking in medicines and resources, did everything humanly possible for our wounded"[78].

---

[77] Dr. Hübner's notes, B.A.-Militärarchiv, Freiburg, H 91-7/1.
[78] Arbeitsgruppe 13 Pz.Div. op.cit. p.211

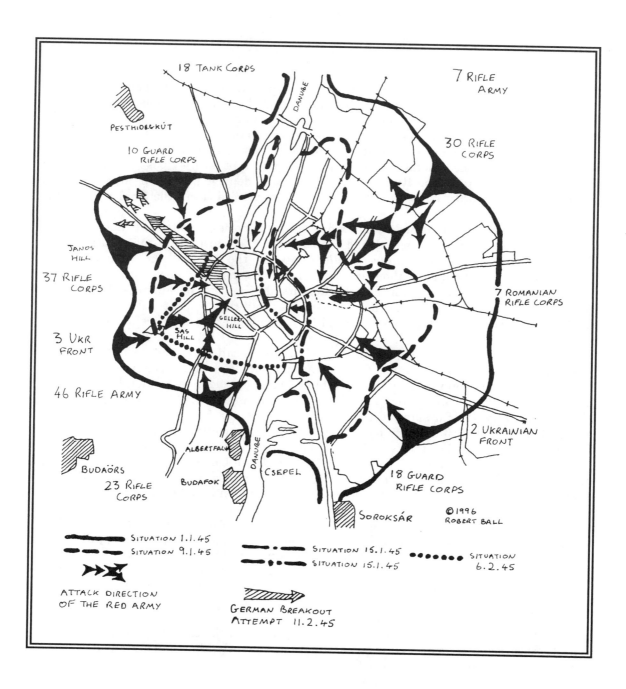

**The Battle of Budapest. The Siege of the City Centre Between 16th
December 1944 and 13th February 1945**

To the Bitter End

The Battle of Budapest was reaching its conclusion. Early in February, having halted their advance to the north, the Russians decided to alter the focus of their attacks to the south and western zones, where they began to exert renewed pressure. Continuously subjected to harsh punishment by enemy artillery and air strikes, the defenders were bled white in violent combat; the losses on both sides were high but the Germans had launched themselves into the fight with all that they possessed, including the clerks of the staff. The Russians, for their part, deployed all their numerical and mechanical superiority knowing full well that they were dealing the final blow to the Budapest garrison.

As we have seen, it had been a while since the besieged battalions had ceased to be independent tactical units and had restructured their arms in a more rationalised form. In the case of the *Feldherrnhalle* divisions, the men of the regiments and battalions were regrouped a thousand and one times, forming new units whose men were of the most diverse origin. For the Commander-in-Chief of 'Fortress Budapest' it was ever more difficult to make his orders reach the 'Front' and he did not hesitate to make public his fear that the basin would be fragmented into a series of unconnected nuclei of resistance.

By 5th February, the fighting was already localised around what might be termed the last bastion, organised in an area where the last remnants of German artillery were to be found. The first assaults had been repelled, partly thanks to cover of fire afforded by their cannon, but a few hours later, in spite of the bitter resistance of the German artillery, the Russians succeeded in opening a way through. On 9th, having lost more than half their artillery pieces, Wolff's soldiers could no longer prevent the Russians from occupying the Gellért hegy, situated on the same bank of the Danube. However, despite the latest retreat, the Commander-in-Chief of the Fortress himself recognised that in the state of malnutrition and weariness in which his troops found themselves, in the face of almost fifty days of siege, his men had displayed almost super-human behaviour[79].

The resistance of the Budapest garrisons was reaching its end. At 1550 on 11th February 1945, von Pfeffer-Wildenbruch sent the following message; "Our supplies have run out, to the last cartridge. The question now is whether to capitulate or try to escape from the siege by fighting. Consequently, I am going on the offensive with the last remaining men still capable of fighting." For Schmidhuber, as for many of those besieged, the order arrived too late. Nevertheless, all preferred to die in an attack than be exterminated in a useless defence.

As the Commander of the 'Fortress' had predicted, the exit from Budapest would have to be carried out as discreetly as possible; consequently, they had already destroyed any remaining heavy weapons, which had fallen silent some time since, through lack of ammunition. The *Feldherrnhalle* divisions had immobilised their armoured vehicles in compliance with these orders. According to the notes of the provisional Commander of the Panzer Division *Feldherrnhalle*, eight 'panther' tanks, six self-propelled *Hummel* cannon and around twenty-five armoured half-tracks had been blown up the previous night[80].

During the afternoon of the 11th, armed only with rifles, machine guns and grenades, the remains of the *Feldherrnhalle* divisions abandoned their positions on the outskirts of the Gellért hegy and, following the agreed instructions, split into several

---

[79] Part of the IX SS-Geb.Korps, dated 10.2.1945, reproduced in the work of G. Maier, op.cit. p.112.
[80] Peter Gosztony <u>Endkampf an der Donau 1944/45</u> (1969) München, p.318.

groups so as to carry out the breakthrough manoeuvre. This consisted, no more, no less, of taking advantage of the darkness of the night to mount a surprise attack on the enemy lines which surrounded the city to the north-west, opening a breach through which the garrison, in several waves, could cover tens of kilometres through the enemy rearguard until they reached the German lines in the Csömör sector. As we can see, more than a game of possibilities, it was a genuinely desperate jump in the dark.

As per usual, a *Feldherrnhalle* unit, in fact, the Pz.Nachrichten Abteilung *Feldherrnhalle* of the Panzer Division *Feldherrnhalle*, together with its opposite number from the 8th SS-Kavallerie Division was to be deployed in the northern zone, near the destroyed Margitsziget bridge, with the aim of protecting the rearguard. All the wounded who were unable to move remained in Budapest, together with a group of first aid staff, amongst whom was the previously mentioned Chief Medical officer of the Panzer Division *Feldherrnhalle*, *Oberfeldarzt* Dr. Hübner.

A short while before the start of the manoeuvre, planned for 2000 hrs on 11th February 1945, the Commanders of the besieged units met to put the finishing touches to the plans. With the tranquillity of those who know their destiny, the meeting of the commanders took place in a relaxed atmosphere, in which they partook of a good few tots of Schnapps. All were convinced that their lives were on the line. A short while later, the troops of the fragmented *Feldherrnhalle* divisions set out. As they had planned, the greater part of the 13th Panzer Division *Feldherrnhalle* and some grenadiers belonging to the II/Panzergrenadier Regiment *Feldherrnhalle* under the command of *Generalmajor* Schmidhuber, tried to infiltrate the zone to the north-west of the Bécsi ut but scarcely had they navigated their way through the deadly anti-tank ditches, than all the fury of the Russian artillery reigned down on them. There was no doubt about it; the enemy had been waiting for them.

Within the space of a few minutes, virtually all of the group had been massacred. *Generalmajor* Schmidhuber was to die as he led his men and together with him, several of his best officers, amongst them his Chief of Operations, *Oberstleutnant* Arthur von Ekesparre, who had been recently awarded the Knight's Cross; the commander-in-Chief of his Artillery Regiment, *Oberstleutnant* Kucklick and *Major* Pabst of the 13th Panzer Aufklärungs Abteilung were also killed. The few survivors were quickly captured. Other attempts in the same sector were similarly unsuccessful and sealed the fate of the men from the two Waffen-SS divisions. In full view of all this, the group led by *Oberstleutnant* Joachim Helmut Wolff, some six hundred men, (mostly belonging to the Panzer Division *Feldherrnhalle*, together with a large group of grenadiers from Schöning's regiment), marched on their own initiative, following a different route to that which led off in a westerly direction, through the Budakeszi zone. There they were more fortunate and after a desperate fight, managed to cross the Russian positions and escape into open land.

Between 18-20,000 Germans men and a number of Hungarians had tried to break the siege. More than three-quarters of them had succumbed without even reaching their target. The deep anti-tank ditches which surrounded the city had become insurmountable death traps for hundred of unfortunate defenders with whose bodies they were now littered. Many others were gunned down by the concentrated artillery fire and enemy aircraft. In small groups, the survivors slowly fell into the Russian hands. If you were Hungarian you could still join the divisions which fought along-side the Red Army; if you wore the Feldgrau you could count yourself lucky not to be shot by your captors.

In addition to the group led by Wolff, another 4,000 Germans had managed to infiltrate Russian lines. However, the task was not over; now they had to cross the entire enemy rearguard. Once the break had been achieved, the survivors of the *Feldherrnhalle* units opened up a route towards the Zsámbék, looking for the protection of the woods and ravines. A little while after they reached the German lines, *Oberstleutnant* Wilhelm Schöning was wounded and *Oberfeldarzt* Dr. Seeger was entrusted with transporting him through no-man's land. When, on 14th February, they reached the lines of *General* Balck, the group under *Oberstleutnant* Wolff, whose health had deteriorated after the last efforts, gathered together 661 men. Among the ranks, apart from the wounded *Oberstleutnant* Schöning, were *Oberstleutnant* Boensch, Commander of the *Feldherrnhalle* artillery Regiment and the first officer of the 8th SS-Kavallerie Divisional Staff, *SS-Sturmbannführer i.G.* Mitzlaff. They were soon to learn that theirs had been the only group to be successful.

On successive days, a few more survivors joined them; in total 785 men - barely two per hundred - was all that remained of the Budapest garrison. Approximately half of them belonged to the *Feldherrnhalle* divisions. The disaster had even exceeded what they had suffered on the outskirts of Minsk seven months earlier. A veteran from the 13th Panzer Division *Feldherrnhalle* wrote an account which might serve as an epitaph to the fallen men from both units; "These men fulfilled their duty during a terrible siege against enemy forces which were vastly superior in number. They fought, convinced that they did so for the good of the Fatherland and for her they sacrificed their lives"[81].

Thus far, whenever the heroic resistance in Budapest has been mentioned, it has been accredited to the Waffen-SS, while, in most cases, the contribution of the *Feldherrnhalle* division has been minimised. There are several reasons why this has happened. Firstly, the fact that the troops under siege in Budapest operated under the command of an SS Corps has led many to believe, erroneously, that the Fortress garrison was exclusively composed of Waffen-SS men. This impression has been perpetuated due to the fact that the interest that such units engender has led on many occasions to a distortion of the truth, and biased judgements. And finally, we should not forget the almost complete ignorance that exists regarding the elite *Feldherrnhalle* units, an ignorance whose roots form part of the legend that surrounds these hardened formations.

As we have been able to see, having outlined the events of one of the most terrible sieges that took place during World War II, the real spinal column of the defence of 'Fortress Budapest' was composed of the men of the *Feldherrnhalle* divisions. It should not be forgotten that these were the only two Panzer divisions that were to be found there, while the Waffen-SS divisions, both cavalry, could not compete with the firepower afforded by the former's Panther tanks and assault cannon. For obvious reasons, it was to them that von Pfeffer-Wildenbruch resorted each time they had to shore up their fronts or launch a key counter-attack. Consequently, it should not appear at all strange that during the 50 days of siege, its soldiers obtained, in addition to the Oak Leaves awarded to Schmidhuber and Schöning, a total of 13 Knight's Crosses, 9 German Crosses in Gold, and three mentions in the Army's Roll of Honour. All of which leads us, for the sake of historical justice, and in no way to the detriment of the soldiers of the SS, to vindicate the key role played in these combats by the *Feldherrnhalle* soldiers; whose men, for the second time, sacrificed themselves in a hopeless fight, displaying the spirit of sacrifice which made their epic achievement one of the most heroic episodes of contemporary military history.

---

[81] <u>Arbeitsgruppe 13 Pz.Div.</u>, op.cit. p.212.

Chapter V

In the Face of the Russian Tide

The 'Division-Gruppe Pape'

As we know, on 21st January 1944, when the troops defending the Budapest zone were about to be surrounded, the Commander of the Panzer Division *Feldherrnhalle, Generalmajor* Günther Pape, had received an order to abandon the sector and make his way westwards, with his staff and some other elements from his Division. According to Rolf O.G. Stoves, in addition to the Füsilier section from his staff, Füs.Staffel/Stab Pz.Div.*Feldherrnhalle*, a *Feldherrnhalle* Artillery Abteilung (which must have been the II/Pz.Art.Rgt.*FHH* for the I remained in Budapest under the command of *Hauptmann* Klein), he was also accompanied by an anti-tank company and an engineering company[82].

These troops made their way to a zone situated to the north-west of Velencei tó where, integrated into the III Panzerkorps of the 6th Army, they were designated as Sperrverband/III Pz.Korps (literally, Blockade Formation), which might be translated as the Combat Formation of the III Panzerkorps). This unit was commanded by *General der Panzertruppen* Hermann Breith, under whose orders the *Feldherrnhalle* divisions had operated to the east of Budapest.

On 24th December 1944, they were joined by other men in the zone situated to the north-east of Szekesfehervar; two Panzer Kampfgruppen belonging to the 3rd and 6th Panzer Divisions, a battalion of *Panther* tanks belonging to the Panzer Lehr Abt.130 and, finally, part of the I Battalion of the 26th Panzer Regiment. Together with the men who accompanied Pape, these troops constituted the 'Division-Gruppe Pape', known simply as the 'Gruppe Pape'.

Until the beginning of the year, these men had been responsible for the defence of the sector located to the east of Mor; there they had awaited the arrival from Poland of the IV SS-Panzerkorps, (*SS-Obergruppenführer und General der Waffen-SS* Herbert Otto Gille), which was to serve as the spearhead for 'Konrad 1', the first operation mounted to liberate the besieged garrison in Budapest. On 1st January 1945, within 'Konrad 1', the 'Gruppe Pape' was deployed to the north-west of the capital, protecting the right flank of the IV-SS Pz.Kp. to whose command it was answerable. Its aim was to cross through the Felsőgaya passes and reach the extreme north-east of the Velencei tó in Kápolnásnyék.

Initially, the tanks of the 5th SS Panzer Division *Wiking* (*SS-Brigadeführer und Generalmajor der Waffen-SS* Helmuth Becker), advanced, irresistible, whilst Pape's men

---

[82] Rolf O.G. Stoves <u>Die Gepanzerten und Motorisierten Deutschen Großverbände 1935-45</u> (1986) Podzun-Pallas-Verlag Freidberg, p.248.

took Felsőgaya. However, as the days passed, their progress was slower and more costly. Finally, when they had navigated almost half of the route, the advance came to a stand-still in the Bicske-Zsámbék sector[83]. On 8th January, the Rescue Operation was suspended and begun once again under the name 'Konrad 2', further to the south. The 'Gruppe Pape' which had suffered very few casualties despite having lost 3 *Jägdpanthers* and 9 Assault Cannon, did not participate, but remained in the Kocs region, exactly where they had begun their manoeuvre on 1st January[84].

According to the Army Group South Operations map, Pape's Stub. took part in the third rescue operation, launched on 12th January to the north of Balaton; they were among the forces entrusted with reducing the pressure, exerting pressure in a southerly direction towards Cece - the right flank of the main movement, recently taken-over by the 3rd and 5th Panzer Divisions of the Waffen-SS[85]. Be that as it may, their participation must have been very limited for, by the middle of the month, they would be withdrawn to the zone to the north-west of Komárom, where they began to prepare the reconstruction of the unit, whose fate, in the wake of the failed rescue operations, was sealed in Budapest. As they awaited the ominous conclusion, some of the units that composed Pape's formation were mobilised to reinforce the defence of the sector of the Front close to Komárom. Eventually, during the second half of February, these men were added to the scarce survivors of the siege of Budapest to form the nucleus of the veterans of the future Panzer Division *Feldherrnhalle* 1.

Towards the Panzerkorps *Feldherrnhalle* (Autumn 44-Spring 45)

The creation of the Panzerkorps *Feldherrnhalle* should be situated within the context of the plans elaborated by the German High Command during the autumn of 1944; the rather ambitious aim of which was to reconstruct the strength of its armoured units. This was to be carried out by means of the creation or reorganisation of the armoured corps in a new structure which would reflect the lack of trained men and materiél from which the Wehrmacht was suffering. The divisions destined to be involved in this programme would lessen their support and service corps, etc., which were to be unified as units belonging to the Corps.

Initially, this new structure, of which there were plenty of critics[86], was to be adopted by four Corps; the existing XXIV (16th and 17th Panzer Divisions), and the XL (19th and 25th Panzer Divisions), as well as the new Corps composed from the elite divisions. According to these plans, the Panzergrenadier Division *Großdeutschland* and the Panzergrenadier Division *Brandenburg* would become the Panzerkorps *Großdeutschland*[87]. Equally, the 13th Panzer Division, now the 13th Panzer Division *Feldherrnhalle*, together with the Panzer Division *Feldherrnhalle*, would unite in a new Panzerkorps to be known as the Panzerkorps *Feldherrnhalle*. At the end of November it

---

[83] For a detailed insight into these rescue operations, I refer the reader to the work of Georg Maier <u>Drama zwischen Budapest und Wien</u> (1985) Munin Verlag, Osnabrück, part I, chapter 2, "Das Ringen um Budapest", pp. 21-134.
[84] As per operations maps (RH 19V/76 dated 2.1.45), (RH 19V/. dated 10.1.45) (RH 19V/. dated 22.1.45), Bundesarchiv/Militärarchiv, Freiburg, Germany.
[85] Ibid.
[86] Among them was *General der Panzertruppen* Walther K. Nehring, who commanded one of those corps, the XXIV. See the work of Wolfgang Paul <u>Panzer General Walther K. Nehring</u> (1986) Motorbuch-Verlag, Stuttgart, Germany, pp. 178-179.
[87] Regarding the Panzerkorps Großdeutschland, I refer the reader to the work of *Major* Spaeter <u>Panzercorps Großdeutschland. Berichte und Bilder über das Erleben, Einsätze, die Männer und Kampfräume</u> and <u>Panzerkorps Großdeutschland. Bilddokumentation</u>, published in 1988 and 1984 respectively. There are also references to this unit in the works <u>Die Einsätze der Panzergrenadier Division Großdeutschland</u> by the same author, published in 1986 and <u>Panzergrenadier Division Großdeutschland</u> by Horst Schreiber, all of them published by Podzun-Pallas-Verlag, Friedberg, Germany.

English-language readers can now turn to the first two volumes of a projected three volume series by Helmut Spaeter <u>The History of the Panzerkorps Großdeutschland</u> Vol 1 1992, Vol2 1995, J J Federowicz, Manitoba, Canada.

was established that both *Feldherrnhalle* divisions would begin their reorganisation under the command of General Kommando IV (Command Team of IV Corps), which had been created on 10th October from the remains of the IV Corps[88]. This command apparatus, whose units had been sketched-out in a similar manner, was headed by *General der Panzertruppen* Ulrich Kleemann, a veteran of the Afrika Korps who had been awarded the Knight's Cross with Oak leaves[89].

Nevertheless, the military crisis which came to a head on the south-eastern front in October 1944 had led to the entry into combat of the units assigned to him, although they were structured as Kampfgruppen. The maelstrom of fighting which developed from that date in that sector would involve these sections, which as divisions would be besieged and annihilated in Budapest. As a result, whilst the XXIV Panzerkorps or the Panzerkorps *Großdeutschland* had been established at the end of autumn 1944, the Panzerkorps *Feldherrnhalle* would not be thus set up until much later.

Meanwhile, to Kleemann's IV General Kommando were subordinated Volksgrenadieren from Infantry divisions and Waffen-SS units from infamous Panzer divisions[90]. However, in spite of the fact that in official documents they would be designated as IV Panzerkorps, as of 27th November 1944 their men were permitted to wear the insignia with the rune of the wolf on their epaulettes, and the brown band which identified them as *Feldherrnhalle* soldiers on their cuffs[91].

Eventually, by the end of March, when the remains of the Panzer Division *Feldherrnhalle* and the 13th Panzer Division *Feldherrnhalle*, elevated to the category of divisions, (even though they were to be reduced in the planned version), and became the

---

[88] This Corps originated in 1934 by the expansion of the 4th Reichswehr Division. It fought in the Polish, French and Russian campaigns, in the latter case as part of the Army Group South, and was destroyed at Stalingrad. Reconstructed in summer 1943, it again operated in the southern sector of the Eastern Front and was once again destroyed at the end of September 1944. On 10 October it was finally reconstructed, then as the IV Panzerkorps, later becoming the Panzerkorps *Feldherrnhalle*.

[89] For more details on his biography, see Appendix E: *Feldherrnhalle* Generals.

[90] Different orders of battle of the IV Panzerkorps/Panzerkorps *Feldherrnhalle* between November 1944 and March 1945:

2nd December 1944
Source: Kriegstagebuch HG Süd, (Peter Gosztony, Der Kampf um Budapest 1944/45, Studia Hungarica, München and Zurich, 1964). Order of Battle of Army Group South
IV Panzerkorps (attached Army Group Fretter-Pico (6th Army and 3rd Hungarian Army))
1st Panzer Division
46th Infantry Division
76th Infantry Division
357th Infantry Division
4th SS-Panzergrenadier Division *Polizei*
18th SS-Panzergrenadier Division *Horst Wessel*

7th January 1945
Source: Bundesarchiv Militärarchiv: RH 19V/45. Order of Battle of Army Group South
IV Panzerkorps (attached Army Group South (8th Army))
Division Gruppe Fischer
Kampfgruppe 46
24th Panzer Division
4th SS-Panzergrenadier Division *Polizei*

5th March 1945
Source: Kriegstagebuch HG Süd/Kriegsgliederung der HG Süd
Panzerkorps *Feldherrnhalle* (attached Army Group South (8th Army))
221 Volksgrenadier Division
46th Volksgrenadier Division
357th Infantry Division

[91] An annotation in a war diary dated 27th November 1944 states that all the members of this Panzerkorps could wear the distinctive band on their cuffs and the insignia on the epaulettes. J. Bender & W. Odegard Uniforms, Organisation and History of the Panzertruppe (1980) R. James Bender Publishing, San José, California, USA, p. 65.

Panzer Division *Feldherrnhalle* 1 and Panzer Division *Feldherrnhalle* 2, and were placed under the command of Kleemann, the *Feldherrnhalle* denomination would begin to make sense and although it had been prescribed the previous autumn, it had only just begun to be applied to the Corps[92].

However, the first action carried out by the soldiers of the *Feldherrnhalle* under the command of *General der Panzertruppen* Kleemann was to take place during the second half of February of 1945, before the planned Panzer Division *Feldherrnhalle* 1 and Panzer Division *Feldherrnhalle* 2 had even been organised.

Counter-attack at the *Esztergom* Bridgehead

Early in 1945, the Russians had succeeded in establishing an important bridgehead on the northern bank of the Danube, to the north-west of the city of *Esztergom*, a key base from which to launch a later attack on Vienna, second capital of the Reich. Aware of the dangers, by mid-February Army Group South proposed to exploit the advantages yielded by the enemy deployment for its absolute elimination. One of the two great units destined to carry out this operation, encoded 'Südwind' (Wind from the south), would be the Panzerkorps *Feldherrnhalle*, which was at the time part of the 8th Army (*General der Infanterie* Hans Kreysing).

Under Kleemann's command, the 44th Reichsgrenadier Division *Hoch und Deutschmeister* (*H.u.D.* henceforth), its left flank protected by the 211th Volksgrenadier Division, (*Generalleutnant* Johann Heinrich Eckhardt) and the 46th Volksgrenadier Division (*Generalleutnant* Erich Reuter), were to open a route from the north-west of the bridgehead so as to advance along a diagonal route towards the south-east, following the Seldin-Mackas-Nána axis. This manoeuvre was to provide the break-through by means of which the tanks of the I SS-Panzerkorps *Leibstandarte SS Adolf Hitler* (*SS-Gruppenführer der Waffen-SS* Hermann Preiss) would attack. Finally, the advance of the 711th Infantry Division (*Generalleutnant* Josef Reichert) would complete the action from the south.

A contingent which came from the already lost *Feldherrnhalle* divisions was to operate on the right flank of the Panzerkorps *Feldherrnhalle*. There, under the command of *Generalmajor* Pape, virtually all the survivors of these two units had been gathered together. Forming the most compact group amongst them were the remains of the 'Gruppe Pape', which had been disbanded in mid-January, to which had been added some of the survivors of the division who had recently escaped from Budapest. In addition, under the command of its former Head of Operations, there was also the so-called 'Kampfgruppe Schöneich' where the survivors of the 13th Panzer Division *Feldherrnhalle* were concentrated[93]. These forces were identified globally as the 'Kampfgruppe Pz.Gren.Div.*Feldherrnhalle*'[94].

By their side was also one of the formations destined for the future Panzerkorps *Feldherrnhalle*. This unit came from the 503rd Schwere Panzer Abteilung, which from

---

[92] In spite of the concession of the name at such an early date as 27th November, on several occasions, even the official documentation continues to refer to them as IV Panzerkorps - I refer the reader to quote 90 - however, in the parts where reference is made to operations against the Gran bridgehead, (Op. Südwind 17/26.02.45), it is referred to as the Pz.Korps.*Feldherrnhalle*.

[93] One of the veterans of the 13th Panzer Division *Feldherrnhalle* confirmed to the author the participation of survivors of this division in the fighting around Gran. (Letter H.W. d: 9.1.1990)

[94] This denomination, although genuine, is totally inappropriate since the Panzergrenadier Regiment had, since November, been converted into a Panzer Division (with a Panzer Regiment). Nevertheless, I have been able to ascertain that in spite of this fact, in Army documentation there was a tendency to continue referring to it as the Pz.Gren.Div.*FHH, e.g.* in the Kriegsliederung of HG Süd of 2.12.44 (Kriegstagebuch HG Süd) as reproduced by Georg Maier, op.cit. p. 486; in the Kriegsliederung of the garrison of Fortress Budapest at the end of 1944. Ibid. p. 490 etc. There are also certain references to the effect that these forces were identified simply as 'Kampfgruppe *Feldherrnhalle*', Rolf Stoves op.cit. p. 249.

the start of January had taken on the *Feldherrnhalle* denomination[95]. This was one of the most veteran Tiger formations, created in mid-1942, and had first gained experience on the Russian Front, confronting the Allied vanguards in Normandy. Since the previous October, it had been deployed in Hungary where, in view of the recent offensives, it had not lacked the opportunity to demonstrate its value as a combat force.

Early in 1945, *Hauptmann* Dr. Nordewin von Diest-Koerber, former head of the 3rd Company, had taken charge of the cited Battalion. Under his command, during the second week in January, it had operated in the Zámoly zone, fleetingly subordinated to the 23rd Panzer Division, (*Generalmajor* Josef von Radowitz).

Now, its 25 impressive Königstigers were lined up in the Fürt region, to the south-east of the sector occupied by the 44th Reichsgrenadier Division *H.u.D.* forming the spearhead of Kleemann's troops.

In the early hours of the morning of 16th February, Operation 'Südwind' got underway. A little while later, the Tigers advanced into no-man's land as an intense barrage of fire pounded the enemy positions. As they navigated the anti-tank ditches in front of them, *Hauptmann* von Diest-Koerber's tank was hit. The Commander of the s.Pz.Abt *Feldherrnhalle* received a severe head wound and had to hand over the command to *Hauptmann* Wiegand. Although the attack had caught the Russians by surprise, the soldiers of the *H.u.D.* met with fierce resistance in Seldin. Consequently, *Generalmajor* Pape, who was in the same zone, received the order to march with his troops to provide back-up. On 18th February the obstacle was overcome and the men of the *Feldherrnhalle* progressed at a good pace on both sides of the Kölköbut highway.

In spite of the anti-tank defences and the minefields, the *Feldherrnhalle* 'Königstigers' made such good progress that on the afternoon of 18th they received the order to proceed immediately to the outskirts of Muzsla, opening a route through enemy positions. This town was 40 kms from their final objective and the liaison point with the I SS-Panzerkorps *Leibstandarte SS Adolf Hitler* had been fixed there, causing the definitive collapse of enemy resistance in the bridgehead.

Contrary to what might have been supposed from the forcefulness of the earlier advances, this action was not exactly going to be easy. A few hours later the Tigers were confronted by a fearsome pounding from the enemy's anti-tank pieces. Before long, the ranks of the battalion began to suffer heavy losses. In spite of all this, the deadline envisaged for achievement of the objective was met. Their forces had been reduced to a mere four tanks; the rest had been destroyed or were in need of repair.

On the 22nd, these forces played a key part in one of the most glorious episodes of their unit when, with great determination, they held their ground and bore the brunt of a furious Russian counter-attack until the Infantry arrived. Their brilliant action, together with the intervention of the Waffen-SS units, facilitated the satisfactory culmination of Operation 'Südwind'. On 26th February, the German Command noted; "The penetration achieved by the enemy in *Esztergom* has been wiped out by means of a lively counter-attack...the enemy has suffered 4,000 dead and 700 prisoners, losing 90 combat tanks and 334 destroyed or captured cannon."[96]

The distinguished conduct of the men of the s.Pz.Abt.*Feldherrnhalle* was recognised by the award of the following decorations; to *Oberleutnant* Richard Freiherr von Rosen, von Diest-Koerber's substitute at the head of the 3rd Company and injured in

---

[95] This is the OKH order Gen.d.H., Org.Abt.Nr.I.16698.44 g AHA Nr 65266 (?) of 21st December 1944. For more information on this unit, see E. Klein and W. Kühn <u>Tiger. Die Geschichte einer legendären Waffe 1942-45</u> (1987) Motorbuch verlag, Stuttgart, Germany, pages 251-255.

This is now available in English as E. Klein and W. Kühn <u>Tiger. The History of a Legendary Weapon 1942-1945</u> (1989) J J Federowicz, Manitoba, Canada.

[96] Kriegstagebuch der OKH, from 26th February 1945.

the early combat, the *German Cross in Gold* and to *Leutnant* Paul Linkenbach, a mention in the Army's Roll of Honour. Moreover, 14 of the men received the Iron Cross, First Class and 9 were awarded the War Merit Cross, also First Class.

All of this added importance to the role of Pape's men. However, as regards the relative importance which the intervention of the remains of the destroyed *Feldherrnhalle* divisions had in Operation Südwind, the great fighting spirit of a few men who had just a short while ago been present during the tragedy in Budapest where many thousands of their comrades had died, stands out particularly; all the more so when amongst them were some of the survivors who had escaped from the inferno scarcely a couple of days previously. Following their intervention in Südwind, while the s.Pz.Abt.*Feldherrnhalle* recovered in Csősz, the other men were transferred to the *Nové Zámky* zone where the planned process of reconstruction of the *Feldherrnhalle* divisions was to take place in line with the new structures[97].

Feldherrnhalle Recruits on the *Vistula* and the Oder

In mid-January, the Red Army once again went on the offensive in the *Vistula*. Following phenomenal artillery preparation, a giant offensive got underway which would stretch from the Balkans to the Carpathian mountains. Its final objective was the destruction of German forces in the East and the conquest of Berlin. However, in the full knowledge that the start of the operations was totally in his hands, and so as to ensure the development of the central thrust of the attack, the Soviet Generals used considerable numbers of forces in the first instance to ensure their flanks; a manoeuvre which was designed to annihilate the German forces deployed in Silesia and East Prussia. The war had reached the zones where, with the exception of the Ersatz und Ausbildungs Regiment *Feldherrnhalle* - billeted in Berlin/Güterfelde - reserve units for the *Feldherrnhalle* Division were located.

Within old Prussia, the majority of the 'Ersatz' units from the division were concentrated in the town of *Elbing*. The Ersatz und Ausbildungs Regiment *Feldherrnhalle* and the III (Pi.u.Nachr.) Abteilung *Feldherrnhalle* were located in the 'Mudra Quarters'; the Pz.Tr.Ers.u.Ausb.Abt.*FHH* in the 'Unger Quarters', and the Art.Ers.u.Ausb.Abt.*FHH* in the 'Gallwitz' and 'Danzinger' Quarters. Moreover, the II (Füs)/Ers.u.Ausb.Rgt.*FHH*, together with the Staff of the Ersatz Brigade *Feldherrnhalle* were billeted in the former quarters of the Imperial Hussars of Langfuhr, on the outskirts of *Danzig*[98]. In the face of the huge offensive unleashed by the Russians, parts of these reserve units were mobilised and sent, as emergency units (Alarmeinheiten), to reinforce fronts that drew ever nearer. From then onwards, all the training and reserve services of the oldest of the *Feldherrnhalle* divisions were incorporated into those of the former 13th Panzer Division *Feldherrnhalle*, situated in Magdeburg and Parchim[99].

Meanwhile, thanks to their vast material and human superiority, after four days of bitter resistance the Russians managed to break through the desperate German resistance and perforate the Front in many places. On 17th January, *Warsaw* fell and they approached *Breslau*, on the banks of the Oder. In just 12 days the Russians had covered more than 300 kms and against them the Germans sent their very last men, composed for the most part of the oldest and youngest men of the Volkssturm.

---

[97] According to the personal notes of *Generalmajor* Dr. Franz Bäke, future Commander-in-Chief of the 2nd Pz.Div.*Feldherrnhalle*, on 24 February came the order to begin the reconstruction of the division. It may be that the reconstruction of the Pz.Div.*Feldherrnhalle* may also have been ordered at the same time.
[98] From information supplied by Klaus Woche and the Kameradschaft der Angehörigen der ehemaligen 60 Inf. Div. (mot) und deren *Feldherrnhalle* Nachfolgeverbände.
[99] G. Tessin, op.cit.vol.XIV, p. 80.

Distributed in companies and assault battalions, the recruits and training staff of the Panzer Division *Feldherrnhalle*, together with other units, were either divided into swiftly-organised Combat Groups or were integrated into the garrisons which defended German bastions on the *Vistula*. Thus, the Art.Ers.u.Ausb.Abt.*Feldherrnhalle* fought whilst integrated into the Kampfgruppe Nagerl whilst the Pz.Ers.u.Ausb.Rgt.*Feldherrnhalle* marched into combat as part of the Becker and Kinder Kampfgruppen. Days later, two of its battalions were assigned to the Gruppe Schirmer (XXII Corps), while a third would be wiped out as it confronted the Russians in *Marienburg*. Also in *Marienburg*, the reserves of the *Feldherrnhalle* defended the towns of *Thorn*, *Graudenz* and *Elbing*, which had been on the front line since the end of January.

On 26th, the Russian vanguards had reached the bay of *Danzig*, isolating the troops defending East Prussia. The *Feldherrnhalle* soldiers deployed in *Elbing* contributed to the most decided counter-attack that was to be mounted in the zone, eventually covering more than half the distance that separated them from their isolated comrades, but the failure of the assaults launched from the east would nullify their efforts. Most of the 'Fortresses' on the *Vistula* would become besieged early in February. Inside, *Feldherrnhalle* soldiers put up a furious defence of their native country, repelling the attacks of a far superior enemy for many days. *Thorn* and *Graudenz* resisted for a whole month; *Elbing* lasted 18 days and *Marienburg* would not fall until 9th March. In this defensive battle, several officers and soldiers distinguished themselves, being mentioned in the Army Roll of Honour[100].

From the end of January, several contingents of the II (Füs)/Ers.u.Ausb.Rgt.*Feldherrnhalle* were also amongst the forces which resisted in *Danzig*. Finally, the last remaining men hiding in the *Hela* Peninsula would not give themselves up until 9th May 1945 itself. The majority of the Ers.u.Ausb.Brig.*Feldherrnhalle* units were lost in these battles. However, remaining men were involved in the confrontations which took place along the Front at the Oder. There is evidence that a battalion from the Pz.Tr.Ers.u.Ausb.Rgt.*Feldherrnhalle*, probably grouped with the remains of the Regiment that was known as 'Kampfgruppe Roeske', confronted the enemy vanguards as they advanced on Berlin in the Küstrin zone. On 19th February this unit was to lose its commander, *Hauptmann* Gerd Roeske, who was mortally wounded as he fought at the front of his men near the town of Reitwein, on the banks of the river. He was posthumously awarded the Knight's Cross for his courageous conduct.

Later on, the remaining men from his battalion would be sent to the Fallingbostel Training Ground where, having been reorganised and re-equipped, they were integrated into the Panzer Division *Clausewitz*, as II/(gem.) Pz.Rgt. *Clausewitz*[101]. However, the recruits of the Panzer Division *Feldherrnhalle* were not the only soldiers bearing the dark band that were to confront the great offensive of January 1945; reserve units from the 13th Panzer Division *Feldherrnhalle* were also mobilised and sent into this fight as independent formations. Such is the case of the Panzergrenadier Ausbildung Bataillon 66 *Feldherrnhalle* situated in Ludwigslust and Parchim, whose men constituted the Alarmbataillon 8/9, later named the Alarmbataillon *Feldherrnhalle*.

At the head of this formation was *Oberleutnant* Karl Bentin, a veteran officer of the 66th Panzergrenadier Regiment who was convalescing, having been badly wounded in the Dnyestr at the end of March. Bentin himself recounts how the unit was organised;

---

[100] For more information, see the appendix entitled 'Heroes of the '*Feldherrnhalle*' units of the German Army'.

[101] Organised early in April 1945, this division was operating between 11th and 14th April against the Americans in the Uelzen zone, being destroyed the following week. Remaining men were sent to the 12th Army. For more information see R Stoves, op.cit. p. 244.

"In November 1944, I was discharged from the Military Hospital (reserve Lazaret) in *Moravsky Beroun*/Ostsudetenland and I made my way to Ludwigslust (where the reserve unit for the Pz.Gren.Ausb.Btl.66 was situated). There I was declared fit for service - something you could bet on then. At that time they were organising the Alarmbataillon 8/9 and I was to be entrusted with its command. The Alarmbataillon was composed of three companies commanded by young subalterns. A more senior subaltern, a reservist from *Danzig* called Karl Rabe, became my adjutant. In mid-January 1945, the Head of the Ludwigsust Billet gave me the order to march...so we boarded the railway-carriages, our mission to take up positions in the Polish Corridor."[102]

The battalion was destined for the garrison of 'Fortress *Schneidemühl*'. As its commander tells us; "The first thing we did here was to expel the Russians who were occupying the German customs buildings. Over the course of the following days, the enemy assaulted our positions with greater forces and the support of assault cannon".

At the end of January, the positions defended by Bentin's men held firm. The fearlessness which they demonstrated during the course of these battles and the courage with which their commander conducted them was to be recognised by the OKH, which held them up as an example for their comrades. At the same time they were authorised to incorporate their denomination '*Feldherrnhalle*' into their name[103]. During subsequent battles, on 10th February 1945, *Oberleutnant* Kurt Bentin would be seriously wounded in his thorax - an injury that would take him out of the war once and for all. Two days later he was awarded the Knight's Cross. On 14th, the *Schneidemühl* Fortress fell into the hands of the Russians.

The former Ersatz Brigade *Feldherrnhalle* had virtually been reduced to the men of the Güterfelde Grenadier Ersatz Bataillon *Feldherrnhalle*, the unit which, since 1940, had channelled the march to the Front of volunteers from the SA; its men were also incorporated into the Berlin garrison and would die fighting to defend the German capital until the end of April 1945.

---

[102] *Oberleutnant* a.D. u. Kdr. Alar.Btl.*FHH* K.Bentin in a letter to the author. References to this unit may be found in G. Tessin op.cit. vol.XIV, p.226.
[103] Ibid.

Hauptmann Haas at the head of the recruits of the *Panzerwaffe* trained in his company, the Panzertruppe Ersatz und Ausbildungs Abteilung *Feldherrnhalle*. Danzig 1.5.44

The face of an elite. Grenadiers and tankmen of the *Feldherrnhalle*. Note the SA-Wehrabzeichen on their tunics, a decoration obtained on passing through the SA pre-military formation courses.

Hauptmann Pohl, commander of the Ersatz und Ausbildungs Abteilung *Feldherrnhalle*, examines a young recruit in the prescence of *Oberstleutnant* Heinrich Drewes, leader of the Ersatz Brigade *Feldherrnhalle* from August 1944.

SA-Brigadeführer Kübler together with *Hauptmann* Pohl during an
inspection visit to the recruits of the Ersatz Brgade *Feldherrnhalle*.

SA-Brigadeführer Kübler together with *Oberstleutnant* Ritter von Eberlein,
commander of the Infanterie/Grenadier Ersatz Bataillon *Feldherrnhalle* at
Güterfelde.

Schepmann saluting a group of convalescents of the Feldherrnhalle . The Obergefreiter shaking hands with him is wearing the Danzig Cross, 1st Class.

Major Gehring, commander of the III/Pz.Rgt.4 (13 Pz.Div.FHH) in Hungary 1944.

Oberleutnant Kurt Bentin who, leading the recruits of the 13th Panzer Division *Feldherrnhalle*, covered himself with glory during the battles which occurred in the 'Fortress Schneidemühl'.

Hauptmann Nordwein von Diest-Koerber, commander of the Panzer battalion of the Panzerkorps Feldherrnhalle. He was awarded the Knight's Cross whilst fighting with his *Königstigers* on the Hungarian Front.

CHAPTER VI

Panzerkorps *Feldherrnhalle*

Phoenix II. March 1945

Towards the end of February 1945, the reconstruction of the destroyed *Feldherrnhalle* divisions began to the west of *Nové Zámky*. As has been mentioned, this was involve a series of changes with regard to the former tactical structure of the divisions. Firstly, their respective Panzer Regiments were to be composed of a tank battalion and a grenadier battalion, drawing on the structure of the Panzerbrigades of 1944.

It had also been planned to unite the remains of the Füsilier regiments from both divisions in a *Feldherrnhalle* Corps Füsilier Regiment, which would form a part of the nucleus of Panzerkorps troops, whilst the number of infantry regiments from the divisions was to be reduced by half. This regiment was to come from the mobilisation of the Feldersatz Battalion *Feldherrnhalle* and the 13th Panzer Division *Feldherrnhalle*. However, the grave numbers of casualties suffered in Hungary would prevent its creation.

Thus, the survivors from the Infantry units of the Panzer Division *Feldherrnhalle* would become the 1st Panzergrenadier Regiment *Feldherrnhalle* and the remains of the 66th and 93rd Panzergrenadier Regiments would remain grouped in the 2nd Panzergrenadier Regiment *Feldherrnhalle* which would constitute the only large infantry units of the new divisions.

The Artillery Regiments were also debilitated; the Panzerkorps Artillerie Abteilung *Feldherrnhalle* in favour of the Corps Artillery. The men would now be reduced to two battalions with two Batteries of heavy cannon and four of light cannon for regiment. The 685th Engineer Regiment (Pionier Regiment 685), initially destined for the Panzerkorps as the Pz.Pionier Stab. *Feldherrnhalle*, was sent to Styria and its place taken by the 678th Pz. Pionier Regiment.

Moreover, at as late a date as April 1945, the Korps Maschinengewehr Battalion Panzerkorps *Feldherrnhalle* (Machine Gun Battalion for the Pz.Kp.*Feldherrnhalle*) was established, which originated from the renaming of the 429th Korps Maschinengewehr Battalion. The divisional units of signals, engineers, reconnaissance, anti-tank, anti-aircraft defence and others were organised as simple companies whilst the rest of the services remained grouped as units in the Corps.

Someone passed the comment that, rather than the creation of an Panzerkorps, what had in fact been organised was a reinforced Panzer Division. It is true that the relative optimism with which the Germans looked towards the south-eastern front early in March 1945, and the priority which the units deployed were given in terms of assignment of men and materiél, aided the process of reconstruction of the

Feldherrnhalle units; but it is no less certain that the German command erred on the side of caution.

On 23rd March, came the official decree on the change of denomination; the former Panzer Division *Feldherrnhalle* would become the Panzer Division *Feldherrnhalle* 1 and the 13th Panzer Division *Feldherrnhalle* would be known as the Panzer Division *Feldherrnhalle* 2.

The veteran *Generalmajor* Günther Pape would continue at the Front. Under his command were some of his old comrades such as *Oberst* Boensch, artillery commander and the courageous *Oberstleutnant* Wolff, as officer in charge of his grenadiers.

Oberst Franz Bäke who had, from mid-January, commanded the 106th Panzerbrigade *Feldherrnhalle*, (a unit which had operated as an independent formation on the Western Front and where the *Oberst* had good friends), was chosen to replace Schmidhuber who had died whilst trying to escape from the siege of Budapest.[104]

Nevertheless, although for his new soldiers this officer who had just turned forty-six years of age was totally unknown, he was a true hero of the 11th Panzer Regiment, the unit with which he had been awarded the Knight's Cross with Oak leaves and Swords which now adorned the collar of his black tank uniform[105]. He would soon gain a solid reputation amongst his troops.

One of the strongest units within the Panzerkorps and which, in spite of its short service as a *Feldherrnhalle* unit, managed to gain great prestige as a combat formation, was the Schwere Panzer Abteilung, whose modern *Königstiger* tanks, great, heavily armoured beasts with a powerful 88 mm cannon had already given ample proof of its fearlessness during the elimination of the *Esztergom* bridgehead. Now its strength was composed of thirty-one tanks organised in only two companies.

Retreat Behind the Thaya

Early in April 1945, the Wehrmacht fought, supported only by the momentum generated by five and a half years of war. Since Stalingrad, the Allies had rejected any type of negotiated peace and the German response of total war, proposed as a great sacrifice that would allow the Third Reich to gain a quick and definitive victory, had already been dragging on for two years. The experts knew that from the point of view of armaments production, Germany had already lost the war.

The latest offensives, the counter-attack in the Ardennes in the west and *General* Dietrich's counter-offensive in the Balaton, had been the swan song of the Wehrmacht. The great German tragedy was now reduced to trusting in a few 'miracle weapons' which would never succeed as talismans over the possibilities which would open up in the event of a rupture of the Allies in which, in their desperation, they believed.

During the first few days of spring of 1945, the English and Americans had crossed the Rhine and advanced towards the heart of Germany; a Germany whose cities had been reduced to a pile of rubble by the bombardments.

The news which reached them from the East was no better. To the north, the Russians had crossed the Oder and were at the gates of Berlin; and to the south, on the Front where the *Feldherrnhalle* divisions had fought, in the wake of the previously-mentioned failure of the 6th SS Panzer Army, the Red Army had once again gone on the offensive, expelling the Germans from Hungary.

---

[104] For more information on this unit, I refer the reader to Appendix B: *Feldherrnhalle* in the West. The 106th Panzerbrigade *Feldherrnhalle*.

[105] For more information I refer the reader to Appendix E: *Feldherrnhalle* Generals.

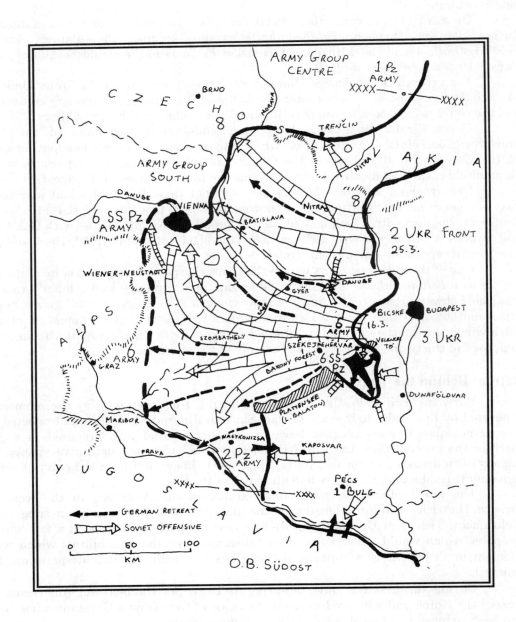

Russian Offensive on Vienna (Late March - Early April 1945)

Kreysing's 8th Army now took shelter behind the Thaya whilst the 6th was pushed back to the Alps. The commander of the *Feldherrnhalle* units, which were still in the process of reorganisation in the *Nitra-Nové Zámky* zone, were well aware of their dangerous position. This was confirmed by the demonstrations mounted by the Commander-in-Chief of the Panzer Division *Feldherrnhalle* 2, *Oberst* Dr. Franz Bäke who, during a visit to the s.Pz.Abt.*Feldherrnhalle*, on 23rd-24th March, openly confessed that he believed the Russians would not waste much time in breaking through the Front at *Esztergom*, behind which they then found themselves.

On 25th March, the long-awaited Soviet offensive began. The Soviet vanguards forced a passage through from the Leitha in Brück and, having capturing Wiener Neustadt, they launched the assault on Vienna. Further to the north the Front was deeply broken by powerful Soviet thrusts in the sector where the Panzerkorps *Feldherrnhalle* were located. Before long, Kleemann's units were overrun by the Soviet vanguards; if the enemy succeeded in consolidating their positions behind them, the fate of the Panzerkorps was unmistakably sealed.

So as to avoid their total destruction, the *Feldherrnhalle* soldiers made a desperate attempt to open up a route to the west, often involving themselves in fierce confrontations with the powerful forces of the Soviet rearguard.

The Panzer Division *Feldherrnhalle* 1 hastily abandoned *Nové Zámky*, while the Panzer Division *Feldherrnhalle* 2 and von Diest-Koerber's 'Tigers', which had already been reintegrated into his post, retreated to *Nitra*, whose defensive positions remained entrusted to the infantry.

Once outside *Nitra*, the 'Königstigers' were deployed, forming a line of resistance against which their persecutors were dashed to pieces. This gave Kleemann the time he required to organise an adequate retreat of his men.

At the beginning of April, the Panzer Division *Feldherrnhalle* 2 had entrenched itself in the Smolenice-Binocz pass where, having crossed the *Trnava* sector, the majority of the Corps was to converge. The rearguard was to be protected by the Tigers of the s.Pz.Abt *Feldherrnhalle*.

On 3rd April, near the town of Nadas, von Diest-Koerber's tanks, reinforced with some armoured vehicles and two anti-aircraft tanks (Flakpanzer), bore the enemy pressure for many hours. Later on, close to Marvaor, they repeated the exploit. Then they retreated, following the Lanstorf-Zistersdorf route.

Meanwhile, thanks largely to its own sacrifice, the Panzerkorps *Feldherrnhalle* succeeded in crossing the mountainous barrier of the Small Carpathians, behind which the Thaya ran, and on whose right bank the German lines were to be found.

In the Ramparts of the South-West

On 5th April, already officially incorporated into Army Group South and known as 'Ostmark' (*Generaloberst* Lothar Rendulic), Kleemann's Panzerkorps, once again subordinated to Kreysing's 8th Army, was deployed in the *Lundenburg*-Zistersdorf-Hohenau zone, some 25 kms to the north-east of Vienna. There they prepared their defence with such determination that the Russians were unable to repel them until the second half of April when the fall of Vienna allowed them to concentrate their efforts on them alone.

During that time, in spite of the directives from their superiors in favour of defensive operations, and in the course of the good job that they were doing with this in mind, the *Feldherrnhalle* soldiers did not lose any opportunity to mount small local

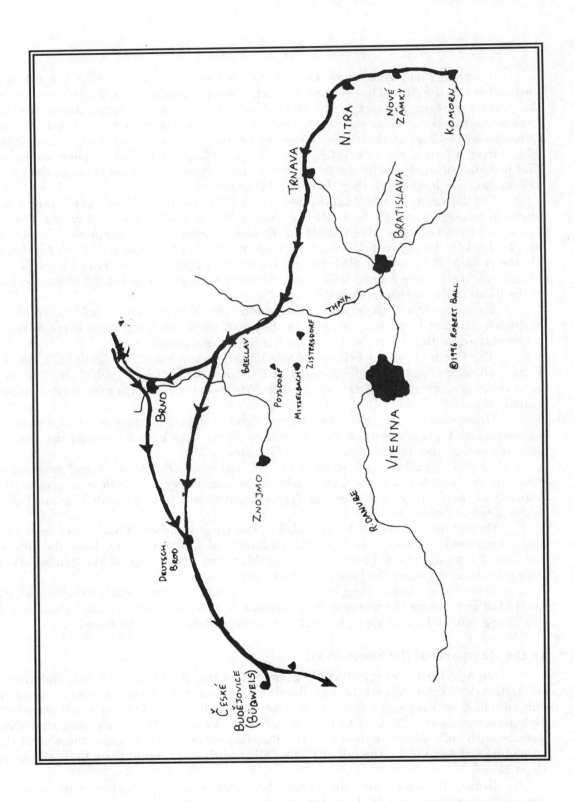

The Panzerkorps *Feldherrnhalle*, April - May 1945

counter-attacks. Proof of this can be seen in the action undertaken by the Panzer Division *Feldherrnhalle* 2 to which a battalion of tanks from the 24th Panzer Division had been subordinated as reinforcement (*Major* Zahn).The counter-attack, which inflicted a harsh defeat on the enemy vanguards, contributed to cementing the prestige of the recently promoted *Generalmajor* Franz Bäke among the soldiers of his new division.

Nevertheless, it was not the launch of his first offensive action that won Bäke the goodwill of his men, but the fact that he did not mount actions which placed the soldiers who had to carry them out in a difficult position. It was said that he was an officer who knew perfectly well what was possible and what was not. Thus, when he was asked to sacrifice his unit for no good reason, in the conquest of the heights of Zeiselberg, where violent combat had already occurred and heavy casualties sustained, on his own initiative *Generalmajor* Bäke decided to continue with the retreat of his unit. Kleemann gave tacit approval of his behaviour and there were no recriminations.

Consequently, it is hardly strange that when reminiscing about those days, lamenting the fact that the High Command seemed to live in an unreal world, they only had words of praise for their *General*. One of them would write; "...as a result of these actions and the resistance that we put up at the cost of few casualties, thanks to the expertise of our commander, we became one of the formations most respected by the enemy."[106]

During the second half of April, the retreat quickened. However, on the 21st, the armoured Russian vanguards penetrated almost 4 kms into the Front occupied by the Panzerkorps, specifically between the s.Pz.Abt.*FHH* and the Panzer Division *Feldherrnhalle* 2, cutting off Bäke from his comrades.

Immediately, the Commander of the s.Pz.Abt. *Feldherrnhalle* took his place at the front of a number of tanks and assault cannon and managed to wipe out the enemy penetration. The courageous *Hauptmann* Nordewin von Diest-Koerber, who with his 'Königstigers' had succeeded in destroying ten Russian tanks in the course of the action, was decorated with the Knight's Cross.

These events coincided with the total collapse of the Wehrmacht. The divisions under siege in the Ruhr had given themselves up, just like the units on the Italian Front. The English had arrived at the Elbe and the Russian and American vanguards had met up in Torgau, dividing in two the German territory which had still not been occupied. Even the Führer himself had left a Berlin that was all but in enemy hands. In spite of all this, the soldiers of the *Feldherrnhalle* divisions continued to fight.

At the beginning of May, the Panzer Division *Feldherrnhalle* 1 left the Panzerkorps and was deployed on the right wing of Army Group Centre (*Generalfeldmarschall* Ferdinand Schörner), as a force aggregated to the XXIV Panzerkorps under *General der Artillerie* Walter Hartmann. At this stage, Pape's men continued to stand firm in the face of the enemy and succeeded in repelling more than one hundred attacks in the space of a few hours[107].

Kriegsende

Nevertheless, the Third Reich, as well as its exhausted combat units, had only a few hours to live. Conscious of this, Kleemann's greatest worry was now to lead his men to the west. His forces were now composed of the Panzer Division *Feldherrnhalle* 2 (which, due to the heavy losses it had sustained, was now identified only as Kampfgruppe Pz.Div.*Feldherrnhalle* 2), Kampfgruppe 211, (previously the 211th

---

[106] Arbeitsgruppe 13 Pz. Div. op.cit. p.215.
[107] E. Klein, op.cit. p.47.

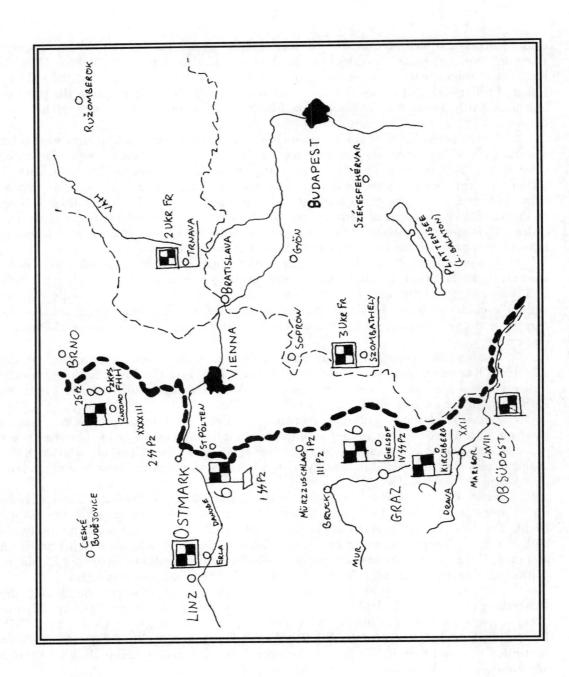

The Eastern Front, 4th May 1945

Volksgrenadier Division), the 357th Assault Unit[108], the remains of the 25th Panzer Division and the 44th Reichsgrenadier Division *Hoch und Deutschmeister*, also reduced to a weakened Kampfgruppe.

After the experience of several years of combat on the Eastern Front and in common with many German units, the soldiers of the *Feldherrnhalle* divisions preferred to surrender to the Americans than be subjected to the atrocities known to occur following capture by the Russians. To this end, on 2nd May, its columns began to retreat towards the *České Budějovice* sector. Ironically, an 'extraordinary calm' would accompany them during several days of retreat. However, on the 7th a powerful bombardment shook the zone occupied by Kleemann's columns and again led to serious confrontations with Russian forces.

During the course of the last battles in which the Panzer Division *Feldherrnhalle* 1 participated in its sector, *Generalmajor* Pape was severely injured. He was forced to relinquish his post to the commander of the 1st Panzergrenadier Regiment *Feldherrnhalle, Oberstleutnant* Wolff, who, from then on, would lead his men to the north of Linz.

Their comrades of the Panzer Division *Feldherrnhalle* 2, who, two days before the war was to end would receive what was to be their last T-34, were also marching in this direction in an orderly formation. All of them were to meet up with the vanguards of the 7th Army of the United States which, coming from France, caught up with them from behind. The notes of the Commander of the s.Pz.Abt.*Feldherrnhalle* allow us to illustrate these events with testimonies; "We retreated without resting towards *České Budějovice*...our vehicles moved in a large column which marched towards the west. A Tiger with serious mechanical problems had to be pushed into a ditch where it could be blown up. Our vehicles were overloaded to the absolute limit with our unfortunate infantry soldiers and the women and children who were fleeing towards the west of Germany. During the afternoon, we reached the out-lying areas of *České Budějovice*. We halted several kilometres from the outskirts of the town.

I learned from the liaison officer who accompanied me that the Czechs from *České Budějovice* had managed to seize several cannon from the retreating German units, with which they were trying to block our escape route. I immediately ordered two of our Königstigers to march towards the city and take the outlying areas. They fired several shots over the positions occupied by the Czechs who rapidly fled, abandoning their pieces. This action opened up the route for our Panzerkorps.

On the morning of 10th May, we crossed the town heading in a westerly direction by means of the main road (the German capitulation had been signed two days previously). We moved at a slow pace, with our last Königstigers acting as the vanguard of our Corps."[109]

Nevertheless, in spite of Kleemann's intention to come to an agreement with the Americans regarding the surrender of his troops, the Panzerkorps *Feldherrnhalle* was unable to surrender to the 'Yankees', as they had envisaged until that point. The truth is that when Kleemann appeared before them, they merely informed him that they would accept no capitulation from his unit, since when the document of general surrender had been signed, they had been deployed in the Soviet zone.

Oberst i.G. Hans Schöneich, Bäke's Head of Operations, managed to contact the American *General* Butler. However, he too failed to obtain any guarantee; on the contrary, all the demands which were raised made him suspect that, once they had been disarmed, they would be handed over to the Russians.

---

[108] According to all available sources, this unit is probably the 357th Infantry Division, possibly in the form of a Kampfgruppe.

[109] N von Diest-Koerber, Memoirs, quote reproduced in the work of E. Klein and V. Kühn, op.cit. p.255.

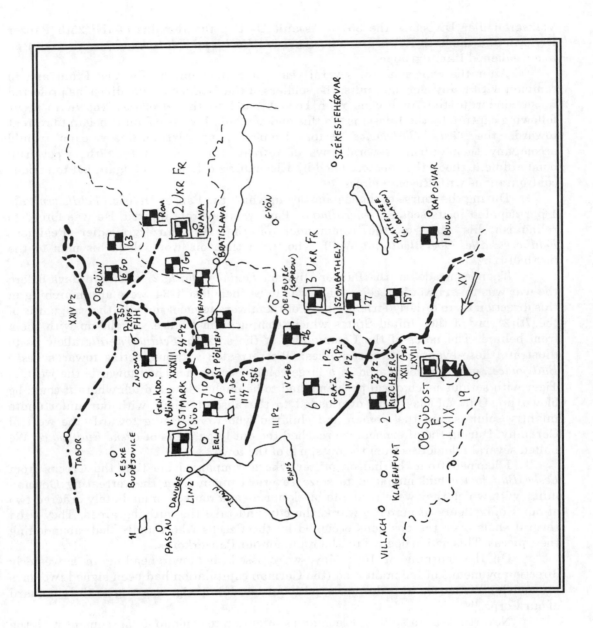

The Eastern Front, 6th May 1945

When the senior officers of the Panzerkorps *Feldherrnhalle* learned how their proposals had been received, they decided to disband their units. Von Diest-Koerber has recently given us an emotional account of those last moments; "I ordered my soldiers to leave the column and to gather in the woods which were to our right. Approximately an hour later, 400-450 men, amongst them 10-12 officers, had gathered together. I said a few words of farewell and awarded the Iron Cross to all those who had been nominated. Straight away I warned them of their immediate future...my last orders ended with thanks for so many years of unerring camaraderie.

"The company clerks handed out the Wehrpass discharge, dated 9th May 1945, with all the promotions awarded. I personally said goodbye to all my officers and they, in turn, shook the hands of all the members of their respective companies. The vehicles were destroyed in the woods (amongst them the two Königstigers), or were used for a few more kilometres only to be abandoned later on...Then we broke up into groups of ten to twelve men."[110]

Similar scenes were repeated in the rest of the great Panzerkorps *Feldherrnhalle* units. Thus, distributed in small groups and following their last instructions, the *Feldherrnhalle* soldiers would try to deceive the American units by marching through the woods until they reached Bavaria. Once there, they were to give themselves up individually, declaring that they had found themselves there at the end of hostilities.

In this manner, many of the *Feldherrnhalle* soldiers managed to escape Russian captivity, handing themselves over to the western Allies; others, on the other hand, came to realise that their last efforts had been in vain for, within just a few days, their captors handed them over to the Red Army. Amongst this number were all those who had been unfortunate enough to fall into the hands of the Czechs. Many of these courageous soldiers were never to return from the soviet prisons and work camps.

The fate of the last of the Wehrmacht's great *Feldherrnhalle* units had not been any more honourable either. There had been no massive desertions, or mutinies, or any other symptom of decomposition, but as its veterans would recall with pride many years later; "Although [the soldiers] knew exactly how the war would end, they resisted the harshness of the battles and personal needs and remained firm in their discipline [in a genuine expression of the camaraderie]."[111]

In the Allied concentration camps, together with hundreds of thousands of comrades, the *Feldherrnhalle* soldiers were disarmed and registered as prisoners of war. Their uniforms were swiftly denuded of all insignia and emblems. The Wehrmacht eagle, epaulettes and stripes were removed from their jackets; within just a few minutes these men would swell the numbers wearing the internment camps' mass feldgrau uniform. On some of the sleeves they came across the remains of the brown bands with the inscription '*Feldherrnhalle*' in silver thread, which had identified them from Narva to Budapest, from Vitsyebsk to Stalingrad, from the Volkhov to the Tisza and from Mahilyov to Nyíregyháza...Names which spoke volumes of the war record of one of the most charismatic units of the German army; a unit that, paradoxically, has reached us as a forgotten elite.

---

[110] Ibid.
[111] Arbeitsgruppe 13 Pz. Div. op.cit. p.214.

APPENDIX A

Feldherrnhalle Units of the German Army

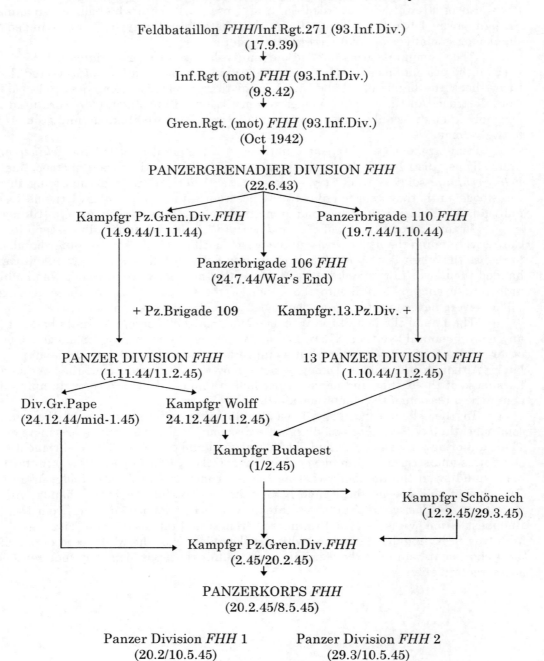

Feldbataillon *FHH*/Inf.Rgt.271 (93.Inf.Div.)
(17.9.39)

Inf.Rgt (mot) *FHH* (93.Inf.Div.)
(9.8.42)

Gren.Rgt. (mot) *FHH* (93.Inf.Div.)
(Oct 1942)

PANZERGRENADIER DIVISION *FHH*
(22.6.43)

Kampfgr Pz.Gren.Div.*FHH*
(14.9.44/1.11.44)

Panzerbrigade 110 *FHH*
(19.7.44/1.10.44)

Panzerbrigade 106 *FHH*
(24.7.44/War's End)

+ Pz.Brigade 109

Kampfgr.13.Pz.Div. +

PANZER DIVISION *FHH*
(1.11.44/11.2.45)

13 PANZER DIVISION *FHH*
(1.10.44/11.2.45)

Div.Gr.Pape
(24.12.44/mid-1.45)

Kampfgr Wolff
24.12.44/11.2.45)

Kampfgr Budapest
(1/2.45)

Kampfgr Schöneich
(12.2.45/29.3.45)

Kampfgr Pz.Gren.Div.*FHH*
(2.45/20.2.45)

PANZERKORPS *FHH*
(20.2.45/8.5.45)

Panzer Division *FHH* 1
(20.2/10.5.45)

Panzer Division *FHH* 2
(29.3/10.5.45)

APPENDIX B

Feldherrnhalle in the West. The 106th Panzerbrigade *Feldherrnhalle*

Virtually all the great *Feldherrnhalle* formations were to stand out as combat forces among the troops fighting on the Eastern Front. The only soldiers of these elite units which confronted the Allied forces in the West were those belonging to an independent armoured formation known as 106th Panzerbrigade *Feldherrnhalle*[112]. This unit began to be established at the end of July 1944, in the Training Ground at *Mielau* (Wehrkreis I. East Prussia), from a group of survivors of the Panzergrenadier Division *Feldherrnhalle* concentrated there.

During the summer, its staff was chosen from among the recruits of the Ersatz Brigade *Feldherrnhalle* and from training personnel from the Panzer arm. At the end of August, the Brigade had completed its preparation, and, in addition to the units belonging to the nucleus of troops of the Brigade, was able to count on the Panzer Abteilung and the Panzergrenadier Bataillon prescribed for this type of formation.

The tank battalion, known as the Panzer Abteilung 2106 *Feldherrnhalle*, was composed of five companies, whose men came from the Pz.Tr.Ers.u.Ausb.Abt.*Feldherrnhalle*, billeted in *Elbing*, as well as the Pz.Ers.Abt.10/18[113]. Each of these companies was equipped with eleven Pzkpfw V *Panther* tanks. In addition, there was one Supplies Company (Versorgungs Kp. or V-Kp.) and a company of Assault Guns (schw.Sturmgeschützen Kp.) equipped with eleven Sturmgeschütz IV's. Finally, the 46 tanks of the Abteilung were placed under the command of one of the most charismatic soldiers of the *Feldherrnhalle*; *Hauptmann* Erich Oberwöhrmann, who has already been mentioned on account of his outstanding combat history on the Eastern Front. *Oberleutnant* Heyder occupied the post of adjutant and *Leutnant* Knauss served as his Orders Officer.

The reinforced Panzergrenadier Bataillon 2106 *Feldherrnhalle* was initially structured around the 'Ebenrode' Group; 347 soldiers and 100 vehicles from the lost Panzergrenadier Division *Feldherrnhalle* which was completed with new recruits from the Ers.u.Ausb.Rgt.*Feldherrnhalle* from *Elbing*. Under its Commander, *Hauptmann* Münzer, it marched with a Maintenance Company (V-Kp.) and eight of Panzergrenadiers equipped with armoured vehicles (78 medium vehicles m.SPW, 14 20 mm Flak and 75 mm Pak SPWs), two of them reinforced with rockets.

The Brigade was completed by the Staff Company (Stab Kp.) with 16 SPWs and Panthers, an Armoured Engineer Company, (Pz.Pi.gp.2106) equipped with 22 60-ton trucks, a Repair Company (Wkst.Kp.) with 24 trucks and a small medical section (San.Zug).

The distinguished *Oberst* Dr Franz Bäke, who had been awarded the Knight's Cross with Oak Leaves and Swords with the 11th Panzer Regiment (6.Pz.Div.)[114] was chosen to command the Brigade. *Hauptmann* Ewald Bartel, who would later be awarded the Knight's Cross, was chosen as his Adjutant and *Oberleutnant* Calliess was selected as Orders Officer.

On 31 August 1944, whilst their comrades from the 110th Panzerbrigade *Feldherrnhalle* and the Panzergrenadier Division *Feldherrnhalle* knew of their new

---

[112] The work of Friedrich Bruns <u>Die Panzerbrigade 106 *Feldherrnhalle*. Eine dokumentation über den Einsatz im Westen vom Juli 1944-Mai 1945</u> 2nd edition (1983 & 1988) Celle, Germany, constitutes a very detailed study with an abundance of documentary references to this unit.

[113] R. Stoves, op.cit. p.321.

[114] For more information on this officer, see the appendix entitled '*Feldherrnhalle* Generals'.

destinations on the Hungarian front, the soldiers and vehicles of the 106th Panzerbrigade *Feldherrnhalle* left the *Mielau* camp in the direction of the Western Front.

Following the Allied victory in Normandy, the defeated German columns retreated to the frontiers of the Reich, unable to put up any resistance worthy of the name. In line with the stunning advances made by their armies during the summer of 1944, there were more than a few Allied commanders who believed that the war would easily be over in a few weeks. Obsessed by their task of maintaining the front, and aiming to reinforcing it, the Germans began to send units from other sectors.

Thus, early in September, the 106th Panzerbrigade *Feldherrnhalle* was transferred to the Trier sector where it initially remained as a reserve force of the 1st Army (*General der Infanterie* Kurt von der Chevallerie), which operated within Army Group G (*General der Panzertruppen* Balck). They were to establish a line of resistance at any price and the soldiers of the 106th Panzerbrigade *Feldherrnhalle* were launched into a counter-attack very quickly in the Briey-St.Privat-Marville zone. Having resisted for several days, the 106th Panzerbrigade *Feldherrnhalle* retreated towards the south of Luxembourg. It was to be during this movement that they would win their first key trophies. Along their route they ran into an American Armoured Battalion which, taken unawares, was destroyed close to Oberkorn-Dippach; 26 tanks and 8 enemy armoured vehicles were destroyed.

During the second fortnight in September, Bäke's men were subordinated to the XIII SS-Corps (*SS-Gruppenführer und Generalleutnant der Waffen-SS* Hermann Priess), and were involved in several defensive and counter-attack actions which occurred in Lorraine, specifically in the Pont-à-Mousson bridgehead, in the Moselle where it operated with some elements from the 3rd Panzergrenadier Division (*Generalmajor* Hans Hecker), Pournoy-la-Grasse this time with the 17th SS-Panzergrenadier Division *Götz von Berlichingen* (*SS-Standartenführer* Thomas Müller) or Château-Salins.

During these operations, Bäke had to face the grave loss of his two battalion commanders, Panzergrenadier *Hauptmann* Münzer and one of the most brilliant *Feldherrnhalle* Panzer officers, *Hauptmann* Oberwöhrmann, both of whom were captured by the enemy. The joy which sprang from the award of the first Knight's Cross to a member of the unit, *Stabsfeldwebel* Oskar Moser of the 2nd Company of the Panzer Abteilung 2106 *Feldherrnhalle*, was no recompense.

Although they had been unable to prevent the enemy from reaching the frontiers of the Reich, the Wehrmacht did not retreat in the west. The retreating combat had ended with the arrival of new units and German resolve once again reappeared. Finally, with the setback suffered by the Allies in Arnhem, war propaganda could again give some reality to their efforts to bolster the courage of the combatants.

At the end of September, having stayed for several days in a garrison in the zone close to Coutures, the 106th Panzerbrigade *Feldherrnhalle* transferred to Lening in order to start the journey by train to the St.Dié-Laval sector immediately. With this transfer would begin its transfer to the orders of the 19th Army (*General der Infanterie* Friedrich Wiese) to which a depleted Army Group G had entrusted the task of defending the south of Alsace. The subordination of the 106th Panzerbrigade *Feldherrnhalle* to the 19th Army was to last almost until February 1945.

Throughout the month of October, at the service of the LXXXV Corps, (*General der Infanterie* Baptist Kneiss), it would provide ample proof of its counter-attack power along the length of the front covered by Wiese, highlighting its actions in Cornimont and Mortagne.

Then, after a period of rest, and already as a unit under the LXIV Corps, (*Generalleutnant* Hellmuth Thumm), it fought in the 'Falkenberg Line' beside St. Avold.

On 19th November it would be transferred by rail to the Saarbrücken sector, being deployed as a reserve for the Army Corps to the north-west of Schlettstadt. There, placed on the defensive near the town of Bar, it succeeded in destroying a key armoured enemy incursion.

During those last November days, all commented on the exploits led by *Gefreiter* Josef Fink, a section leader who served in the 8th Company of the Panzergrenadier Bataillon 2106 *Feldherrnhalle*, who, armed with only a Panzerfaust, had managed to wipe out seven of the attacking tanks. His valiant action would earn the Brigade its second *Ritterkreuz*. However, the was little time for celebration as the 19th Army had fallen into a trap that would cost it 30,000 men and would force it to withdraw towards the Reich all the other men, among whom figured the 106th Panzerbrigade *Feldherrnhalle*. From then on, they were looking for miracles. To this end, all the troops of the 19th Army, including the LXIV Corps to which Bäke's soldiers were subordinated, were put under the direct orders of *Reichsführer-SS* Himmler. In order to stave off the invasion of sacred German soil, the Führer put more trust in 'loyal Heinrich' than in the abilities of his Generals.

Throughout the months of December and January, the 106th Panzerbrigade *Feldherrnhalle* dedicated itself to the defence of the bridgehead at Colmar; the only one that the Germans still retained before the Rhine, on Alsacian territory. Early in December, this basin came under pressure from the north and the south from large enemy forces which, in spite of their repeated assaults, failed to bring down the resolute German defence. Had the miracle occurred?

During these combats, the 106th Panzerbrigade *Feldherrnhalle* would demonstrate itself to be one of the units which contributed most to the defensive success. A short while afterwards, two officers received the Knight's Cross. One of them was *Hauptmann* Ewald Bartel, Commander of the Panzergrenadiers and the other the replacement for Oberwöhrmann at the head of the Panzer Abteilung, *Hauptmann* Paul Te-Heesen, who received the award posthumously.

The failed offensive in the Ardennes was undoubtedly the last demonstration of German offensive power on a large scale, but the events that took place in Colmar still allowed the German troops to launch a substantial attack.

There were too few Allied troops in Alsace to achieve definitive results, which, together with the controversial strategic retreat carried out in the region on their part, facilitated the launch of 'Operation Nordwind' by the 19th Army; an operation with which Himmler attempted to cut off and annihilate the enemy army deployed in front of them. The main movement of this attack fell, among other infantry units, to the 106th Panzerbrigade *Feldherrnhalle*. However, in spite of some early successes, two weeks later the offensive stagnated. This was, again, a cruel reality.

A few days previously, *Oberst* Franz Bäke, Commander of the 106th Panzerbrigade *Feldherrnhalle*, had left the unit so as to take charge of the new Panzer Division *Feldherrnhalle* 2 which was being organised in the East; the officer destined to replace him was *Major* Bernhard von Schkopp who, as the new Commander, was only present during the last stages of Operation 'Nordwind', for he was taken prisoner during the course of a counter-attack which took place on 22nd in the outskirts of Colmar.

Two days later the enemy, now reinforced, again launched itself at the bridgehead at Colmar. This time, the Germans were not so lucky. Under the command of their Commander, *Oberstleutnant* Heinrich Drewes, the tanks and soldiers of the *Feldherrnhalle* came to blows with the Allied vanguards in the outskirts of the city, where the Panthers took a good number of Shermans. Nevertheless, the fate of the bridgehead was sealed and the Germans had no alternative but to retreat across the Rhine.

The *Feldherrnhalle* was relieved on 8 February. On the following day, the Allies celebrated the elimination of the bridgehead. The greatest tribute to its defenders are the comments made by some Allied and neutral Generals regarding its performance during these battles.

After a brief rest, in mid-February the men of the 106th Panzerbrigade *Feldherrnhalle* were transported by rail to Köln where, early in March, they again went into action. But the Rhine front was broken and accompanied by Army Group B under *Generalfeldmarschall* Mödel, the 106th Panzerbrigade *Feldherrnhalle* became besieged in the so-called 'Ruhr Basin', a 'Kessel' of strategic proportions. In spite of all of this, the soldiers of the *Feldherrnhalle* continued to fight. They did so near Bonn, in the Altenkirchen zone and in the outskirts of Haiger. Eventually they retreated to the southern zone of the basin where at the end of April, they capitulated together with 325,000 men from Army Group B. The *Feldherrnhalle* soldiers' adventure in the west was at an end.

Oskar Moser, Platoon leader of
the 2/Pz.Abt.106 *FHH*.

Gefreiter Josef Fink, Group leader,
Pz.Gren.Btl.106 *FHH*.

Hauptmann d Res Ewald Bartel,
commander of the Pz.Gren.Btl.106
FHH.

Hauptmann Paul Te-Heesen,
commander of the 2106th Panzer
Battalion *Feldherrnhalle*, who fell
during combat on 9th January
1945.

Oberstleutnant Dr Heinrich Drewes,
commander of the Panzerbrigade 106
Feldherrnhalle.

Leutnant Klaus Voß

(Right) *Oberleutnant* Richard Werbs, Signals Officer,
Panzerbrigade 106 *Feldherrnhalle*.

Visit of *SA-Stabschef* Wilhelm Schepmann to the Pz.Bde 106 *FHH* in Mielau. 29.8.44.
(Top) Behind him in black uniform is the leader of the unit, *Oberst* Dr Franz Bäke.
(Middle) Schepmann reviewing the unit.
(Bottom) Schepmann talking to veterans and young recruits.

(Above and right)
Panzerkampfwagen V
Panther.

(Left) *Obergefreiter*
Kurt Ferch. Gun
commander in the Flak
platoon of the Panzer
Abteilung. Somewhere
near Bötzingen
(Kaiserstuhl)

On the Friedensplatz in Bonn

The HQ Radio Car
(Centre) Brigade
Commander *Oberstlt*
Drewes
(To his left) AdjutantLt
Richter
(To his right) *Gefr* (Fhjuffz)
Bruns
(Back) *Fw* Hulle, Car
commander

(Left and Overleaf)
The Battle in Agidienberg
One of the Brigade's
Sturmgeschütze

One of the Brigade's
Panzers under cover

Panzergrenadiers with a Flak-mounted half-track

News-sheet of the Panzerbrigade 106 Feldherrnhalle.

APPENDIX C

109th Panzerbrigade *Feldherrnhalle*

This unit had been organised at the end of July 1944, at the Grafenwöhr Training Ground, from elements which had come from the 25th Panzer Division, the 133rd Reserve Panzer Division and recruits from the Military Districts of Lower Bavaria (Wehrkreis VII), Franconia (Wehrkreis XIII) and from Upper and Lower Austria (Wehrkreis XVII).

The 109th Panzerbrigade *Feldherrnhalle* had also been transferred to Hungary to complete its preparation and receive its heavy weaponry, in much the same way as the 110th Panzerbrigade *Feldherrnhalle* in the Örkény Training Ground (Hungary).

Its command was initially entrusted to *Oberstleutnant* Baier, who would later be replaced by one of the most competent officers of the Panzergrenadier Division *Feldherrnhalle*, *Oberstleutnant* and future Ritterkreuzträger Joachim Helmuth Wolff.

At the outset, its men had served to 'guarantee', from the south of Budapest, the continuity of the unsteady alliance with Hungary. However, by mid-October, it had been transferred to the east of the Tisza as a combat force. From this moment on, its actions follow the usual pattern, for there would be parallels with the other *Feldherrnhalle* divisions.

At the end of October, having crossed the Tisza, the Panzerbrigade proceeded with its unification with the Kampfgruppe Panzergrenadier Division *Feldherrnhalle* and, on 1 November 1944, it became the Panzer Division *Feldherrnhalle*.

APPENDIX D

Insignia and Emblems

Part 1. SA-Standarte *Feldherrnhalle*

The SA-Standarte *Feldherrnhalle* wore standard SA uniform with the addition of special badges and insignia in order to emphasise the special nature of the unit. These consisted of the *Feldherrnhalle* Cuff-title, Collar Patch, Gorget, Shoulder Badge and special Steel Helmet Insignia. This appendix is only intended as a brief overview, for further information the reader is advised to consult the bibliography.

Cuff-Title (*Armelstreifen*)

This consisted of a strip of brown material 43.5 cm long by 2.7 cm wide, embroidered with straight trim in grey or silver cotton thread 2 mm from each edge. In the centre was the inscription *Feldherrnhalle* in silver Sütterlin script. This title was initially prescribed in 1936 for the exclusive use of the SA-Standarte *Feldherrnhalle*, but was later worn by the Army *Feldherrnhalle* units.

It was worn on the left cuff of all uniforms including the greatcoat.

Two examples of the *Feldherrnhalle* Cuff-title

Feldherrnhalle Collar Patch

For all ranks below SA-Standartenführer the right-hand collar patch was of a special design incorporating the 'wolf-rune' symbol. Most SA units wore facing colours to their patches and kepis according to their respective Gruppe (District). However, the SA-Standarte *Feldherrnhalle* wore a special Carmine Red backing.

The *Feldherrnhalle* Gorget (*Ringkragen*)

The *Feldherrnhalle* Gorget was worn as a part of the uniform and consisted of a steel gorget finished in 'new silver'. The central device of an eagle and swastika and the outer rim were finished in polished gilt.

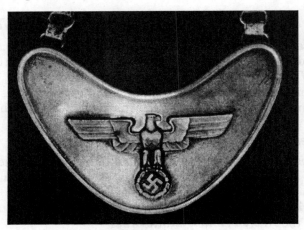

The *Feldherrnhalle* Gorget (Courtesy of Cassell plc and Brian L Davis)

Steel Helmet Insignia

Like all SA units the SA-Standarte *Feldherrnhalle* wore a swastika and shield device on the steel helmet. However, they were also given a special symbol of a shield with a depiction of the *Feldherrnhalle* and the wolf-rune.

(Left) The *Feldherrnhalle* steel helmet insignia and (right) their appearance on a surviving helmet

SA-Standarte Feldherrnhalle Uniforms

Two types of SA Service Jacket showing the positioning of the insignia described

Men of the SA-Standarte Feldherrnhalle. Note the collar patch and steel helmet device

The SA Greatcoat

Men of the SA-Standarte Feldherrnhalle wearing (left) the Greatcoat during a parade in Vienna and (right) the SA Service Jacket

Part 2. German Army *Feldherrnhalle* Units

The *Feldherrnhalle* units of the German Army wore standard Army uniforms but with certain items of insignia from the SA uniform to retain the firm link with the parent formation. As the war progressed, however, the number of men actually from the SA diminished and the insignia came more to represent the traditions of the old units and to show their elite status.

The insignia included the *Feldherrnhalle* Cuff-title, Gorget and Shoulder Strap Badge. These units also used formation symbols (usually referred to as Divisional Signs), painted on the sides of their vehicles.

Cuff-Title (*Armelstreifen*)

This was identical to the item worn by the SA-Standarte *Feldherrnhalle* from 1936. Unlike most of the cuff-titles of elite Army units, it was worn on the left cuff, in the style of National-Socialist paramilitary units such as the SA and SS. On the Dress Uniform (Waffenrock), it was placed 7.5 cm above the cuff decoration. On the Field Service Uniform (Dienstrock), it was placed 15 cm from the cuff and on the Greatcoat (Mantel), 1 cm above the upper edge of the turn-back cuffs.

The title was initially prescribed in 1936, for the exclusive use of the SA-Standarte *Feldherrnhalle*, finally appearing on the Army feldgrau jackets on the 9th August 1942 when, by order HM 42 N.770 it was decided that it should become the emblem of the former 271st Infantry Regiment, now with the denomination of Infantry Regiment *Feldherrnhalle*, as well as the reserve units which drew, for the most part, on the mentioned SA Standarte.

A short while later, the 120th Regiment of the 60th Motorised Infantry Division, whose losses at the end of 1942 had also been made up from among the recruits coming from this SA unit, was also permitted to wear it.

Some months later, its use was extended to the members of the new Panzer-Grenadier Division *Feldherrnhalle*, the two previously-mentioned regiments and its reserve Brigade. When this unit was destroyed during the summer of 1944, all the new formations created from its survivors, the Kampfgruppe Panzer-Grenadier Division *Feldherrnhalle*, the 110th Panzerbrigade *Feldherrnhalle* and the 106th Panzerbrigade *Feldherrnhalle*, continued to wear it.

During the following autumn, following the unification of the 110th Panzerbrigade *Feldherrnhalle* with the destroyed 13th Panzer Division, it also became the emblem of what was now known as the 13th Panzer Division *Feldherrnhalle*.

Finally, in accordance with order OKH/Org.Abt.I/ 20430/44, of 27th November 1944, even before it had been formally organised, this title would adorn the uniforms of all the personnel belonging to the planned Panzerkorps *Feldherrnhalle*.

The *Feldherrnhalle* Gorget (*Ringkragen*)

The *Feldherrnhalle* Ringkragen was used in the army on parade occasions by those Army personnel acting as an 'Honour Guard' for units from the 60th Panzer-Grenadier Division *Feldherrnhalle* and the 271st Infanterie Regiment *Feldherrnhalle*.

The gorget used by these units was identical to that used by the elite SA unit of the same name. It was worn by these army troops as a mark of distinction which, along with the *Feldherrnhalle* cuff-title and special SA. shoulder strap insignia, emphasised the direct links these army units had with the National-Socialist Sturmabteilung formation.[115]

Shoulder Strap Badge (*Abzeichen auf Schulterklappen*)

The *Feldherrnhalle* Kampfrune

This insignia, known as the *Feldherrnhalle* Kampfrune, was later also taken into use by the SA-Standarte *Feldherrnhalle*. It consisted of a metallic badge - although there were versions in cloth - consisting of the SA runic symbol on three horizontal and one vertical 'wolf-rune'; a combination of the emblem worn by members of the SA-Standarte *Feldherrnhalle* on the right collar patch of their jackets and overcoats with the traditional runic symbol, which could be seen on the canopy which covered the Residenzstrasse during the commemorative celebrations of the 'March of 1923'.

There were three types; gold for officers, silver for NCOs and bronze for the rank and file. Its introduction in the Army dates from the beginning of June 1943 and its use extended, in the same way as that of the cuff-title, throughout the *Feldherrnhalle* units.

(Right) The *Feldherrnhalle* Kampfrune as used on the shoulder strap, in this case that of an Oberfeldwebel

---

[115] The section on the *Feldherrnhalle* Gorget is taken from B L Davis <u>German Army Uniforms and Insignia 1933-1945</u>, 1971, Lionel Leventhal Ltd, with the permission of the copyright holders, Cassell plc. In his otherwise excellent book, Mr Davis has unfortunately made an error in his unit designation "60th Panzer-Grenadier Division *Feldherrnhalle*", which did not exist, and, of course, the insignia was presumably also worn by the later Panzer units.

Divisional Signs

As if in an attempt to emphasise the new nature of the Panzer-Grenadier Division *Feldherrnhalle*, the former emblem of the 60th Motorised Infantry Division, (from whose survivors it had been raised), was abandoned once and for all. Thus, the crosses of the old German city of Danzig by which it had been identified until then, would be replaced with a black emblem in the centre of which was the new symbol of the wolf-rune in yellow. This was to be seen as much on vehicles there as on those of the units which originated there.

On the other hand, the 13th Panzer Division *Feldherrnhalle*, later the Panzer Division *Feldherrnhalle* 2 continued to use the Division's traditional symbol, a yellow sun-wheel.

One of the most characteristic symbols of the *Feldherrnhalle* units is without doubt, that of its Heavy Panzer Battalion (schwere Panzer Abteilung *Feldherrnhalle*), which reproduced the head of a tiger on a yellow background, a clear reference to the Panzer VI *Tiger* tanks which constituted its basic armament. This had originally been the symbol of the 503rd Schwere Panzer Abteilung, from which the unit was created.

Panzer-Grenadier Division
Feldherrnhalle

13th Panzer Division
13th Panzer Division *Feldherrnhalle*
Panzer Division *Feldherrnhalle* 2

(Left) 503rd schwere Panzer Abteilung
Schwere Panzer Abteilung *Feldherrnhalle*

Part 3. Luftwaffe *Feldherrnhalle* Units

The *Feldherrnhalle* units incorporated into the Luftwaffe wore their standard SA-Standarte *Feldherrnhalle* uniform with the addition of a Luftwaffe eagle and swastika above the right breast. They also wore the standard Luftwaffe blue uniform with the same insignia, including their SA collar patches.

All Feldherrnhalle insignia was worn, including the gorget, although the swastika and shield steel helmet badge was replaced by the Luftwaffe eagle type. For further illustrations, see Appendices I and J.

The SA uniform with Luftwaffe insignia applied.

The Luftwaffe Breast Eagle

(Left) The Luftwaffe *Feldherrnhalle* steel helmet insignia and (right) their appearance on a surviving helmet

Men of the *Feldherrnhalle* in Luftwaffe Uniform. Note the mixture of SA, SA-Standarte
Feldherrnhalle and Luftwaffe insignia.

APPENDIX E

Feldherrnhalle Generals

Generalmajor Dr. Franz Bäke

Born on 28th February 1898 in Schwarzelfels, on 19 May 1915 he was admitted as a volunteer to the Imperial Army and served as an NCO in Fusse.Rgt.7.

On 1st December 1937, he served as a *Leutnant der Reserve* in the Aufklärungs Abteilung 6 of the of the 6 *Leichte Division*, later the 6th Panzer Division. On 1st November 1939, he was promoted to the rank of *Oberleutnant* and posted to the 1st Kompanie of the Pz.Abt.65.

On 1st February 1941 he began a period of service with the 11th Panzer Regiment of the 6th Panzer Division as Orders officer, achieving the rank of *Hauptmann* three months later. After a period at the front of a Pz.Staffel of his regiment, he returned to his former assignment until, on 1st April 1942, he took charge of the II Bataillon. Four months later he was appointed *Major der Reserve* and on 11 November he was awarded the *Knights Cross*.

On 14 July 1943, he finally headed the 11th Panzer Regiment and on 1st August, he was awarded the *Oak Leaves*. Three months later he was appointed *Oberstleutnant der Reserve*. On 21st February 1944, he was awarded the Swords for the Knights Cross and on 1st May he became an *Oberst*.

On 13th July 1944, he took charge of the 106th Panzerbrigade *Feldherrnhalle* in this post; a position in which he would remain until the following 12th January. His last post was at the front of the 13th Panzer Division *Feldherrnhalle* where he became *Generalmajor* a few weeks before the end. He survived the war, and died in an accident on 12th December 1978.

Generalmajor Werner Froemert

Born on 15th May 1899, in Oppeln. On 4 February 1918 he enrolled in the Marine Schule in Flensburg. On 1st October 1920 he became *Leutnant* of the Reichswehr's 7th Infantry Regiment. On 10th November 1938, he began to serve as the Head of Training at the Wiener Neustadt Academy.

At the beginning of the war he headed the II Battalion of the 217th Infantry Regiment where he remained until 31st March 1941. On 15th April of this year he served within the OKH, being promoted to *Oberstleutnant* on 1 November.

On 1st September 1942, he became the Wehrmacht's representative to the Oberste SA Führung. On 1st June 1943 he was promoted to the rank of *Oberst* and, three months later, he headed the *Feldherrnhalle* Ersatz Brigade of *Danzig*. On 1st July he was promoted to *Generalmajor*, and died just 27 days later.

General der Panzertruppen Ulrich Kleemann

Born on 23rd March 1892 in Lagensalza. He enrolled as a Fahnenjunker in the Imperial Army on 23rd October 1911. He fought in the World War I, as an officer in the 21st Dragoon Regiment, later remaining in the Reichswehr.

On 1st October 1934 he was appointed Commander of the 1st Kradschützen Battalion and on 1st March 1936 he was promoted to the rank of *Oberstleutnant*.

He was to march to the Front with this unit. Later, in January 1940, he took charge of the 3rd Schützen Brigade. On 1st November 1941, he was appointed a *Generalmajor* serving in North Africa with the 90th Leichte Division with whose command he was entrusted between 19th April 1941 and 14th July 1942 and with which he would be awarded the Knight's Cross on 13th October.

Later, he headed the Sturm-Division Rhodos, where on 1 April 1943, he was promoted to *Generalleutnant* and with which he would be awarded the Oak Leaves.

Finally, on 1st September 1944, he was appointed *General der Panzertruppen* and took charge of the IV Panzerkorps, later the Panzerkorps *Feldherrnhalle*. He survived the war and settled in Oberursel.

Generalleutnant Otto Kohlermann

Born on 17th February 1896 in Magdeburg. Enrolled in the Army as a Fahnenjunker on 3rd July 1914 and fought in the First World War as an officer in the 66th Fa.Regiment, later serving in the Reichswehr.

On 1st October 1936, with the rank of *Major*, he was bound for the 5th Beobachtung Abteilung. Just one year later he was promoted to the rank of *Oberstleutnant*, the grade at which he began the Second World War.

During the first month of the conflict, he was sent to the Versuchs Stab der Artillerie Schule (Experimental General Staff of the Artillery Academy), and three months later, having being promoted to *Oberst*, on 1st December 1940, he took charge of the 4th Artillery Regiment. On 8th January 1942 he became the Artillery Commander of the 129th Infantry Division where he would earn the Knights Cross which he was awarded on 22nd February 1942.

Three months later, on 15th May, he was placed at the head of the 60th Motorised Infantry Division, being appointed *Generalmajor* the following 1st July. He survived the disaster suffered by his unit at Stalingrad and was to be at the forefront of the process of reconstruction of that unit as the Panzergrenadier Division *Feldherrnhalle*, which he commanded from 15th May 1943 to 3rd April 1944. The counter-attacks at Vitsyebsk took place under his command.

His last posting with the Wehrmacht was as Höhere Küsten Artillerie Kommandeur West of Supreme Head of the Artillery on the West Coast. He survived the war and settled in Augsburg.

Generalmajor Günther Pape

Born on 14th July 1907 in Düsseldorf. He enrolled in the Army on 1st April 1927, serving as a *Leutnant* in the 5th Reserve Regiment. On 1st January 1938, he became the Head of the 2nd Kompanie of the 3rd Kradschützen Battalion of the 3rd Panzer Division, the unit with which he was to receive his baptism of fire. From 12th June 1941, he led the I Battalion of the 394th Schützen Regiment and on 1st September, already a *Major*, he took charge of the Pz.Aufklärungs Abt.3, still with the 3rd Panzer.

On 10th February 1942, he received his first important decoration; the German Cross in Gold. On 6th August of this year, he became the interim commander of the 394th Schützen Regiment, being confirmed in the post as commander the following September - the day on which he was promoted to the rank of *Oberst*. On 5th July of the following year he was badly wounded. His heroic performance was recognised on 15th September with the award of the Knights Cross.

After a considerable period of convalescence, in August 1944 he was admitted to the course for future divisional commanders and on 14th September he became the provisional commander of the reconstituted *Feldherrnhalle* division.

On 1st December, he was confirmed in the post as Commander, receiving his promotion to *Generalmajor* and four days later was mentioned in the Army Roll of Honour. In mid-January 1945, he left his post to take charge of the Kampfgruppe which operated under the name of the 'Gruppe Pape', which was to rescue him from the siege of Budapest where his division was annihilated.

Following the reorganisation of the unit as the Panzer Division *Feldherrnhalle* 1, he led the unit until the conclusion of the war.

His career continued later on in the Bundeswehr where, between 1957 and 1960 he was destined to lead the Panzertruppenschule in Munster at the rank of *Brigadegeneral*. He died at 78 years of age.

Generalmajor Gerhard Schmidhuber

Born on 9th April 1894 in Dresden. He enrolled as a volunteer in the Army on 1st April 1914 and fought at the rank of *Leutnant der Reserve* in the 177th Infantry Regiment, being discharged on 21st February 1920.

He returned as a *Hauptmann* on 15th July 1934, joining the 10th Infantry Regiment. On 10th November 1938, he became the commander of the 2nd Kompanie of the 103rd Infantry Regiment. When the Second World War broke out, he was already at the front of II Battalion of the mentioned Regiment.

On 1st July 1941 he was promoted to *Oberstleutnant* and on 1st April he became *Oberst*. The following month, he left the 103rd Regiment and, as of 1st June 1942, joined the Pz.Truppen Schule.

On 11th July of the following year, he headed the 304th Panzergrenadier Regiment with which we would be awarded the Knights Cross. He remained in this unit until 1st February 1944, when he enrolled on the course for future divisional commanders. Following a short period with the 7th Panzer Division, on 9th September 1944 he became the interim commander of the 13th

Panzer Division. At the beginning of October he was appointed *Generalmajor* and he took charge of the reconstituted 13th Panzer as its commander.

His unit was besieged in Budapest, and he with it, and on 21st January 1945 he added the Oak Leaves to his Knights Cross. On 11th February 1845 he was mortally wounded whilst trying to break the siege.

Generalmajor Friedrich Karl von Steinkeller

Born in Deutsch Krone, he enrolled in the Army as a Fahnenjunker on 19th August 1914. On 8th May 1915 he served as a *Leutnant* in the Third Ulan Regiment, being discharged on 24th November 1919.

He again joined the Reichswehr on 1st July 1934 at the rank of Rittmeister, posted to the XV Panzer Korps as Adjutant on 1st November 1938. This was the unit with which he would go to war.

On 17th October 1939 he was placed at the head of the 7th Kradschützen Battalion (7th Panzer Division), being promoted to *Oberstleutnant* on 1st September 1941 and distinguishing himself sufficiently for the German Cross in Gold, which he was awarded on 25th May 1942. From the previous 1st May, he led the 7th Panzergrenadier Regiment of the same division, a post in which he was to remain until 15th January 1944. On 31st March 1943 he was awarded the Knights Cross and, the following day, was promoted to the rank of *Oberst*.

During the second fortnight of January 1944, he took part in the course for future divisional commanders and on 3rd April of that year he commanded the Panzergrenadier Division *Feldherrnhalle*, leading the combat in Narva and the defence of the Dnyepr against the Soviet offensive of summer 1944 during the course of which his division was besieged and destroyed. On 8th July he was captured by the Russians. He was freed on 9th October 1955 and settled in Hanover.

APPENDIX F

Feldherrnhalle Reserve Units

1. Ersatzeinheiten (Replacement Units)

Replacement Unit	Field Unit	Recruiting Area	Barracks
5 Kp/Ers.Btl.9 (17.9.39?)	III *FHH*/Inf.Rgt.271 (93 Inf.Div.)	Berlin/Kreis Teltow	Güterfelde
6 Kp/Ers.Btl.9 (24.4.42)	III *FHH*/Inf.Rgt.271 (93 Inf.Div.)	Berlin/Kreis Teltow	Güterfelde
Inf.Ers.Btl.*FHH* (Until 23.9.42 split into two Battalions)	Inf.Rgt.*FHH* (93 Inf.Div.)	Berlin/Kreis Teltow	Güterfelde
Inf.Ers.Btl.*FHH* (23.9.42 - previously Gren.Ers.Btl.*FHH*)	Inf.Rgt.*FHH* (93 Inf.Div.)	Berlin/Kreis Teltow	Güterfelde
Inf.Ausb.Btl.*FHH* (23.9.42 - previously Gren.Ausb.Btl.*FHH*)	Inf.Rgt.*FHH* (93 Inf.Div.)	*Arnswalde*	
Gren.Ers.Btl.*FHH* (Until 8.4.43 when amalgamated with Gren.Ausb.Btl.*FHH*)	Gren.Rgt.*FHH* (93 Inf.Div.)	Berlin/Kreis Teltow	Güterfelde
Gren.Ausb.Btl.*FHH* (Until 8.4.43 when amalgamated with Gren.Ers.Btl.*FHH*)	Gren.Rgt.*FHH* (93 Inf.Div.)	*Arnswalde*	
Ers.u.Ausb.Btl.*FHH* (8.4.43)	Gren.Rgt.(mot) *FHH* (60 Inf.Div. (mot))	Berlin	

Ersatz Brigade *Feldherrnhalle* (1.9.44)/Wehrkreis II

The Brigade was destroyed in West Prussia. Reorganised from the Military Academies (Offizier Bewerber Schule) at Parchim and Magdeburg

Staff		*Danzig*	Langfuhr
Ers.u.Ausb.Rgt.*FHH*		*Elbing*	Mudra
Pz.Tr.Ers.u.Ausb.Btl.*FHH*		*Elbing*	Unger
Art.Rrs.u.Ausb.Abt.*FHH*		*Elbing*	Gallwitz/ Danziger

Ersatz und Ausbildungs Regiment *Feldherrnhalle* (mot) (1.9.43)

Mobilised as an Alarmeinheit on 10.2.45 and thrown into the struggle in East Prussia, forming part of the Kampfgruppen Becker und Kinder etc.

I (Pz.Gren)/Ers.u.Ausb.Rgt.*FHH* (Part of Ers.u.Ausb.Btl.*FHH*, finally integrated into Pz.Div.Clausewitz)	Gren.Rgt.(mot) *FHH*	*Elbing*	Mudra
II (Füs)/Ers.u.Ausb.Rgt.*FHH* (From Ers.Btl.120)	Füs.Rgt.(mot)	*Danzig*	Langfuhr
III (Pi.u.Nach.)/Ers.u.Ausb.Rgt.*FHH* (From 15.3.44)	Nach.Abt.*FHH* & Pi.Btl.(mot) *FHH*	*Elbing*	Mudra

Panzertruppen Ersatz und Ausbildungs Abteilung *Feldherrnhalle* (1.9.43)

Pz.Komp./Pz.Tr.E.u.A.Abt.*FHH*	Pz.Abt.(sp.Pz.Rgt.) *FHH*	*Elbing*	Mudra
Pz.Jäg.Kp./Pz.Tr.E.u.A.Abt.*FHH*	Pz.Jäg.Abt.*FHH*	*Elbing*	Mudra
Pz.Aufkl.Ausb.Kp./Pz.Tr.E.u.A.Abt. *FHH*	Pz.Aufkl.Abt.*FHH*	*Elbing*	Mudra

Artillerie Ersatz und Ausbildungs Abteilung *Feldherrnhalle* (1.9.43)

Art.Ers.u.Ausb.Abt.*FHH*	Pz.Art.Rgt.(mot) *FHH*	*Elbing*	Gallwitz/ Danziger

2. Feldersatzeinheiten (Field Replacement Units)

Feldersatz Bataillon *Feldherrnhalle*

Formed 1943 and consisting of 4 companies. Destroyed in July 1944 in the Mahilyov sector.

Feldersatz Regiment *Feldherrnhalle*

Projected as a regiment attached to the nucleus of troops forming the Panzerkorps *Feldherrnhalle* 27.11.44. Never actually formed. Units were to be:
    I/Felders.Rgt.*FHH* (Felders.Btl.*FHH*)
    II/Felders.Rgt.*FHH* (Felders.Btl.13)

Alarmbataillon 8/9

Formed with 4 companies from the ersatz units of the 13th Pz.Div.*FHH*. Destroyed in February 1945 at Schneidemühl.

Panzergrenadier Regiment 1030 *Feldherrnhalle*

Formed to make up the losses of the Pz.Gren.Rgt.93 in June/July 1944. Destroyed in August 1944 in the southern Ukraine.

I Panzergrenadier Bataillon *Feldherrnhalle* (Pz.Gren.Ers.u.Ausb.Rgt.*FHH*)

Motorised and equipped with armoured vehicles before being mobilised and intended for the Oder Front. Fought in Reitwein and in the Velzen-Gifhorn zone. Commanded by *Hauptmann* Gerd Roeske (killed 19.2.45, RK 11.3.45). The survivors moved to Lauenburg where they were integrated into the Panzer Division Clausewitz on 6th April 1945.

Panzer Jagd Brigade *Feldherrnhalle*

Intended to form in Parchim and Magdeburg from the reconstituted Ersatz Brigade *Feldherrnhalle*. The organisation of the unit was halted when only a very small part had been formed and it did not see action. Intended units were as follows, each of five companies:

Panzerjagdverband I
Panzerjagdverband II
Panzerjagdverband III

(This and following page) Instructors and recruits of the Ersatz Brigade *Feldherrnhalle*.

APPENDIX G

Heroes of the *Feldherrnhalle* Units of the German Army

(Including those of the 60th Infantry Division (mot) and the 13th Infantry Division/13th Panzer Division)

Knight's Cross Holders of the *Feldherrnhalle* Units of the German Army

Knight's Cross with Oakleaves (*Ritterkreuz mit Eichenlaub*)

Generalmajor	Gerhard Schmidhuber	Kdr 13 Pz.Div.*FHH*	21.1.45
Major d Res	Wilhelm Schöning	Kdr Pz.Gren.Rgt.66	21.1.45
		RK 7.2.44 als Kdr I/Fus.Rgt.*FHH* (mot)	
Oberstleutnant	Herbert Kündiger	Fhr Kpfgr d 13 Pz.Div.*FHH*	21.2.45
		RK 9.12.44 als Major u Kdr I/Gren.Rgt.978	

Knight's Cross (*Ritterkreuz*)

Leutnant der Res	Walther Evers	Fhr 11 Kp d III FeldBtl.*FHH*/Inf.Rgt.271, 93 I.D.	4.12.41
		† 28.12.43 als *Hauptmann* d R u Btl Kdr III/Gren.Rgt.(mot) *FHH*, Pz.Gren.Div.*FHH*	
Major d Res	Wilhelm Schöning	Kdr I/Fus.Rgt.*FHH*(mot), Pz.Gren.Div.*FHH*	7.2.44
		Eichenlaub 7.1.45	
Oberleutnant	Erich Oberwöhrmann	Fhr d Pz.Abt.*FHH*, Pz.Gren.Div.*FHH*	7.2.44
Oberfeldwebel	Herbert Berger	Zugfhr id 10/Gren.Rgt.(mot) *FHH*, Pz.Gren.Div.*FHH*	12.3.44
Hauptmann d R	Hans Arno Ostermeier	Fhr einer Kampfgr im Pz.Gren.Ausb.Rgt.Gleiwitz, Pz.Gren.Div.*FHH*	23.8.44
		Eichenlaub 15.4.45 als Major u Fhr Pz.Gren.Rgt.3 Hermann Göring	
Stabsfeldwebel	Oskar Moser	Zugfhr 2/Pz.Abt.106 *FHH*, Pz.Brig.106 *FHH*	4.10.44
Leutnant	Otto Erdmann	Fhr d 2/Pz.Gren.Rgt.66 *FHH*, 13ᵗʰ Pz.Div.*FHH*	9.12.44
Gefreiter	Josef Fink	Gruppfhr Pz.Gren.Btl.106 *FHH*, Pz.Brig.106 *FHH*	9.12.44
Hauptmann d R	Ewald Bartel	Kdr Pz.Gren.Btl.106 *FHH*, Pz.Brig.106 *FHH*	31.12.44
Hauptmann	Paul Te-Heesen	Kdr Pz.Abt.2106 *FHH*, Pz.Brig.106 *FHH*	13.1.45
Oberstleutnant	Arthur von Ekesparre	Ia id 13 Pz.Div.*FHH*	15.1.45
Rittmeister[116]	? Pabst	Pz Aufkl Abt 13, 13 Pz.Div.*FHH*	15.1.45
Oberstleutnant	Joachim Helmuth Wolff	Fhr Pz.Gren.Rgt.*FHH*, Pz.Div.*FHH*	21.1.45
Oberleutnant d R	Kurt Räder	Fhr I/Pz.Gren.Rgt.*FHH*, Pz.Div.*FHH*	21.1.45
Hauptmann	Helauth Bunge	Fhr II/Pz.Gren.Rgt.*FHH*, 13 Pz.Div.*FHH*	1.2.45
Oberfeldwebel	Johann Stiegler	Zugfhr id Pz.Jäg.Abt.*FHH*, Pz.Div.*FHH*	1.2.45
Oberstleutnant	Paul Krämer	Kdr Pz.Gren.Rgt.93, 13 Pz.Div.*FHH*	7.2.45
Unteroffizier	Emil Ulrich	Gruppfhr id 5/Pz.Gren.Rgt.*FHH*, Pz.Div.*FHH*	7.2.45
Obergefreiter	Karl Schnitteln	Nelder id 6/Pz.Gren.Regt.66, 13 Pz.Div.*FHH*	7.2.45
Oberleutnant	Kurt Bentin	Fhr Btl.8/9.*FHH*	12.2.45
Oberleutnant	Heinz Hamel	Fhr 4/Pz.Gren.Rgt.*FHH*, Pz.Div.*FHH*	12/14.2.45
Oberleutnant	Kurt Müller	Fhr 6/Pz.Rgt.4, 13 Pz.Div.*FHH*	13/14.2.45
Feldwebel	Rudolf Weber	Zugf id 9/Pz.Rgt.4, 13 Pz.Div.*FHH*	14.2.45
Hauptmann	Gerd Roeske	Fhr Btl.*FHH* (Erst Einh *FHH*)	11.3.45
		† 19.2.45 bei Reitwein/Oder	
Oberleutnant	Friedrich Rothe	Fhr 5/Pz.Gren.Rgt.93, 13 Pz.Div.*FHH*	17.3.45
Hauptmann d R	Nordewin von Diest-Koerber	Kdr s.Pz.Abt.*FHH*, Pz.Kps.*FHH*	1.5.45
Hauptmann	Hans Fernau	Kdr I/Pz.Gren.Rgt.*FHH*, Pz.Div.*FHH* 2	9.5.45

---

[116]No references exist for this name in the list of Knight's Cross Holders in the Bundesarchiv, which is available as Gerhard von Seemen Die Ritterkreuzträger 1939-45 Podzun-Pallas-Verlag

The following members of the *Feldherrnhalle* Units of the German Army won their Knight's Cross and/or the Oakleaves/Swords whilst serving in other units.

Oberst	Herbert Böhme	Kdr Blt *FHH* d Inf.Rgt.(mot) 271 (6.40...) u Kdr Gren.Rgt.(mot) *FHH* (.../27.12.43) RK als Major u Kdr III/Inf.Rgt.28 (8ID) †27.12.43 als Oberst u Kdr Gren.Rgt.(mot) *FHH*	19.7.40
General d Panzertr	Ulrich Kleeman	Kdr d Panzerkorps *FHH* (20.2.44/9.5.45) RK als Oberst u Kdr 3 Schutzen Brigade 18.9.42 Eichenlaub als Generalleutnant u Kdr Sturm.Div.Rhodos 16.9.43	13.10.41
Major iG	Waldemar von Gazen/Gaza	Ia i d 13.Pz.Div.*FHH* RK als Oberleutnant 2/Pz.Gren.Rgt.66 Eichenlaub als *Hauptmann* u Fhr e Kpfgr d 13.Pz.Div. (Kdr I/Pz.Gren.Rgt.66) 18.1.43 Schwerten als Major u Fhr Pz.Gren.Rgt.66 3.10.43	18.9.42
Generalmajor	Günther Pape	Kdr Kampfgr.Pz.Gren.Div.*FHH* (8.44/1.10.44) Kdr Pz.Div.*FHH* (1.9.44/24.12.44) Kdr Kpfgr.Pape (Restl Pz.Div.*FHH*) (24.12.44/20.2.45) Kdr Pz.Div.*FHH* 1 (20.2.45/9.5.45) RK als Major u Kdr Kradschutzen Btl.3 10.2.42 Eichenlaub als Oberst u Kdr Pz.Gren.Rgt.394 15.9.43	
Generalleutnant	Otto Kohlermann	Kdr Pz.Gren.Div.*FHH* (15.5.42/3.4.44) RK als Oberst u Arko 129	22.2.42
Generalmajor	Dr Franz Bäke	Kdr Pz.Brig.106 *FHH* (13.7.44/12.1.45) u Kdr Pz.Div.*FHH* 2 (9.3.45/9.5.45) RK als Major d Res u Kdr II/Pz.Regt.11, 6 Pz.Div. Eichenlaub als Major d Res u Kdr II/Pz.Regt.11 1.8.43 Schwerten als *Oberstleutnant* d Res u Kdr Pz.Regt.11 21.2.44	11.2.42
Generalmajor	Friedrich Karl von Steinkeller	Kdr Pz.Gren.Div.*FHH* (3.4.44/8.7.44) RK als *Oberstleutnant* u Kdr d Pz.Gren.Rgt.7 (7 Pz.Div.)	31.3.43
Oberstleutnant	Dr Heinrich Drewes	Kdr Pz.Brig.106 *FHH* (3.2.45/29.3.45) RK als Major u Kdr Kradschutzen Btl.10	24.4.43
Oberst	Albert Henze	Fhr Pz.Gren.Div.*FHH* (13.2.44/13.4.45) RK als Oberst u Kdr Pz.Gren.Rgt.110 id 11 Pz.Div. Eichenlaub 21.2.45 als Kdr Kampfgr.Henze.Feld.Div.21(L)	
Generalmajor	Gerhard Schmidhuber	Kdr 13 Pz.Div.*FHH* (9.9.44/11/2/45)	

Holders of the German Cross in Gold of the *Feldherrnhalle* Units of the German Army

Rank	Name	Unit	Date
Leutnant	Rudolf Bärthel	C d 10 Kp d FeldBtl *FHH* Inf.Rgt.271 (93.Inf.Div.)	2.1.42
Major	Herbert-Asmus Winter	II/Inf.Rgt.*FHH* (93.Inf.Div)	20.11.42
Oberfeldwebel	Herbert Berger	10/Inf.Rgt.*FHH* (93.Inf.Div)	20.11.42
Oberleutnant d R	Walter Baumann	1/Gren.Rgt.*FHH* (93.Inf.Div)	14.4.43
Oberleutnant	Hans Starostzi	5/Pz.Aufkl.Abt.*FHH* Pz.Gren.Div.*FHH*	4.2.44
Leutnant	Josef Schuster	Pz.Jäg.Kp.*FHH* Pz.Gren.Rgt.*FHH*	4.2.44
Oberfeldwebel	Gotthard Strunz	5/Pz.Aufk.Abt.*FHH* Pz.Gren.Div.*FHH*	4.2.44
Oberfeldwebel	Helmut Schmeil	12/Gren.Rgt.(mot) *FHH* Pz.Gren.Div.*FHH*	4.2.44
Leutnant	Edmund Kloss	II/Gren.Rgt.*FHH* Pz.Gren.Div.*FHH*	23.3.44
Oberfeldwebel	Bruno Wolff	4/Gren.Rgt.(mot) *FHH* Pz.Gren.Div.*FHH*	11.4.44
Oberleutnant	August Müller	4/Pz.Abt.*FHH* Pz.Gren.Div.*FHH*	14.5.44
Oberfeldwebel	Karl-Heinz Dahlmeyer	2/Pz.Aufkl.Abt.*FHH* Pz.Gren.Div.*FHH*	15.5.44
Oberfeldwebel	Franz Ross	4/Fus.Rgt.*FHH* Pz.Gren.Div.*FHH*	17.5.44
Oberfeldwebel	Alfred Kringel	1/Gren.Rgt.(mot) *FHH* Pz.Gren.Div.*FHH*	20.5.44
Feldwebel	Julius Schmahlfeld	9/Gren.Rgt.(mot) *FHH* Pz.Gren.Div.*FHH*	20.5.44
Hauptmann	Hans-Georg Schulte	I(Sfl)/Art.Rgt.(mot) *FHH* Pz.Gren.Div.*FHH*	1.6.44
Oberleutnant	Erich Klein	2(Sf)/Art.Rgt.(mot.) *FHH* Pz.Gren.Div.*FHH*	1.6.44
Leutnant d R	Walter Levedag	10/Gren.Rgt.*FHH*	8.6.44
Unteroffizier d R	Felix Bollin	2/Fus.Rgt.(mot)*FHH* Pz.Gren.Div.*FHH*	8.6.44
Oberfeldwebel	Max Finkbeiner	8/Pz.Rgt.4 13.Pz.Div.*FHH*	14.10.44
Unteroffizier	Fritz Willno	4/III Pz.Gr.A.Btl.66.*FHH* Ers.Einh.d. 13.Pz.Div.*FHH* (?) N.K.S.i.Gold 12.2.45	27.11.44
Hauptmann	Hans Fernau	Pz.Gren.Rgt.66/Füh.Res.H.Gr.Süd 13.Pz.Div.*FHH*	13.12.44
Hauptmann d R	Herbert Tauer	9/Pz.Gren.Rgt.66 13.Pz.Div.*FHH*	22.12.44
Hauptmann d R	Ernst Röschmann	I/Fus.Rgt.*FHH* Pz.Div.*FHH*	6.1.45
Feldwebel	Andreas Weltner	2/Pz.Jäg.Abt.*FHH* Pz.Div.*FHH*	7.1.45
Major	Friedrich Sander	Pz.Jäg.Abt.*FHH* Pz.Div.*FHH*	13.1.45
Hauptmann d R	Harald Simon	Ord.Of.1 Pz.Brig.106 *FHH*	13.1.45
Leutnant d R	Karl-Heinz Mielow	Pz.Gren.Btl.106 *FHH* Pz.Brig.106 *FHH*	13.1.45
Hauptmann	Erich Hasenbein	II/Pz.Gren.Rgt.66 13.Pz.Div.*FHH*	20.1.45
Obergefreiter	Evald Holz	Pz.Gren.Rgt.93 13.Pz.Div.*FHH*	20.1.45
Leutnant d R	Lothar Kretzig	3.Pz.Aufkl.Abt.13 13.Pz.Div.*FHH*	4.2.45

Oberleutnant d R	Gabriel Krämer	9/Art.Rgt.*FHH*	9.2.45
		Pz.Div.*FHH*	
Leutnant d R	Werner Schomert	2/Pz.Gren.Rgt.66	9.2.45
		13.Pz.Div.*FHH*	
Hauptmann d R	Paul Rutzke	Gren.Rgt.*FHH*	23.2.45
		Pz.Div.*FHH*	
Oberleutnant	Richard Frhr v Rosen	3/s.Pz.Abt.*FHH*	28.2.45
		Pz.Kps.*FHH*	
Hauptmann d R	Helmuth Friedrich	Adj.Pz.Art.Rgt.13	8.3.45
		Pz.Div.*FHH* 2	
Oberwachtmeister	Willi Eichel	2/Pz.Art.Rgt.13	8.3.45
		Pz.Div.*FHH* 2	
Leutnant	Otto Beyer	2/s.Pz.Abt.*FHH*	18.3.45
		Pz.Kps.*FHH*	
Oberfeldwebel	Nikolaus Ewen	2/s.Pz.Abt.*FHH*	27.4.45
		Pz.Kps.*FHH*	

The following members of the *Feldherrnhalle* units of the German Army won their decoration whilst serving in other units.

Generalmajor	Albert Henze	Fhr als Oberst d Pz.Gren.Div.*FHH*
		(13.2.44/13.4.45)
		DKG 2.3.43 als Oberst u Kdr
		Pz.Gren.Rgt.110
Generalmajor	Fried.Karl	Kdr Pz.Gren.Div.*FHH* (3.4.44/8.7.44)
	v.Steinkeller	DKG 25.5.42 als *Oberstleutnant* u Kdr
		Kradsch.Btl.7 (7.Pz.Div.)
Generalmajor	Gunther Pape	Kdr Kampfgruppe Pz.Gren.Div.*FHH*
		(8.44/1.10.44)
		Kdr Pz.Div.*FHH* (1.9.44/24.12.44)
		Kdr Kampfgruppe Pape
		(24.12.44/20.2.45) u Kdr Pz.Div.*FHH* 1
		(20.2.45/9.5.45)
		DKG 23.1.42 als Major u Kdr
		Kradschutzen Btl.3 (3.Pz.Div.)
Oberstleutnant	Waldemar Ratzel	Kdr Art.Rgt.*FHH* (???/9.6.44)
		DKG 28.7.42 als Major u Kdr
		II/Pz.Art.Rgt.13 (13.Pz.Div.)
Oberstleutnant	Joachim-Helmuth	Kdr Pz.Gren.Rgt.*FHH* (1.11.44/???)
	Wolff	DKG 10.1.43 als *Hauptmann* u Kdr
		I/Gren.Rgt.156 (mot)
Oberstabsarzt	Franz Menke	DKG 17.4.43 als Stabsarzt I/Pz.Rgt.13
Hauptmann	Paul Te-Heesen	Kdr Pz.Abt.2106.*FHH* (8.9.44/9.1.45)
		DKG 18.6.43 als Oblt i d I/Pz.Rgt.11

Holders of the German Cross in Silver of the *Feldherrnhalle* Units of the German Army

Oberfeldwebel	Walter Helmke	Verst.Kp.d I/Pz.Gren.Rgt.93 13.Pz.Div.*FHH*	5.11.44
Oberfeldwebel	Friedrich Leske	Verst.Kp.d Pz.Gren.Btl.*FHH* 106 Pz.Brig.106 *FHH*	12.2.45
Hauptfeldwebel	Otto Hänsel	2/s.Pz.Abt.*FHH*	29.4.45

Holders of the Army Roll of Honour Clasp of the *Feldherrnhalle* Units of the German Army

Leutnant (SA-Stuf)	Wilhelm Maier	11/FeldBtl.*FHH* Inf. Rgt. 271 (93.Inf.Div.)	8.4.42
Hauptmann	WalterHoffmann	1/Gren.Rgt.*FHH* Pz.Gren.Div.*FHH*	17.3.43
Major	Kurt Schmidt	Gren.Rgt.(mot) *FHH* Pz.Gren.Div.*FHH*	7.2.44
Hauptmann (SA-Ostuf)	Leo Maciejewski	I/Gren.Rgt.*FHH* Pz.Gren.Div.*FHH*	5.6.44
Leutnant[117]	Wolfgang Beltzer	Zugfhr i d II/Pz.Rgt.4 24/25.9.44 b Kosjazszeg 13.Pz.Div.*FHH*	5.11.44
Stabsfeldwebel	Arno Herrmann	1/Pz.Abt.106.*FHH* Pz.Brig.106.*FHH*	7.11.44
Oberfeldwebel	Richard Jänicke	3/Pz.Abt.106.*FHH* Pz.Brig.*FHH*	7.11.44
Oberst	Günther Pape	Kdr Pz.Div.*FHH*	5.12.44
Oberleutnant	Max Pichlmaier	C d 1/Pz.Gren.Rgt.66 19.10.44 b Balmaz-Ujvaros 13.Pz.Div.*FHH*	15.12.44
Leutnant	Wilhelm Pfaff	Pz.Gren.Btl.106.*FHH* Pz.Brig.106.*FHH*	7.1.45
Oberleutnant	Willy Büchner	2/Pz.Pi.Btl.*FHH* Pz.Div.*FHH*	5.2.45
Unteroffizier	Karl Hoffmann	2/(s.?)Pz.Abt.*FHH* (?)	5.2.45
Oberfeldwebel	Walter Kempny	1/Pz.Gren.Rgt.*FHH* Pz.Div.*FHH*	5.2.45
Hauptmann	Hartwig Binder	1/Pz.Gren.Ausb.u.Ers.Abt.*FHH* Ers.Brig.*FHH*	25.2.45
Oberleutnant d R	Ulrich Scheske	Pz.Pi.Kp. Pz.Brig.106.*FHH*	25.2.45
Oberleutnant d R	Arthur Martin	2/I.Pz.Gren.Ausb.Btl.*FHH* Ers.Brig.*FHH*	25.2.45
Oberleutnant	Arthur Klauser	1/Pz.Gren.Ausb.Btl.*FHH* Ers.Brig.*FHH*	25.2.45
Oberfeldwebel	Rudolf Tiltsch	Pz.Tr.Ers.u.Ausb.Abt.*FHH*	25.2.45
Leutnant	Paul Linkenbach	s.Pz.Abt.*FHH* Panzerkorps *FHH*	5.3.45
Leutnant d R	Erich Fürlinger	s.Pz.Abt.*FHH* Panzerkorps *FHH*	1945
Major d R	Karl Becker	Art.Ers.u.Ausb.Abt.*FHH* Ers.Brig.*FHH*	1945
Leutnant d R	Wilhelm Bartelborth	2/Pz.Abt. Pz.Brig.106.*FHH*	1945
Unteroffizier	Franz Hampel	Sturm Bataillon *FHH*	1945

---

[117] Decoration awarded in the 13.Pz.Div.*FHH* for action with the old 13.Pz.Div.

Close Combat Clasp Holders of the *Feldherrnhalle* Units of the German Army

Unteroffizier	Fritz Willno	Gruppfhr 3/Pz.Gren.Rgt.66	12.2.44
		DKG 27.11.44 als Unteroffizier u Gruppenfhr i d	
		4/Pz.Gren.A.Btl.66 *FHH*Pz.Gren.Div.*FHH*	
Unteroffizier	Otto Krüger	Pz.Ers.Brig.*FHH*	1944

Knight's Cross Holders of the 13th Infantry Division (mot)/13th Panzer Division

Oberstleutnant	Oskar Radwan	Kdr II/lnf.Rgt.93	19.7.40
		†18.6.42 am Mius	
Generalmajor	Friedrich Wilhelm von Rothkirch und Panthen	Kdr 13 Inf.Div.(mot)	15.8.40
Generalmajor	Walther Düvert	Kdr 13 Pz.Div.	30.7.41
Hauptmann	Albert Brux	Kdr I/Schützen Rgt.66	12.9.41
		Eichenlaub 24.6.44 als Oberst u Kdr Pz.Gren.Rgt.40	
Oberst	Trugott Herr	Kdr 13 Schutz Brigade	2.10.41
		Eichenlaub 9.8.42. als Gen.Major u Kdr 13.Pz.Div.	
		Schwerten 18.12.44. als Gen.d.Pz.Tr. u. Kom.Gen LXXVI Pz.Kps.	
Leutnant	Hans Hermann Sassenberg	Zugfhr i d 2/Pz.Aufkl.Abt.13	23.10.41
		† 25.10.43 als Kp.Chef	
Oberschirrmeister	Fritz Meusgeier	3/Pz.Jäg.Abt.13	15.11.41
Oberst	Eduard Hauser	Kdr Pz.Rgt.4	4.12.41
		Eichenlaub 26.1.44 als Generalmajor u. Kdr l3 Pz.Div.	
Oberstleutnant	Fritz Krämer	Iz 13.Pz.Div.	17.1.42
Oberleutnant	Joachim Voß	Fhr 5/Schutz.Rgt.93	17.5.42
Obergefreiter	Richard Gambietz	Stabskp/Schutz.Rgt.93	27.5.42
		†25.4.44 als Unteroffizier	
Oberstleutnant	Harald Stolz	Kdr Kradschutzen Btl.43	28.8.42
Oberfeldwebel	Fritz Schelhorn	Zugfhr i d Stabskp/Schutz.Rgt.66	4.9.42
Leutnant	Heinz Reverchon	Zugfhr i d 1/Kradschutzen Btl.43	16.9.42
Hauptmann	Herbert Gomille	Kdr II/Pz.Rgt.4	25.10.42
Obergefreiter	Rudi Brasche	Gruppenfhr i d 4/Pz.Gren.Rgt.93	9.11.42
Hauptmann	Joachim Barth	Kdr Pz.Jäg.Abt.13	17.12.42
Generalmajor	Helmut von der Chevallerie	Kdr 13.Pz.Div.	30.3.43
Leutnant	Walter Obst	Fhr 4/Pz.Gren.Rgt.66	30.11.43
		† 10.10.43 bei Oktoberfeld	
Oberst	Friedrich-Erdmann von Hake	Kdr Pz.Rgt.4	30.11.43
Obergefreiter	Wilhelm Schleef	MG-Schutz.1 i d 7/Pz.Gren.Rgt.66	11.12.43
Major	Hartwig	Kdr I/Pz.Gren.Rgt.66	5.1.44
San.Unteroffizier	Manfred Jordan Zugfhr. 1./Pz.Gren.Rgt.66	Zugfhr 4/Pz.Gren.Rgt.66 † 2.8.43	11.1.44
Unteroffizier	Emil Vogler	Kradmeldestaffel im I/Pz.Gren.Rgt.93	24.1.44
Oberleutnant	Rudolf Becker	C 1/Pz.Gren.Rgt.66 †13.10.44 in Ungarn	23.2.44
Hauptmann	Johann Sauer	Kdr II/Pz.Gren.Rgt.93 † 19.5.44 als Major d R	15.5.44
Obergefreiter	Wilhelm Grunge	6ruppenfhr i d 4/Pz.Gren.Rgt.93	3.7.44
Hauptmann	Manfred Wendt	m.F.b I/Pz.Gren.Rgt.66	9.7.44
Hauptmann	Josef Eck	Fhr 4/Pz.Rgt.4	15.7.44
Oberleutnant d Res	Gustav Soldner	C 1/Pz.Gren.Rgt.66	18.7.44

Holders of the German Cross in Gold of the 13th Infantry Division (mot)/13th Panzer Division

Oberleutnant	Waldemar von Gazen	2/Schutzen Rgt.66	15.11.41
Oberfeldwebel	Willi Philipp	1/Schutzen Rgt.66	15.11.41
Major	Friedrich von Hake	Pz.Aufkl.Abt.13	22.11.41
Oberstleutnant	Gerhard Wentscher	Kdr III/Pz.Art.Rgt.13	1.12.41
Hauptmann	Wolfram Montfort	I/Pz.Rgt.4	1.12.41
Oberleutnant	Hans-Georg Biedermann	8/Schutzen Rgt.66	1.12.41
Leutnant d R	Franz Hünnemeier	7/Schutzen Rgt.93	1.12.41
Oberfeldwebel	Hans Georg Lehmann	1/Pz.Aufkl.Abt.13	1.12.41
Oberfeldwebel	Fritz Schelhorn	14/(Pz.Jäg.) Schutzen Rgt.66	9.12.41
Oberleutnant	Joachim Barth	3/Pz.Jäg.Abt.13	19.12.41
Oberleutnant	Erich von Hanstein	1/Pz.Rgt.4	19.12.41
Major	Kurt Polster	Kdr d II/Schutzen Rgt.66	2.1.42
Major	Fritz Albrecht	Kdr I/Pz.Art.Rgt.13	14.1.42
Major i G	Fritz Krämer	Ia 13.Pz.Div.	29.1.42
Hauptmann	Herbert Gomille	5/Pz.Rgt.4	14.2.42
Oberstleutnant	Job von Raczek	Kdr d Schutzen Rgt.66	14.2.42
Oberfeldwebel	Hieronimus Hilski	3/Kradschutzen Btl.43	14.2.42
Leutnant	Kurt Hebäcker	4(MG)/Schutzen Rgt.66	21.2.42
Oberstleutnant	Gottfried Scholz	Kdr Schutzen.Rgt.93	20.3.42
Oberleutnant	Karl August Weisbach	2/Pz.Aufkl.Abt.13	20.3.42
Feldwebel	Wilhelm Hoetz	2/Pz.Gren.Rgt.66	20.3.42
Oberstleutnant	Ewald Hohmann	Kdr II/Pz.Rgt.4	14.4.42
Oberleutnant	Bernhard Gehring	2/Pz.Rgt.4	5.5.42
Hauptmann	Otto Steiner	3/Schutzen Rgt.93	25.5.42
Hauptmann	Erich Schmidt	3/Pz.Rgt.4	30.5.42
Unteroffizier	Paul Skotz	2/Schutzen Rgt.66	3.6.42
Oberleutnant	Klaus Lehmann	4/Schutzen Rgt.66	2.7.42
Major	Waldemar Ratzel	Kdr II/Pz.Art.Rgt.13	28.7.42
Oberleutnant	Hans Rahn	3/Kradschutzen Btl.43	26.8.42
Leutnant d R	Woldemar Jentsch	III/Pz.Rgt.4	12.9.42
Oberst	Dr Walter Kühn	Kdr Pz.Art.Rgt.13	19.9.42
Oberleutnant	Günter Baranek	Pz.Pi.Btl.4	19.9.42
Oberleutnant	Thilo Wolff von der Sahl	4/Kradschutzen Btl.43	19.9.42
Oberfeldwebel	Hermann Oertel	1/Kradschutzen Btl.43	19.9.42
Feldwebel	Lothar Peters	1/Pz.Pi.Btl.4	19.9.42
Major	Werner Niedick	Kdr d III/Pz.Rgt.4	20.9.42
Oberfeldwebel	Otto Topp	4/Pz.Gren.Rgt.66	20.9.42
Feldwebel	Artur Guddat	2/Pz.Rgt.4	25.9.42
Major d R	Wilhelm Moritz	Kdr I/Pz.Gren.Rgt.93	14.10.42
Hauptmann	Fritz Kucklick	Kdr I/Pz.Art.Rgt.13	14.10.42
Oberleutnant	Eick	1/Kradschutzen Btl.43	14.10.42
Feldwebel	Wilhelm Gericke	1/Pz.Gren.Rgt.66	14.10.42
Feldwebel	Roman Simon	1/Kradschutzen Btl.43	14.10.42
Oberleutnant	Fritz Roth	5/Pz.Rgt.4	31.10.42
Oberleutnant d R	Johann Sauer	7/Pz.Gren.Rgt.66	5.11.42
Unteroffizier	Franz Kanngiesser	Stab.Kp./Pz.Gren.Rgt.66	5.11.42
Unteroffizier	Herbert Scheider	7/Pz.Gren.Rgt.93	5.11.42
Oberfeldwebel	Heinz Gückel	7/Pz.Rgt.4	5.11.42
Oberfeldwebel	Alwin Haberland	5/Pz.Rgt.4	13.11.42
Oberfeldwebel	Willy Heinrich	6/Pz.Rgt.4	13.11.42
Oberleutnant	Heinz Renk	6/Pz.Rgt.4	24.11.42
Oberleutnant	Horst Moll	2/Pz.Rgt.4	24.11.42
Leutnant	Willibald Witzani	1/Pz.Pi.Btl.4	28.11.42
Leutnant	Ottokar Hinz	3/Pz.Rgt.4	8.12.42
Unteroffizier	Adolf Aichele	2/Pz.Gren.Rgt.66	13.12.42
Hauptmann	Helmuth Giersdorf	I/Pz.Gren.Rgt.93	8.1.43
Oberleutnant d R	Rudi Schmidt	1/Pz.Jäg.Abt.13	8.1.43
Oberleutnant	Fritz Schöck	9/Pz.Rgt.4	8.1.43
Oberfeldwebel	Alois Hemmelmann	6./Pz.Rgt.4	8.1.43

Feldwebel	Otto Szagun	5/Pz.Rgt.4	8.1.43
Oberfeldwebel	Otto Giercke	3/Pz.Art.Rgt.13	20.1.43
Oberfeldwebel	Walter Rennert	3/Pz.Gren.Rgt.66	20.1.43
Oberfeldwebel	Fritz Wopp	8/Pz.Gren.Rgt.66	20.1.43
Feldwebel	Otto Lehmann	5/Pz.Gren.Rgt.66	20.1.43
Major	Albert Brux	Kdr Kradschutzen Btl.43	23.1.43
Leutnant d R	Hans-Heini Roozk	4/Kradschutzen Btl.43	21.2.43
Oberfeldwebel	Helmut Schumann	1/Pz.Gren.Rgt.66	21.3.43
Hauptmann	Reinhard Morell	1/Pz.Rgt.4	29.3.43
Hauptmann	Johannes Steinberg	II/Pz.Gren.Rgt.66	29.3.43
Oberleutnant	Hans Joachim Ladicke	2/Pz.Gren.Rgt.66	29.3.43
Oberfeldwebel	Friedrich Münz	2/Pz.Gren.Rgt.66	29.3.43
Oberleutnant	Dietrich Mielke	4/Kradschutzen Btl.43	30:4.43
Oberfeldwebel	Walter Michel	2/Pz.Gren.Rgt.66	6.7.43
Unteroffizier	Otto Kubitza	2/Pz.Gren.Rgt.93	10.7.43
Oberfeldwebel	Hermann Kochan	4/Pz.Gren.Rgt.66	13.7.43
Feldwebel	Kurt Wogeck	1/Pz.Gren.Rgt.93	13.7.43
Oberleutnant	Manfred Wendt	5/Pz.Gren.Rgt.93	20.8.43
Feldwebel	Kurt Fickendey	I/Pz.Gren.Rgt.66	20.8.43
Stabsarzt	Dr. Norbert Broichmann	St.Arzt d Pz.Gren.Rgt.66	28.8.43
Oberleutnant	Willy Dondl	5/Pz.Rgt.4	7.10.43
Oberleutnant	Gustav Soldner	1/Pz.Gren.Rgt.66	29.10.43
Leutnant	Rudolf Becker	1/Pz.Gren.Rgt.66	29.10.43
Unteroffizier	Friedrich Sadowski	5/Pz.Gren.Rgt.93	21.11.43
Obergefreiter	Hans-Georg Borde	2/Pz.Gren.Rgt.93	21.11.43
Hauptmann	Rudolf Schröter	III/Pz.Art.Rgt.13	5.12.43
Oberfeldwebel	Kurt Schacher	6/Pz.Rgt.4	5.12.43
Leutnant d R	Günther Gruß	8/Pz.Rgt.4	8.12.43
Leutnant d R	Hans Georg Koch	8/Pz.Gren.Rgt.66	8.12.43
Unteroffizier	Ernst Matthes	7/Pz.Gren.Rgt.66	8.12.43
Oberstleutnant iG	Helmut Möller-Althaus	Ia 13.Pz.Div.	15.12.43
Stabsfeldwebel	Hermann Ecke	1/Pz.Gren.Rgt.93	13.1.44
Stabsgefreiter	Rudolf Stelzer	3/Pz.Gren.Rgt.93	13.1.44
Major	Franz von Wiecki	Kdr d II/Pz.Gren.Rgt.93	16.1.44
Hauptmann	Horst Joachim Störmer	Adj Pz.Gren.Rgt.66	16.1.44
Oberleutnant	Arno Tietz	5/Pz.Gren.Rgt.66	20.1.44
Oberfeldwebel	Hinrich Meyerdierks	10(Fla)/Pz.Gren.Rgt.66	27.1.44
Hauptmann	Hans Joachim Rodatz	I/Pz.Gren.Rgt.66	4.2.44
Feldwebel	Jakob Meyer	4/Pz.Gren.Rgt.93	17.2.44
Oberleutnant d R	Walter Schulze	Chef d 4 He.Flak Abt.271	23.2.44
Hauptmann d.R	Heinz Böttcher	5/Pz.Art.Rgt.13	5.3.44
Oberleutnant d R	Paul Großkopf	4/Pz.Art.Rgt.13	5.3.44
Oberleutnant	Heinz Albert	Pz.Pi.Btl.4	12.3.44
Oberfeldwebel	Frizt Bauersfeld	7/Pz.Gren.Rgt.93	23.3.44
Oberst	Friedrich-Karl Barth	Kdr d Pz.Gren.Rgt.93	1.6.44
Hauptmann	Hans-Georg von Gusovius	Kdr II/Pz.Rgt.4	1.6.44
Leutnant d R	Paul Willing	3/Pz.Gren.Rgt.93	15.6.44
Oberfeldwebel	Franz Arndt	9/Pz.Gren.Rgt.93	20.6.44
Oberstleutnant	Alexander von Oppen	Kdr Pz.Gren.Rgt.66	28.6.44
Leutnant	Kurt Bentin	5/Pz.Gren.Rgt.66	28.6.44
Hauptmann d R	Anton Taschner	Pz.Aufkl.Abt.13	2.7.44
Oberleutnant d R	Joachim Graf Kalckreuth	2/Pz.Aufkl.Abt.13	2.7.44
Oberfeldwebel d R	Otto Drebenstedt	6/Pz.Gren.Rgt.93	2.7.44
Fahj.Oberfeldwebel	Anton Heine	Stab Kp/Pz.Gren.Rgt.66	8.7.44
Hauptmann	Hellmut Bunge	2/Pz.Gren.Rgt.66	14.7.44
Feldwebel	Johann Grötsch	3/Pz.Gren.Rgt.66	14.7.44
Oberleutnant	Helmut Eckoldt	Adj II/Pz.Gren.Rgt.66	21.7.44
Hauptmann	Hans Joachim Hildebrandt	I./Pz.Gren.Rgt.66	10.8.44

Holders of the Army Roll of Honour Clasp of the 13th Infantry Division (mot)/13th Panzer Division

(sp.13.Pz.Div.*FHH*/Pz.Div.*FHH* 2)

Leutnant	Heinz Süßengut	Schutz.Rgt.93	22.7.41
Leutnant	Hans-Horst Borg	1/(Pz.Spah)Pz.Aufkl.Abt.13	19.8.41
Leutnant	Otto Freytag	Ord.Offz. I/Art.Rgt.13	20.9.41
Unteroffizier	Josef Trybura	1/Pz.Jäg.Abt.13	6.11.41
Leutnant	Wilhelm Wiese	Zugfhr i d 2/Schutz.Rgt.66	8.12.41
Leutnant	Leo Witter	Zugfhr 2/Schutz.Rgt.93	4.5.42
Oberfeldwebel	Ernst Hauschild (mit seine sMG Gruppe)	4/Schutz.Rgt.93	4.5.42
Unteroffizier	Erwin Trapp	4/Schutz.Rgt.93	21.6.42
Leutnant	Manfred Wendt (mit seinen Zuge)	Zugfhr i d 4/Pz.Gren.Rgt.93	19.11.42
Obergefreiter	Horst Brauner	9/Pz.Rgt.4	7.1.43
Obergefreiter	Ernst Hillert	Zugfhr i d 1/Pz.Pi.Btl.4	7.1.43
Uberfeldwebel	Willy Fetting	Zugfhr 5/Pz.Rgt.4	26.2.43
Hauptmann	Horst Moll	Chef d 2/Pz.Rgt.4	17.7.43
Leutnant	Rudolf Becker	Zugfhr d 1/Pz.Gren.Rgt.66	7.8.43
Feldwebel	Jakob Pech	Halbzugfhr i d 6/Pz.Rgt.4	7.8.43
Unteroffizier	Günther Mews (mit seine Gruppe)	Gruppfhr 2/Pz.Gren.Rgt.93	27.8.43
Major	Günther Baranek	Kdr Pi.Btl.4	27.2.44
Hauptmann	Johann Sauer	Kdr I/Pz.Gren.Rgt.66	27.2.44
Major	Johannes Steinberg	Fhr d. I/Pz.Gren.Rgt.66	7.7.44
Oberleutnant	Werner Schmutz	Chef d 3 (Sfl)/Pz.Art.Rgt.13	7.7.44
Oberleutnant	Herbert Gutschmidt	Chef d 3 (Sf.)/Pz.Art.Rgt.13	25.7.44

Knight's Cross Holders of the 60th Infantry Division (mot)

Leutnant	Rolf Schneege	Pi Zugfhr Stabs.Kp/Inf.Rgt.120 (mot)	14.5.41
Oberstleutnant	Rudolf Petershagen	Kdr II/Inf.Rgt.120 (mot)	20.7.41
Hauptmann	Erich Schröter	Kdr I/Inf.Rgt.120 (mot)	8.9.41
		†als Major 26.5.42	
Oberst	Karl-Albrecht Groddeck	Kdr Inf.Rgt.120 (mot)	8.9.41
		†als Gen.Lt. u Kdr 161I.D.	
Genralleutnant	Friedrich Georg Eberhardt	Kdr 60 I.D. (mot)	31.12.41
Major	Georg Hesse	Fhr III/Inf.Rgt.120 (mot)	31.12.41
		† 22.9.42 nördl. Stalingrad	
Oberarzt d R	Dr Horst Wilcke	Truppenarzt III/Inf.Rgt.120 (mot)	25.7.42
Hauptmann	Karl Willig	Fhr II/Inf.Rgt.120 (mot)	25.7.42
		Eichenlaub 18.1.43	
Feldwebel	Albert Dressel	Zugfhr i d 3/Pz.Abt.160 sp i Pz.Abt.106.*FHH*	13.10.42
		† als Oberfeldwebel i d Pz.Abt.106.*FHH*	
Oberleutnant	Fritz Sacha	Chef 2/Pz.Jäg.Abt.160	20/5.1.43
	Franz Klitsch	Kp C i d Gren.Rgt.120 (mot)	22.1.43
Obergefreiter	Fritz Mette	Gruppenfhr i d 9/Gren.Rgt.92	22/5.1.43

The following members of the 60 Infanterie Division (mot) won their decoration whilst serving in other units.

Oberst	Dr Hans Böelsen	Kdr A.A.160	17.9.43
		RK als Kdr Pz.Gren.Rgt.111 (11 Pz.Div.)	
Hauptmann	Wilhelm H J von Malachowski	Batterie Offz/Art.Rgt.(mot) 160 (1.8.40/12.6.41)	30.1.42
		RK als Oberleutnant u Battr.Chef i d Sturmgesch.Abt.189	
		Eichenlaub 8.6.42	

Holders of the German Cross in Gold of the 60th Infantry Division (mot)

Leutnant	Heinrich Halmschlag	4/Inf.Rgt.120 (mot)	18.10.41
		EBS 5.10.42 als Obit d 4/Inf.Rgt.120 (mot)	
Oberfeldwebel	George Martin	Inf.Rgt.120 (mot)	18.10.41
Hauptmann d R	Dr Gerd Hillger	I/Art.Rgt.160 (mot)	15.11.41
Oberstleutnant	Dr Hans Boelsen	Kradsch.Btl.160 (mot)	17.11.41
Oberleutnant	Gunther Jaenike	8/Inf.Rgt.92	17.11.41
Oberfeldwebel	Wilhelm Maddei	Stab.Kp/Inf.Rgt.120 (mot)	17.11.41
Rittmeister d R	Ernst Coelle	2/Aufkl.Abt.160	1.12.41
Oberfeldwebel	Herbert Hess	1/Aufkl.Abt.160	26.12.41
Oberleutnant	Wilhelm Schöning	10/Inf.Rgt.120 (mot.) sp Kdr *FHH* Einh	14.2.42
		RK 7.2.44 als Major d R u Kdr I/Fus.Reg.*FHH* (mot)	
		Eichenlaub 21.1.45 als Major d R u Kdr Pz.Gren.Rgt.66 (13.Pz.Div.*FHH*)	
Oberst	Georg Heinrich Zwade	Inf.Rgt.92 (mot)	28.2.42
Oberleutnant	Otto Meyn	I/Inf.Rgt.92	14.4.42
Oberleutnant	Alfons Leibold	Pi.Btl.160 (mot)	9.7.42
Oberleutnant	Johannes Teichert	Kradsch.Btl.160	9.7.42
Oberfeldwebel	Fritz Moede	II/Inf.Rgt.92 (mot)	9.7.42
Hauptmann	Gert Pfeiffer	Inf.Rgt.92 (mot)	3.8.42
Oberstleutnant	Walter Hollaender	Mg.Btl.9	18.10.42
Oberfeldwebel	Richard Friemelt	2/Kradsch.Btl.160	27.10.42
Oberleutnant	Dietrich Behrend	1/Kradsch.Btl.160	14.10.42
Unteroffizier	Richard Lewrenz	1/Inf.Rgt.120 (mot)	14.10.42
Oberleutnant	Fritz Sacha	Pz.Abt.160	18.10.42
Gefreiter	Karl Altmann	3/Pz.Jäg.Abt.160	18.10.42
Oberleutnant	Wilhelm Zunker	II/Inf.Rgt.120 (mot)	27.10.42
Oberfeldwebel	Hans Wolfshausen	3/Kradsch.Btl.160	27.10.42
Hauptmann	Kurt Schmidt	II/Inf.Rgt.120 (mot)	6.11.42
Oberleutnant	Gotthard Janello	Kradsch.Bt.160	6.11.42
Oberleutnant d R	Eberhard Rabe	II/Inf.Rgt.92 (mot)	6.11.42
Oberleutnant d R	Wilhelm Benwitz	Inf.Rgt.120	15.11.42
Oberfeldwebel	Arno Herrmann	1/Pz.Abt.160	21.1.43
Oberstleutnant iG	Ernst Stübichen	60.Inf.Div (mot)	23.1.43
Feldwebel	Alfred Jahnke	2/Pz.Abt.160	29.1.43
Oberst	Walther Kaegler	Art.Rgt.160 (mot)	18.6.43

The following members of the 60th Infantry Division (mot) won their decoration whilst serving in other units.

Oberst	Hans A v Arenstorff	SR 79	14.1.42
Oberleutnant	Werner Grün	Pz.Rgt.5	25.3.42

Holders of the Army Roll of Honour Clasp of the 60th Infantry Division (mot)

(sp.Pz.Gren.Div.*FHH*/Pz.Div.*FHH*/Pz.Div.*FHH* 1)

Unteroffizier	Hermann Kalkreuth	2/lnf.Rgt.92	6.11.41
Major	Hans Wolfgang von Fabeck	Aufkl.Abt.160 (mot)	28.11.41
Oberleutnant	Otto Meyn	3/Inf.Rgt.92	28.11.41
Oberleutnant	Willi Casseabum	6/Inf.Rgt.120 (mot)	8.2.42
Hauptnann	Martin Schönberger	I/Inf.Rgt.92 (mot)	4.5.42
Leutnant	Johannes Teichert	2/Kradsch.Btl.160	4.5.42
Feldwebel	Benno Grabrucker	12/Inf.Rgt.120 (mot)	21.6.42
Oberfeldwebel	Siegfried Gröppler	3/Inf.Rgt.120 (mot)	15.7.42
Oberleutnant	Heinrich Hamlschlag	4/Inf.Rgt.120 (mot) DKG 18.19.41 als Leutnant 4/Inf.Rgt.120 (mot)	5.10.42
Hauptmann	Georg Wilhelm Schöning	III/lnf.Rgt.120 (mot) DKG 14.2.42 als Oberleutnant u Kdr 10/Inf.Rgt.120 (mot) RK 7.2.44 als Major d R u Kdr I/Fus.Rgt.*FHH* (mot) Eichenlaub 21.1.45 als *Oberstleutnant* d R u Kdr Pz.Gren.Rgt.66	5.10.42
Oberfeldwebel	Gerhard Kroll	12/Inf.Rgt.120 (mot)	16.10.42

APPENDIX H

Orders of Battle

Panzergrenadier Division *Feldherrnhalle* (22 June 1943)

Divisional Commander

Generalmajor Otto Kohlermann (15.5.42 - 3.4.44)
Oberst Albert Henze RK mit EL, DKG (acting 13.2.44 - 13.4.44)
Generalmajor Friedrich Carl von Steinkeller RK, DKG (3.4.44 - 8.7.44)

Staff (Begleit Kompanie)

Ia *Oberleutnant* Felsch

Füsilier Regiment (mot) *Feldherrnhalle*

Oberst von der Hagen
Major Georg Wilhelm Schöning RKT

Formed on 15 April 1943 from the survivors and reservists from the 120th Infantry Regiment (mot) (Inf.Rgt. (mot) 120) destroyed in Stalingrad. From these men the I Battalion and the 14th Company were organised, being completed at the beginning of April with a unit coming from the 92nd Infantry Regiment (mot) (Inf.Rgt. (mot) 92), specifically the regimental Staff, the III Battalion and the 13th Company. On 20 June, it was officially converted into the Füsilier Regiment (mot) *Feldherrnhalle* (Füs.Rgt. (mot) *FHH*).

Regiment Stab
I/Füs.Rgt. (mot) *FHH* (*Major* Georg Wilhelm Schöning RKT)
II/Füs.Rgt. (mot) *FHH*
III/Füs.Rgt. (mot) *FHH*
Schweres Infanterie Geschütz (Selbstfahrlafette) (sIG Sfl)
Panzer Jäger Kompanie (Pz.Jg.Kp.)

Grenadier Regiment (mot) *Feldherrnhalle*

Oberst Herbert Böhme RKT
Major Heinrich Drewes RKT

This regiment, with a great SA tradition, was ceded by the 93rd Infantry Division. It was the new denomination adopted by the 271st Infantry/Grenadier Regiment (Gren.Rgt.271), a unit which had been organised in Jüterbog in October 1939 and which had gained experience in the western campaign and on the Russian Front. It had the peculiarity of having a battalion, the III/Gren.Rgt.271, almost exclusively composed of volunteers who came from the SA-Standarte *Feldherrnhalle*, a title which was officially given to the Regiment on 9 August 1942, making it the very first *Feldherrnhalle* unit in the Wehrmacht. On 17 February 1943, this unit left the 93rd Infantry Division, (*AOK* 16. Lovat), to contribute to the reconstruction of the destroyed 60th Infantry Division (mot). On 20th June 1943, it was officially assigned to the new *Feldherrnhalle* Division.

Regimental Staff
I/Gren.Rgt. (mot) *FHH*
II/Gren.Rgt. (mot) *FHH*

III/Gren.Rgt. (mot) *FHH* (*Hauptmann* Walter Evers RKT)
Schweres Infanterie Geschütz (Selbstfahrlafette) (sIG Sfl)
Panzer Jäger Kompanie (Pz.Jg.Kp.)

Panzer Artillery Regiment (mot) *Feldherrnhalle*

Oberst Walter Kaegler
Oberstleutnant Ratzel

This unit was initially formed from the remains of the 160th Artillery Regiment (mot) and contained the Regimental Staff and the I and II Battalions with 6 Feldhaubitze Batteries and elements of the destroyed 891st Panzergrenadier Regiment. On 22 June 1943, it received the denomination Artillery Regiment *Feldherrnhalle*.

Staff Battery (*Oberleutnant* Henke[118])
I/Art.Rgt. (mot) *FHH* (*Hauptmann* Hans Georg Schulte[119])
    1 Battery (*Oberleutnant* von der Heydt - Killed Feb 1944)
    2 Battery (*Oberleutnant* Erich Klein)
    3 Battery (*Leutnant* Seher - killed February 1944)
II/Art.Rgt. (mot) *FHH* (*Major* Froese)
III/Art.Rgt. (mot) *FHH* (*Hauptmann* Haber)

Panzer Abteilung *Feldherrnhalle*

Oberleutnant Erich Oberwöhrmann RKT

At the end of March, the remains of the 160th Panzer Abteilung returned to France. These gathered together the Staff (Stab/Pz.Abt.160) and the re-organised 1st Company (1/Pz.Abt.160). It was reconstituted and armed with the Sturmgeschütze III and IV, receiving the new *Feldherrnhalle* denomination.

Staff
1/Pz.Abt.*FHH*
2/Pz.Abt.*FHH*
3/Pz.Abt.*FHH*

Panzer Aufklärungs Abteilung *Feldherrnhalle*

The unit was furnished by the Krampnitz Academy for Panzer Troops II.

Panzerspähwagen Company
Panzeraufklärungs Company
Panzeraufklärungs Company
Schwere Schützenpanzerwagen (SPW) Company

Nachrichten Abteilung (mot) *Feldherrnhalle*

Fernsprech Kompanie (Telephone Company)
Funk Kompanie (Radio Company)
Nachrichten Kolonne (Signals Column)

---

[118] Died at the end of January 1944, replaced by Ziegler
[119] DKG died at the beginning of February 1944, replaced towards the end of the month by the acting commander of the 2 Battery, *Oberleutnant* Erich Klein and then by *Hauptmann* Habst

Pionier Bataillon (mot) *Feldherrnhalle*

1 Pionier Kompanie
2 Pionier Kompanie
3 Pionier Kompanie
Brückenkolonne "K"

Heeres Flak Abteilung *Feldherrnhalle*

Consisting of Batteries of Anti-Aircraft guns, previously known as He.Flak.Abt 282 (282nd Army Flak Battalion)

Division Naschschubtruppen *Feldherrnhalle* **(Di.Na.Fü.** *FHH***)**

Supply columns

Verwaltungsdienste (Administrative Services)

Sanitätsdienste (Medical Services)

Feldpostamt (Field Post Office)

Kampfgruppe Panzergrenadier Division *Feldherrnhalle*

Kampfgruppe Leader
Oberst Günther Pape RK m EL

Staff
Ia *Oberleutnant* Schöneich

Panzergrenadier Regiment *Feldherrnhalle*
Stab/Pz.Gren.Rgt.*FHH*
I/Pz.Gren.Rgt.*FHH*
II/Pz.Gren.Rgt.*FHH*
III/Pz.Gren.Rgt.*FHH*
Schwere Infanterie Geschütz (Motorisierte Zug)
Pionier Kompanie

Artillerie Regiment (mot) *Feldherrnhalle*
Stab/Art.Rgt.(mot) *Feldherrnhalle*
I (Sfl)/Art.Rgt.(mot) *FHH* (*Hummel*)
II/Pz.Art.Rgt.(mot) *FHH*
III/Pz.Art.Rgt.(mot) *FHH*

Panzerjäger/Sturmgeschütze Abteilung *Feldherrnhalle*
1/Pz.Jäg.Abt.*FHH*
2/Pz.Jäg.Abt.*FHH*
3/Pz.Jäg.Abt.*FHH*

Support Units
Panzer Nachrichten Kompanie
Panzerjäger Kompanie (PAK)
Pionier Kompanie

110th Panzerbrigade *Feldherrnhalle*

Commander
Oberstleutnant Georg Wilhelm Schöning RK m EL

Staff
Füsilier (Sfl) Kompanie/Stab Pz.Brig 110
Equipped with 16 armoured personnel carriers (SPW)

Panzer Abteilung 2110
Formed mainly with personnel from the Panzer Ersatz Abteilungen 10 and 18, and equipped with 36 Panthers and 4 Flakpanzers (A-A Tanks).

1/Pz.Abt.2110
2/Pz.Abt.2110
3/Pz.Abt.2110
Schwere Panzerjäger Kompanie (Sfl) 2110

Panzergrenadier Bataillon 2110 (Gepanzerte)
This battalion obtained its personnel in part from the veterans of the I (gp)/Pz.Gren.Rgt.*FHH* and the I (Sfl)/Art.Rgt.(mot) *FHH, the main* majority coming from the Replacement (Ersatz) units and equipped with 85 armoured personnel carriers (SPW - Schützen Panzerspahwagen).

1/Pz.Gren.Btl.(gp) 2110
2/Pz.Gren.Btl.(gp) 2110
3/Pz.Gren.Btl.(gp) 2110
4/Pz.Gren.Btl.(gp) 2110
5/Pz.Gren.Btl.(gp) 2110
Schwere Infanterie Geschütz Kompanie (Mot Zug) (150mm sIG)
Flak Zug (Sfl)

Support Units
Panzer Pionier Kompanie (gepanzerte) 2110 (5 platoons (Züge); equipped with 35 light APCs (le.SPW)
Brigade Versorgung/Nachschub Kompanie 2110
> **Kw.Kol.60t** (60 tonne capacity supply column)
> **Sanitäts Zug**
> **Werkstat Zug** (Workshop Platoon)
> **Flak Zug** (A-A Platoon)

13th Panzer Division *Feldherrnhalle*

Divisional Commander

Generalmajor Gerhard Schmidhuber RK m EL, DKG (Killed 11.2.45)

Staff

Ia *Oberstleutnant* Arthur von Ekesparre RK

Panzergrenadier Regiment 66

Formed by the fusion of the HQ of the Pz.Brigade 110 *FHH*, the Panzergrenadier Regiment 2110 *FHH* and the remains of the Panzergrenadier Regiment 66, originally part of the 13th Panzer Division.

Regiment Stab
I (gp)/Pz.Gren.Rgt.66
II/Pz.Gren.Rgt.66

Panzergrenadier Regiment 93

Following the new OKH directives on the formation of the new Panzerkorps *Feldherrnhalle*, the personnel of this regiment - from the reorganisation of the infantry of the 13.Pz.Div.*FHH*, together with the personnel of the Pz.Füs.Rgt.*FHH* of the Pz.Div.*FHH*, were supposed to have formed the new Füs.Rgt.*FHH*. However, this did not come to fruition because, as mentioned, the formation of the Panzerkorps was suspended due to the entry into combat of the units intended for it.

Regiment Stab
I/Pz.Gren.Rgt.93
II/Pz.Gren.Rgt.93

Panzer Artillerie Regiment (mot) 13

Formed by making up to strength the remnants of the old Artillery Regiment 13 of the 13th Panzer Division.

Regiment Stab
I/Pz.Art.Rgt.(mot) 13
II/Pz.Art.Rgt.(mot) 13
Panzer Haubitzen Batterie

Panzer Regiment 4

Consisted of two battalions; the first being the Panther Abteilung from Panzerbrigade 110 *Feldherrnhalle*, the second being the remnants of the old Pz.Rgt.4 (13th Panzer Division) made up to strength.

I/Pz.Rgt.4
II/Pz.Rgt.4

Panzer Aufklärungs Abteilung 13

Unit furnished by Wehrkreis XVII (Northern Austria).

1/Pz.Aufkl.Abt.13
2/Pz.Aufkl.Abt.13
3/Pz.Aufkl.Abt.13
4/Pz Aufkl.Abt.13

Panzer Pionier Bataillon 4

Heeres Flak Abteilung 271 (mot Zug)

Support Units (previously Pz.Brig.110 *FHH*)

Panzer Pionier Kompanie (gepanzerte) (ex-2110 probably integrated into Pz.Pi.Btl.4).

The medical, service and maintenance services were integrated with those of the 13th in the new divisional services.

Panzer Division *Feldherrnhalle*

Divisional Commander

Oberst (*Generalmajor* from 1.12.44) Günther Pape RK m EL, DKG, EBS (1.9.44/11.2.45)
Oberstleutnant Joachim Helmuth Wolff RK (21.12.44/11.2.45)

Staff

Ia *Oberstleutnant* Hans Schöneich

Panzergrenadier Regiment *Feldherrnhalle*

Oberstleutnant Joachim Helmuth Wolff RK[120]

Reconstructed from remnants of the Gren.Rgt.(mot) *FHH*, temporarily as I (gp)/Gren.Rgt.(mot) *FHH*, to which were added the effectives of a Jäger Bataillon *Feldherrnhalle*, organised in the spring of 1944 by Wehrkreis IV (Dresden), and young recruits from the Ersatz Brigade *Feldherrnhalle*. Originally formed part of the Kampfgruppe *Feldherrnhalle* and on the formation of Pz.Div.*FHH* [(through the absorption of Pz.Brig109)], ceded one of its battalions (III/Pz.Gren.Rgt.*FHH*) to the Fusilier Regiment to bring it up to strength.

Regiment Stab
I/Pz.Gren.Rgt.*FHH* (*Oberleutnant* Kurt Räder RK)
II/Pz.Gren.Rgt.*FHH* (*Hauptmann* Helmuth Bunge RK)
III/Pz.Gren.Rgt.*FHH* [121]
Schwere Infanterie Geschütz Kompanie (Mot Zug)
Pionier Kompanie

Panzer Füsilier Regiment *Feldherrnhalle*

The unit received the name of the old Füs.Rgt.(mot) *FHH* practically annihilated in Byelorussia. The regiment was formed taking as its base formations of Panzerbrigade 109. Among these was Pz.Gren.Btl 2109 to which was added the HQ Company, the Stab/Pz.Brig.109, as well as Schwere Infanterie Geschütz Kompanie 2109 and the cadre of troops from the brigade. The addition of the effectives of III/Pz.Gren.Rgt.*FHH* provided an element of continuity with the traditions of the *Feldherrnhalle* units. In the plan for the new Pz.Korps *Feldherrnhalle*, it was planned to unify this regiment with the Pz.Gren.Rgt.93 (13.Pz.Div.*FHH*) to constitute the Korps Füs.Rgt.*FHH*; however, the formation of this had to be postponed, and with it the proposed amalgamation due to the fact that these divisions were hurriedly thrown into combat.

Regiment Stab
I/Pz.Füs.Rgt.*FHH*
II/Pz.Füs.Rgt.*FHH*.
III/Pz.Füs.Rgt.*FHH*.
Schwere Infanterie Geschütz 2109 (Mot Zug)
Pionier Kompanie

Panzer Artillerie Regiment *Feldherrnhalle*

Formed from the Artillerie Abteilung (mot) of the Kampfgruppe duly completed with the addition of new reserves who were particularly concentrated in the heavy III Abteilung. The nucleus consisted of a large group of veterans, men who had returned from the central sector of

---

[120] This officer previously commanded Pz.Brig.109 (R.Stoves)
[121] This battalion later transferred to Pz.Füs.Rgt.*FHH*

the Eastern Front in *Hauptmann* Lepach's group, to which were added men returning from convalescence or leave. However, the majority were drawn from the Ersatz units of the Regiment, the Art.Res.u.Ausb.Abt.*FHH* of *Elbing*. As one of its officers commented: "For the most part they were young volunteers from Berlin or Prussia who had received a good training. First in the Wehrabteilungen and then in the Ersatz unit in *Elbing*".

Stabsbatterie
I (*Hummel*)/Pz.Art.Rgt.*FHH* (*Hauptmann* Erich Klein)
II/Pz.Art.Rgt.*FHH* (*Hauptmann* Lange)
III (schw)/Pz.Art.Rgt.*FHH*

Panzer Regiment *Feldherrnhalle*

Unit organised from the Sturmgeschütze Abteilung of the Kampfgruppe *Feldherrnhalle* which was converted into the II Abt. (assault guns) of the Panzer Regiment of the new division.; and Pz.Abt.2109, the armoured nucleus of Pz.Brig.109, which became the I Abt.

Pz. Regiment Stab
I/Pz.Rgt.*FHH*
II/Pz.Rgt.*FHH*

The rest of the units arose from the amalgamation of the troops of this branch-of-service of the two units, filling the gaps with personnel from the reserves.

Panzer Aufklärungs Abteilung *Feldherrnhalle*

Organised from personnel from the Ers.Brig.*FHH*.

1/Pz Aufkl.Abt.*FHH*
2/Pz.Aufkl.Abt.*FHH*
3/Pz.Aufkl.Abt.*FHH*
4/Pz.Aufkl.Abt.*FHH*

Panzer Nachrichten Abteilung *Feldherrnhalle*

Hauptmann Klaus[122]

Organised mainly from the service troops of the Kampfgruppe with the addition of personnel destined for the headquarters of dissolved Pz.Brig.109.

Fernsprech Kompanie (*Oberleutnant* Fritz)
Funk Kompanie

Panzer Pionier Bataillon *Feldherrnhalle*

Hauptmann Kurt (Killed February 1945 north of Zsámbék)

1/Pz.Pi.Btl.*FHH*
2/Pz.Pi.Btl.*FHH*
3 (gepanzerte)/Pz.Pi.Btl.*FHH* (previously Pi.Kp.2109)[123]

Panzer Jäger Abteilung *Feldherrnhalle*

1/Pz.Jäg.Abt.*FHH*
2/Pz.Jäg.Abt.*FHH*

---

[122] Sent on a course for liaison officers in November 1944.
[123] The company commander was wounded in Isaszeg in October 1944 and died in hospital in Budapest.

3 (Sfl)/Pz.Jäg.Abt.*FHH* (previously Jägd-Pz.Kp.2109)

Panzer Flak Abteilung *Feldherrnhalle*
1/Pz.Flak.Abt.*FHH* (88mm)
2/Pz.Flak.Abt.*FHH* (88mm)

Signals Units

Verwaltungsdienste

Medical Services
Division Medical Officer: *Oberfeldarzt* Dr Bulle (Killed in Budapest)
                                       Oberfeldarzt Dr Hübner

Field Post Office

Panzerkorps *Feldherrnhalle*

Corps Commander
General der Panzertruppen Ulrich Kleemann (27.11.44/8.5.45)

Staff
Chief of Staff *Oberst* iG von Natzmer
Ia *Major* iG Haen

Corps Units

Artillerie Kommandeur *Feldherrnhalle*

Pionier Regiment Stab *Feldherrnhalle*
Set up in December 1944 on the basis of the Pionier Regiment 685. This unit was subsequently transferred to Styria and its place taken by Panzer Pionier Regiment 678.

Schwere Panzer Abteilung *Feldherrnhalle* (Tiger Abteilung)
Hauptmann Nordewin von Diest-Koerber

Derived from Panzer Abteilung 503, from the 21st December known as s.Pz.Abt.*FHH*.

1/s.Pz.Abt.*FHH* (*Oberleutnant* Oelmer)
2/s.Pz.Abt.*FHH* (*Hauptmann* Reichsfreiherr von Eichel-Streiber)

Korps Füsilier Regiment *Feldherrnhalle*
Initially it had been intended that the personnel of the old Füs.Rgt.*FHH* of the Pz.Div.*FHH* and Pz.Gren.Rgt.93 of the 13.Pz.Div.*FHH* would unify to form this unit. However, the hurried entry into combat of these divisions and the temporary suspension of the formation of the Panzerkorps *Feldherrnhalle* held up its formation to the autumn of 1944. Finally, after the losses suffered in Budapest, the unit was never set up..

Regiment Stab
I/Kps.Füs.Rgt.*FHH* (Companies 1-4)
II/Kps.Füs.Rgt.*FHH* (Companies 5-8)
9/Kps.Füs.Rgt.*FHH*

Panzerkorps Artillerie Abteilung
I/104
II/104

Panzer Pionier Bataillon 404[124]

Panzer Nachrichten Abteilung 44 (Signals Abteilung)

Panzerkorps Versorgungs Regiment (Logistics Regiment)

Formed 27 November 1944 on the basis of the amalgamation of the service troops of the Pz.Div.*FHH* and the 13 Pz.Div.*FHH*. Due to the losses suffered in Budapest it could only be partly organised.

> **Nachschub Abteilung** *FHH* (Supply)
> **Feldzeug Bataillon** *FHH*
> **Kraftfahrzeuge Instands. Abteilung** *FHH*
> **Sanit.Abteilung 404m** (Medical)
> **Verwaltungs Truppen Abteilung** *FHH*

Korps Maschinengewehr Bataillon Panzerkorps *Feldherrnhalle* (MG Battalion)

Organised in April 1945 on the basis of Korps Maschinengewehr Bataillon 429.

---

[124] The numbers 404 and 44 were applied to units belonging to the cadre of the old IV Panzerkorps.

Panzer Division *Feldherrnhalle* 1 (20.2.-8.5.1945))

Divisional Commander
Generalmajor Günther Pape (20.2.45/8.5.45)
Oberstleutnant Hans Joachim Wolff (April/May 1945)

Staff

Panzer Regiment *Feldherrnhalle* 1
This Panzer Regiment was to reproduce the structure of the previous Panzerbrigades; thus it's first battalion would be a battalion of tanks from Pz.Abt.208, its second battalion formed from Panzergrenadiers.

Regiment Stab
I/Pz.Rgt.*FHH* 1
II (SPW)/Pz.Rgt.*FHH* 1

Panzergrenadier Regiment *Feldherrnhalle* 1
Oberstleutnant Hans Joachim Wolff

Regiment Stab
I(gp)/Pz.Gren.*FHH* 1 (Companies 1-4)
II/Pz.Gren.*FHH* 1 (Companies 5-8)
III/Pz.Gren.*FHH* 1 (Companies 9-12)
13 Schwere Infanterie Geschutz Kompanie
14 Pionier Kompanie

Panzergrenadier *Feldherrnhalle* 2
Never formed.

Panzer Artillerie Regiment *Feldherrnhalle*
Oberstleutnant Bönsch

Composed of two heavy howitzer batteries (Schwere Feldhaubitze Batterie) and four light howitzer batteries (Leichte Feldhaubitze Batterie), spread amongst two battalions.

Regiment Stab
I/Pz.Art.Rgt.*FHH* (Companies 1-3)
II/Pz.Art.Rgt.*FHH* (Companies 4-5)
III(?)/Pz.Art.Rgt.*FHH* (Companies 7-9)

Support Units

Panzer Aufklärungsgruppe *Feldherrnhalle*
Consisted of a reinforced reconnaissance company (verst.Pz.Aufkl.Kp.) equipped with motorcycles (Rad/Kette) and APCs (SPW).

Panzer Jäger Kompanie (Selbstfahrlafette)

Equipped with 10 Jagdpanzer IIIs and three sections of anti-tank guns (schwere Panzer Abwehr Kanone). There are references to the existence in March 1945 of a PzJäg.Abt.1.

Panzer Flak Batterie *Feldherrnhalle*

Composed of three A-A platoons (Flak-Kampfstrupp/gem.Fla.Zug) equipped with 88mm guns.

Verst.Panzer Nachrichten Kompanie *Feldherrnhalle*

Including an armoured section (Funkstaffel (gp)).

Verst.Panzer Pionier Kompanie *Feldherrnhalle*

Equipped with armoured vehicles (SPW) and reinforced with a section of heavy rocket launchers (schwere Werfer Zug), the abbreviation for rocket launchers being 'Wf'.

Versorgungs Bataillon *Feldherrnhalle* (Service Battalion)

Consisting of the following companies:

Nachschub Kompanie (Nach.Kp.)
Versorgungs Kompanie (Versorg.Kp.)
Instandhaltung Kompanie (Inst.Kp.)
Sanitäter Kompanie (San.Kp.)

Panzer Division *Feldherrnhalle* 2 (9.3.45/8.5.45))

Divisional Commander

Oberst/Generalmajor (s.4.45) Dr Franz Bäke (9.3.45/8.5.45)

Staff

gem.Panzer Regiment *Feldherrnhalle* 2

Organised in March 1945. Once again, it followed the structure of Pz.Rgt.*FHH* 1. Thus, it's first battalion consisted of one abteilung of tanks formed from the survivors of Pz.Rgt.4 and replacements from Pz.Abt.219 (Independent troops at the disposition of the Army) and the new replacements from Pz.Ers.Abt.4. For its part, the second battalion consisted of an abteilung of Panzergrenadiers derived from the remnants of Pz.Gren.Rgt.93 and was equipped with armoured vehicles (SPW).

> **Regiment Stab**
> **I/Pz.Rgt.*FHH* 2 (Panthers, Companies 1-4)**
> **II(gp)/Pz.Rgt.*FHH* 2 (Companies 5-8)**
> **III/Pz.Rgt.*FHH* 2 (Companies 9-12)**

Panzergrenadier Regiment *Feldherrnhalle* 3

This was also formed in March 1945 on the basis of regiments 66 (concentrated in the first battalion) and 93 (concentrated in the second) plus new reinforcements.

> **Regiment Stab**
> **I(gp)/Pz.Gren.Rgt.*FHH* 3 (Kompanien 1-4)**
> **II/Pz.Gren.Rgt.*FHH* 3 (Kompanien 5-8)**
> **III/Pz.Gren.Rgt.*FHH* 3 (Kompanien 9-12)**
> **13 Infanterie Geschutz Kompanie**
> **14 Pionier Kompanie**

Panzergrenadier Regiment *Feldherrnhalle* 4

Never formed.

Panzer Artillerie Regiment (mot) 13

Organised in March 1945 on the basis of the survivors of Pz.Art.Rgt.13. Equipped with two heavy howitzer batteries (Schwere Feldhaubitzen Batterien) and two light (Leichte Feldhaubitzen Batterien).

> **Regiment Stab**
> **I (Sfl)/Pz.Art.Rgt. (mot) 13 (Kompanien 1-3)**
> **II/Pz.Art.Rgt. (mot) 13 (Kompanien 4-5)**
> **III/Pz.Art.Rgt. (mot) 13 (Kompanien 7-9 ?)**

Support Units (Id. Pz.Div.*Feldherrnhalle* 1)

Panzer Aufklärungsgruppe 13

Panzer Jäger Kompanie (Sfl) 13

Also Pz.Jäg.Kp.*FHH* 2. Organised in March 1945 reinforcing the remnants of the Pz.Jäg.Abt. with elements from the Ersatz units.

Panzer Flak Batterie 13

Also Heeres Flak Abt.*FHH* 2. Raised from Heeres Flak Artillerie Abteilung 271.

Verst.Panzer Nachrichten Kompanie 13

Verst.Panzer Pionier Kompanie 13

Also Pi.Btl.*FHH* 2, raised from Pz.Pi.Btl.4.

Versorgungs Bataillon 13

Panzerbrigade 106 *Feldherrnhalle*[125]

Brigade Commander

Oberst Dr. Franz Bäke (13.7.44/12.1.45)
Major Berhard von Schkopp (12.1.45/24.1.45)
Oberstleutnant Heinrich Drewes (24.1.45/29.3.45)
Hauptmann Richard Pohl (29.3.45/11.4.45)
Oberleutnant Ernst Matten (19.4.45/4.45)

Staff

St.Kp./Pz.Brig.106 *FHH* (*Oberleutnant* Ernst Matten)

Panzer Abteilung 2106 *Feldherrnhalle*

Hauptmann Erich Oberwöhrmann (7.44/8.9.44)
Hauptmann Paul Te-Heesen (8.9.44/9.1.45)
Oberleutnant Leppla (9.1.45/27.2.45)
Hauptmann Richard Pohl (27.2.45/11.4.45)

> **1/Pz.Abt.2106** *FHH* (*Hauptmann* Wiede)
> **2/Pz.Abt.2106** *FHH* (*Oberleutnant* Körber)
> **3/Pz.Abt.2106** *FHH* (*Oberleutnant* Struck)
> **4/Pz.Abt.2106** *FHH* (*Oberleutnant* Auer)
> **V/Pz.Abt.2106** *FHH* (*Oberleutnant* Schuster)

Panzergrenadier Bataillon 2106 *Feldherrnhalle*

Hauptmann Münzer (7.44/8.9.44)
Hauptmann Bartel (8.9.44/26.12.44)
Hauptmann Bennwitz (26.12.44/24.1.45)
Oberleutnant Hartmann (24.1.45/10.2.45)
Hauptmann Kettmann (10.2.45/18.3.45)
Oberleutnant Sommer (18.3.45/30.3.45)
Oberleutnant Baumgart (30.3.45/10.4.45)
Oberleutnant Pfaff (10.4.45/19.4.45)

> **1/Pz.Gren.Btl.2106** *FHH* (*Oberleutnant* Hobel)
> **2/Pz.Gren.Btl.2106** *FHH* (*Oberleutnant* Papke)
> **3/Pz.Gren.Btl.2106** *FHH* (*Oberleutnant* Anding)
> **4/Pz.Gren.Btl.2106** *FHH* (*Oberleutnant* Büchting)
> **5/Pz.Gren.Btl.2106** *FHH* (*Oberleutnant* Hollfelder)
> **6/Pz.Gren.Btl.2106** *FHH* (*Oberleutnant* Barkschat)
> **7/Pz.Gren.Btl.2106** *FHH* (*Leutnant* Neumann)
> **8/Pz.Gren.Btl.2106** *FHH* (*Oberleutnant* Hartmann)
> **V/Pz.Gren.Btl.2106** *FHH* (*Hauptmann* Pluhm)

Panzer Pionier Kompanie 2106 *Feldherrnhalle*

Hauptmann Scheske

---

[125] The names of the company commanders appearing here are taken from the Order of Battle for 31.8.44 and may have changed subsequently.

Versorgungs Kompanie 2106 *Feldherrnhalle*
Oberleutnant Löffler

Werkstatt Kompanie 2106 *Feldherrnhalle*
Hauptmann Wicke

Panzerbrigade 109

Brigade Commander

Oberstleutnant Baier
Oberstleutnant Joachim Helmuth Wolff

Staff

Panzer Abteilung 2109 (Panthers)

Panzergrenadier Bataillon 2109

Sanitäts Zug (Medical Section)

Werkstätte Zug (maintenance Section)

Flak Zug (A-A Section)

Kraftwagen Kolonne 60 t. (Supply Column)

APPENDIX I

Under the Eagles of the Luftwaffe

Figure 1 A group from the Luftlande Regiment *Feldherrnhalle* during training. The *Feldherrnhalle* cuff-title is just visible on some of their arms.

Origins

The origins of the airborne *Feldherrnhalle* units should be identified with one event which, at the time, may well have seemed relatively insignificant. There is no question that any of the Brownshirts serving in the elite honorary unit of the SA, known as the SA-Standarte *Feldherrnhalle,* could have envisaged that the deference that its *Stabschef* would pay to the head of the new Luftwaffe, Hermann Göring, (to whom he intended to hand over the honorary command of the Standarte), would have such a decisive impact on its future as a military force. Certainly, many different hypotheses may be advanced as to the possible motives which may have led Viktor Lutze to take the step which would place his praetorians under the protection of such an ambitious individual.

One of the greatest experts on the subject, the German researcher Klaus Woche, interprets the gesture as a kind of guarantee that the organisation would have to pay as a result of its former disloyalties; a type of surety demanded by those who were still jealous of the potential threat posed by the SA; a way of exorcising a possible show of strength by the SA, by placing its best men - the only men, moreover, who were armed and barracked - under the careful vigilance of a figure as trustworthy as Göring.

Nonetheless, although at first glance his arguments seem logical, if we bear in mind the consequences of "Operation Kolibri (Hummingbird)", which had led to the disappearance of those who identified with the so-called "Second Revolution", the pacifying effects which the gradual disappearance of unemployment amongst its militants exercised over the attitude of the SA as a group, the drastic reduction (of some 75%) in their numbers, or the consolidation of key counter-weights like the new Army, the State Security Forces, or the SS, we might venture a more precise explanation of the motives underlying this reality. From this new point of view, it may appear more as an initiative originating from within SA circles close to that of *Stabschef*, rather than as a contribution imposed from outside.

We should bear in mind that Lutze had good reasons for feeling grateful towards those at the head of the new National-Socialist state. It should not be forgotten that his rise to the Supreme Command of the SA had been facilitated by the purge of 1934, of which, moreover, Göring had been one of the principle instigators. This appointment, then, was a gesture of face, an offering which proved beyond all doubt that the much-vaunted reconciliation between the SA and the National-Socialist family was firmly cemented and that the "black cloud" which had once thrived amongst its ranks was no more than a memory of the past. On the other hand, at that time, the fact of being able to count on the goodwill of a man like the future *Reichsmarschall* was not without significance.

The former pilot of the famous Jagdgeschwader *Richthofen*, who now enjoyed wide-ranging powers within political and economic field, had been placed at the head of an Air Force in full development and enjoyed the aura of being the successor to the Führer. For Göring, much time had elapsed since the days when, as a recently-joined member of the NSDAP, Hitler had conferred on him the command of the first SA units. However, although from that point onwards his relations with the Brownshirts had not developed any further than those of any other leader of the Party, he liked to recall his former role and, later on, it was not unusual to see him wearing the over-elaborate armband (which during 1923 had distinguished him as the *SA-Führer*) on specific versions of his SA uniform.

Continually fêted with honorary appointments and presidencies, Lutze's gesture did not stand out from his splendid record, although it would, without any doubt, have had special significance for Göring. The name of the unit offered referred to the venerated march of 1923 and, therefore, to the first martyrs of the Movement. Certainly, on that 12th January 1937, the day of his 44th birthday, when he proudly accepted the appointment, Göring was to recall, in a self-satisfied manner, how his participation in that event almost cost him his life; it was no bad thing that these events were remembered now, in the "good times". Thus ensconced in his new office, also

Figure 2 An inspection of the *Feldherrnhalle* men by *Generalinspektor der Luftwaffe* Milch, with *SA-Stabschef* Lutze.

honorary, of *SA-Obergruppenführer*, he added the brown and silver cuff-title, the emblem of the magnificent unit of honour of the organisation, to his uniform.

Nevertheless, the effective command of the SA-Standarte *Feldherrnhalle* remained in the hands of Lutze's former adjutant, *SA-Brigadeführer* Erich Reimann, and whose "honorary" superior lost no time in causing him headaches, as we will see.

The Luftlande Regiment *Feldherrnhalle*

From its establishment in 1935, the Luftwaffe had not ceased to strengthen its numbers under the watchful gaze of Göring's team of specialists. In those days, one of his most ambitious plans was the organisation of a large airborne unit which, later on, was to become the basis for his battle-hardened parachute force.

To raise the required number of men, he mobilised all available forces. The new Division, later to be known as the 7th Flieger Division, was established from the two parachute Battalions which had, until then, been trained separately by the Army and the Luftwaffe, and to which, little by little, were added a series of units which for the most part came from the *General Göring* Regiment (the elite ground regiment of the Luftwaffe). However, there were still huge gaps to fill and before long Göring's officers began to consider the possibility of drawing the first-rate human resources of the SA-Standarte *Feldherrnhalle* into the project.

The suggestion was immediately accepted and thus, on 21st May 1938, an official communiqué from the Oberkommando der Wehrmacht made it known that specific Standarte units would, under Luftwaffe instructors, undergo short, eight-week courses which were to give the trained SA men the specialised training of the airborne forces.

The objective of these courses, was to train the necessary numbers of men so as to be able to set up a new Airborne Regiment whose battalions would be drawn from the re-structuring of Sturmbanne I, II and III of the Standarte.

On 1st June, the Oberkommando der Luftwaffe set the date for the start of these courses. The I Sturmbann from Berlin was to start its training on 1st August, the II, from München, would begin on 1st October and, finally, the III, from Hattingen and stationed in the Ruhr, would begin on 1st December. Thus, early in 1939, the new Luftlande Regiment SA-Standarte *Feldherrnhalle* (Ll.Rgt.SA-St.*FHH*), was ready to go into action if the circumstances required, the plan being that it would operate as a unit subordinated to the Kommandeur der Fallschirmjäger und Luftlandentruppen (Commander of the Parachute and Airborne Troops) *Generalleutnant* Kurt Student.

Once the training period was complete, and during peace time, the battalions of this Ll.Rgt.SA-St.*FHH* would be composed of a Staff (Stab) and four companies: two infantry, one heavy and one of engineers (all motorised). These forces were completed by a motorised signals platoon (Nachrichten Zug (mot)) and a motorcycle despatch-rider platoon (Kradzug).

The first two companies, the motorised infantry (1 & 2 Infanterie Kompanie (Motorisierte)/Inf.Kp.(mot)), each had six sections (Schützentrupps) armed with rifles and light machine-guns (le.MG34), 6 sections of heavy machine guns (Schwere Maschinengewehr Trupps) with s.MG34, one mortar platoon (Granatwerferzug), a signals section (Funkstelle) and a M/C despatch rider section (Kradfahrer). The third Company of heavy infantry (3 schwere Inf.Kp.(mot)) was where the support weapons were concentrated. There were two anti-tank platoons (Pak Zug) equipped with Pak 35/36 37 mm weapons, two anti-aircraft platoons (Flak Zug) armed with 20 mm guns and two further sections equipped with infantry guns (Infanterie Geschütz/IG).

Finally the engineer battalion (4 Pi.Kp.(mot)) was organised into two platoons (1 & 2 Züge) each of which had specialised demolition (Zerstörtruppe), ground clearance (Aufräunungstrupp), fortifications (Sperrtrupp), flame-thrower (Flamenwerfertrupp) and chemical warfare (Gastrupp) sections.

This structure was repeated in the three battalions of the Regiment, which retained *SA-Brigadeführer* Erich Reimann as its commander, who was supported in his work by a Staff, and also having at his disposal, as a core of troops belonging to the Regiment, a motorised signals platoon (Nachr.Zug) and a M/C despatch rider platoon (Kradzug).

Although the command structure of the Regiment and the Battalions, as well as the Signals and Despatch Rider platoons directly subordinated to them, were to retain their structure in peace time as well in war, this was not the case with the Companies.

In the event of war, the men of the four peace-time companies would re-organise into two Airlanding Companies (1st and 2nd Luftlande Kompanie/Luftl.Kp.). Each of these companies used one of the previous Infantry Companies as a base and were reinforced by means of the distribution of the men from the Engineer and Heavy Infantry Companies. Thus, they amounted to six sections armed with rifles and light machine-guns, an anti-tank platoon with two Pak 35/36 37 mm pieces, one anti-aircraft with two 20 mm pieces, one of mortars, one of infantry guns with two 75 mm pieces, one of engineers, a signals team, m/c despatch riders and medical units.

The supply of officers and non-commissioned officers for the Regiment should also have come from the SA-Standarte *Feldherrnhalle*. Nonetheless, although a sizeable proportion were Führers and Unterführers from the SA who, having completed training courses, were awarded the equivalent rank on the Luftwaffe scale, there were particular problems in making up the required number of officers, so it became necessary to sanction the transfer of officers form the Army, the Police and other Luftwaffe units.

The Czech Crisis

During the month of May 1938, German attempts to encourage the wish of the Sudeten minority to join their territory to that of the Reich, met with a declaration of partial mobilisation by the Czech government. It was almost a month since the German Staff, for their part, anticipating potential action against Czechoslovakia, had drawn up a plan of operations which had been dubbed the "Grun" plan. This was the backdrop against which a intense political struggle took place which was to extend throughout the summer and which was to become known as the "Czech Crisis".

As the preparations to set up the 7th Flieger Division continued at top speed, on 20th June, with the specialised training programme scarcely underway, and with the likelihood of an armed conflict growing daily, the Ll.Rgt.SA-St.*FHH* remained officially integrated into the Luftwaffe.

Consequently, the SA ceremoniously swore the oath of allegiance laid down for members of the Wehrmacht in front of their officers so as to immediately receive their new military documentation. From then onwards, they were subject to the legal, economic and welfare regime of the Armed Forces. By now, all questions relating to budget, equipment and armaments were a matter for the Luftwaffe.

Göring's eagles came to adorn the helmets and jackets of these men, giving rise to one of the most peculiar uniforms of the Third Reich. However, in all its actions as a airborne combat force, it had to wear the blue uniform of the Luftwaffe with the *Feldherrnhalle* armband sewn on the left cuff.

The 7th Flieger Division came into being on 1st July. Four days later, *Generalleutnant* Kurt Student took charge. Under his orders were formed the I/Fallschirmjäger Regiment 1 (*Oberstleutnant* Bruno Oswald Braüer), the Army Fallschirmjäger Infanterie Bataillon (*Major* Richard Heidrich), the Luftlande Bataillon *General Göring* (*Major* Sydow), a Company of Infantry Guns (Infanteriegeschütz Kompanie) (*Oberleutnant* Schram) a Medical company (Sanitäts Kompanie) (*Oberstabsarzt* Dr Dierigshofen), the Glider Company (Lastensegler-Kommando) (*Leutnant* Kiess), an Airborne Signals Company (Luft-Nachtrichten-Kompanie) (*Oberleutnant* Schleicher and finally, as forces subordinated to the Division, the Luftlande Regiment *Feldherrnhalle*, (*SA-Gruppenführer* Reimann), the 16th Infantry Regiment (*Oberst* Kreysing) and two Air Transport Groups Lufttransport Kampfgruppe zbV 1 & 2) (*Oberstleutnant* Ziervogel and *Oberstleutnant* von Lindenau respectively).

Figure 3 *Oberleutnant* **Karl Stefan (Tyczka) Tannert, an example of an SA-Standarte** *Feldherrnhalle* **officer who followed a career as a Fallschirmjäger**

Early in the autumn, the "Czech Crisis" appeared to have reached a dead end and, after the latest manoeuvres, the Ll.Rgt.FHH, together with the 7th Flieger Division was placed in a state of maximum alert.

In all of these actions which had been anticipated, Student's forces had had to take on the role of wiping out part of the frontier fortifications which the Czechs had prepared in the Freudenthal/Altvatergebirge zone in the Sudetenland. However, the Munich Conference averted the confrontation altogether, and what had originally been planned as a war aim, became an exercise in tactical training, the objective of which was the occupation of the Freudenthal aerodrome. They were not in Blummenkrieg for nothing (?).

Figure 5 Fallschirmjäger NCO demonstrating the use of the harness during the jump

The SA returned to their barracks without having fired a single shot. Curiously enough, in their first major action, the *Feldherrnhalle* men did not wear their distinctive armbands since, due to the speed with which events had unfolded, they had not been supplied by the service corps.

The disputes between the SA and the Luftwaffe to decide which of them controlled the SA-Standarte *Feldherrnhalle* continued. Initially, Lutze had been tolerant of Göring's management, acknowledging that in times of war, his men would be placed under Göring's orders. But Göring had other ideas. On 28th May 1938, he had made it known, through an official decree, that he commanded the men of the SA-Standarte *Feldherrnhalle* in peace time, as much as in times of war. This had taken the SA commanders by surprise - some of whom felt vexed by the impact of Lutze's 'friendly' gesture.

Nonetheless, the balance could only tip one way, and on 8th September 1938, the Oberkommando der Wehrmacht (OKW) officially sanctioned the manoeuvre begun by Göring four months earlier.

On 27th October 1938, in accordance with the new composition adopted by the SA-Standarte *Feldherrnhalle*, the opportunity arose for young Germans who so desired to do their military service in its ranks. The path towards the entire integration of the unit into the Luftwaffe as one more formation of the Armed Forces appeared relentless.

Meanwhile, in his Headquarters in Berlin-Tempelhof, Student took advantage of the October to December period to complete the organisation of his Division. In November, he was to receive three further Transport Groups and, on 1st January 1939, he was finally able to go ahead with establishing the first Parachute Regiment (Fallschirmjäger Regiment 1).

As we have already seen, the Munich agreement had not signalled the end of the "Czech Crisis", but rather the beginning. The artificial state created by the Treaty of Saint-Germain was on the verge of breaking up. It is true that the problems of the German, Polish and Hungarian

Figure 4 Practical exercises in jumping and landing for the future Fallschirmjäger

minorities had been resolved, but the Slovaks, oppressed since time immemorial by the overbearing Czechs, declared their independence, with German backing. The territory occupied by the Czech majority, Bohemia and Moravia, was now neither a viable political or economic entity and, under pressure from Hitler, it "sought" help from the Reich in establishing a "Protectorate" on its territory.

The Oberkommando der Wehrmacht prepared the military occupation of this area. From early in March, the Ll.Rgt.*FHH* was in a state of alert and on 15th March 1939, the same day as the signing of the agreement over the Protectorate, the second key operation got underway from the Schönwalde aerodrome: the occupation (undertaken together with their comrades from the 7th Flieger Division) of Prague aerodrome. In the same way as on the first occasion, this mission proved bloodless and, eight days later, the Ll.Rgt.*FHH* returned to its quarters. This was to be the last action undertaken by the SA airborne unit.

Surprisingly, on 1st April, the period of subordination of the SA-Standarte *Feldherrnhalle* to the Luftwaffe was officially ended. In addition, the emblems of the Air Forces disappeared from their uniforms and they once again took on their former appearance.

Although it might initially be thought that Lutze had succeeded in holding his own in the face of the all-powerful Göring, a more detailed analysis reveals that this outcome had been agreed.

There is no question that the publicised arrangement whereby military service could be done in the ranks of the SA-Standarte *Feldherrnhalle* would be overturned at an opportune moment by means of a new decree, 1939/S49 Nr. 131; but it is no less significant that this states that the members of the SA-Standarte *Feldherrnhalle* who were of service age would carry out their military obligations in Luftwaffe parachute units. Thus, Göring continued to have the pick of the best men, already with military training, from the Standarte. And as if this wasn't enough, there came another move, even more subtle.

The period between 20 June 1938 and 31st March 1939, was considered to be a period of active military service. In Germany, military service lasted twenty-four months and could not be fragmented. As a result, all the veterans who had belonged to the airborne regiment had to complete the twelve and a half months which remained, in the same way as any Luftwaffe recruit. This meant that all these fine men, already trained and experienced, were to remain in the Luftwaffe as individuals without the SA having any hold over them at all.

Moreover, Göring made out that the cohesion which existed amongst the former companies of the disbanded Ll.Rgt.*FHH* should not be lost and went to great lengths to ensure it was not by incorporating them as a unit into the new battalions of the parachute arm.

Nevertheless, they would still have to undergo the demanding tests which permitted access to this chosen elite. A high percentage passed, ending up in the brand-new Fallschirmjäger Regiment 1. The rest remained in the Regiment *General Göring*, where most were assigned to the Wachtbataillon of the Regiment as a way of capitalising on their excellence as a ceremonial guard unit.

As it was, the veterans of the SA-Standarte *Feldherrnhalle* began to take on recruits from the parachute wing. In June 1939, the first unit of the 2nd parachute regiment was created, (Fallschirmjäger Regiment 2), specifically its 1st Battalion (under *Major* Woster), and two months later the second (under *Hauptmann* Erich Pietzonka) followed. Amongst the ranks were the majority of the SA men from the *Feldherrnhalle*, such that early in the war, about 80% of the men of service age from the Standarte were serving in Fallschirmjäger Regiment 2. However, although these SA volunteers participated in the most glorious actions undertaken by the parachute wing, their successes could not be attributed to the SA, since these men fought as Luftwaffe soldiers, not as members of an SA unit.

Little by little, the attention of the SA command came to focus on the former members of the SA-Standarte *Feldherrnhalle* who fought, initially as a Battalion, and later as a Panzergrenadier Regiment, in the Army and whose links with the SA were publicly recognised by the use of the cuff-title and the name *Feldherrnhalle*, which was eventually to be displayed by a whole Corps.

Although the SA component of this group was always in inverse proportion to its size, it was these *Feldherrnhalle* formations who, for the most part, inspired the SA with the hope of the military glory which it sought.

APPENDIX J

Fallschirmjäger Regiment *Feldherrnhalle*

A few years had to go by before, towards the end of 1942, in an attempt to introduce veterans of the SA-Standarte *Feldherrnhalle* into the parachute branch, the idea of establishing a parachute Regiment composed of SA volunteers and to be named *Feldherrnhalle*, could be studied. To this end, early in 1943, the *München*-based II/SA-Standarte *Feldherrnhalle* was chosen to gather together the SA volunteers destined for the Luftwaffe. In fact, this Sturmbann had moved its barracks from Dresden where, curiously enough, the 2nd Fallschirmjäger Regiment's reinforcement units were also situated.

And so it was that the plan of the SA came to be realised through precisely this Regiment, which, we should remember, had been the unit that at the outbreak of war, had contained most of the veterans of the disbanded Luftlande Regiment *Feldherrnhalle*. On 21st June 1943, the Oberkommando der Wehrmacht (OKW Communiqué No 17390/43 AHA/Ag/E (Ia)/II) echoed this.

In spite of the casualties suffered from that point onwards, by mid-1943 the presence of the former SA had spread throughout many of the German parachute, and airborne, units. They were particularly numerous in some cases, such as that of the Schützen Kompanie zbV of the 1st Fallschirmjäger Regiment. Even so, as far as the men were concerned, it was to be almost a year before the those who were to form the core of the future *Feldherrnhalle* parachute regiment began to be gathered together.

The process was to begin during the summer of 1944 when, thanks to the transfer of a group of recruits from the Fallschirmjäger Ers.u.Ausb.Rgt.1 and volunteers from the SA-Standarte *Feldherrnhalle*, it had been possible to establish the I/Fallschirmjäger Regiment 2 (2nd Fallschirmjäger Division/*Generalleutnant* Lacknert). During the last week of September, the regiment was to enter into combat in Holland under the command of Major Oswald Finzel, and bore huge losses during the course of engagements with the Americans in the Brest sector.

The Luftwaffe High Command was to order the re-establishment of the Division, incorporating as many men as it was possible to take from the reinforcement units in Dresden. The I/ Fallschirmjäger Regiment 2 was to be set up thanks to the large-scale arrival of SA volunteers originating from the II Sturmbann of the SA-Standarte *Feldherrnhalle*. Early in December, under the command of Oberst Meyer-Sach, the Regiment was transferred to Holland together with the remainder of the 2nd Fallschirmjäger Division, being assigned the mission of protecting the coast in the Amsterdam sector. It was there that the oft-quoted presence of the SA volunteers led to the traditional relationship between the Regiment with the Standarte to be finally recognised, for, in mid-December 1944, the 2nd Fallschirmjäger Regiment was to change its name to Fallschirmjäger Regiment *Feldherrnhalle*. At its head was Oberst i.G. Vorwerck.

During the third week of December, the 2nd Fallschirmjäger Division was called upon to defend the front situated between the south and south-west of Arnhem, where they resisted until February 1945, the date on which they had to retreat in the face of the Allied offensive to the south-east of Nijmegen against the Reichswald. For one month, the Fallschirmjäger Regiment *Feldherrnhalle* was deployed in that area and after the start of the Allied offensive, it was to fiercely defend the zone to the west of Goch and Bleijenbeek.

Eventually, during the first week of March, the Regiment crossed the Rhine with the rest of the Division. Upon regrouping in Duisburg, the magnitude of the casualties suffered became clear and, in order to carry out its next mission - the defence of the bank of the Rhine between Wesel and Krefeld - it had to be reinforced by units from the Volkssturm. Even so, the sector assigned to the Division had to be reduced and, in the days which followed, the *Feldherrnhalle* parachutists continued to fortify their stretch of the front in the sector allocated to the Division which included Ruhr-Mundung, the outskirts of Duisburg and the north of Düsseldorf.

During the last week of March, the Regiment stood its ground, but once the American vanguards crossed the Rhine, at Dinslaken, they had to retreat. As a result of the latest battles, the right flank of the Division, where the *Feldherrnhalle* parachutists were located, was cut off, and, in the midst of fierce attacks from armoured units, the Division was to re-group on the Rhine-Herne-Kanal early in April. Nothing seemed to be able to halt the enemy offensive, and once a large breach had opened up to the east of Essen, Oberst i.G. Vorwech received the order to retreat with his men and adopt a fortified position in Gelsenkirchen. A large part of the Regiment, including its Commander, was to be besieged and captured in this city.

Finally, the remainder was to continue fighting for a few more days alongside their comrades from the 2nd Fallschirmjäger Division to the south of Hattingen. Their munitions exhausted, the last parachutists of the Fallschirmjäger Regiment *Feldherrnhalle* were to end their days of fighting in mid-April, very close to the town which, curiously enough, had previously served as the barracks for one of the SA-Standarte *Feldherrnhalle* Sturmbanne.

APPENDIX K

The Oath-Swearing Ceremony of the Infanterie Ersatz Bataillon *Feldherrnhalle*, October 1942[126]

At the beginning of October 1942 the semi-trained volunteers passing out from the *Ausbildungs* battalions of the SA-Standarte *Feldherrnhalle* were reunited again at Güterfelde. There they were concentrated in the so-called Rekruten Kompanie (Recruits

Photograph 1. The procession to the Oath-Swearing Ceremony

Company) of the Inf.Ers.Btl.*FHH*, a unit formed from companies 5 and 6 of Inf.Ers.Rgt.9 from Potsdam on 11th September 1942. This Ersatz battalion must have been organised, according to Neumann's testimony, in two companies, a Recruits Company, whose function was the military preparation of the new soldiers and the a Convalescents Company to concentrate the wounded during the period of recovery.

The commander of the Recruit's Company was *Oberleutnant* Schumacher[127] and his second-in-command *Oberfeldwebel* Bleichert.

The first thing we can identify is the date of the celebration of the act. According to the inscriptions on the reverse of the photographs this took place in October 1942. The programme of instruction took 10 weeks and began with the swearing of the oath. It was from this point that the time of military service was counted.

The scene of the ceremony was the area behind the Palace at Güterfelde which acted as a parade ground. This was arranged in the shape of an gardened ellipse bordered by a fence in the half closest to the building. At the other end, at a clearly lower level, was a stone

Photograph 2. Schumacher (centre) and Bleichert (right) converse with Heuberger

---

[126] This reconstruction is based on the testimony and photographic documentation provided by Reinhold Neumann, one of the recruits who took the oath on that occasion.

[127] *Oberleutnant* **Schumacher**
Commanded the Recruit Company of the Inf.Ers.Btl.*FHH*. Probably an SA veteran. His tunic displayed the ribbons of the Iron Cross 2nd Class and the eastern Campaign Medal, the SA-Sports Badge, the Wound badge in black and two unidentified medals

Photograph 3. Von Eberlein, Mangels and Evers stand before the Parade

podium 15-18m wide and a little over 3m tall with a handrail and accessed from the rear. The front was adorned with an imposing Nazi eagle. As a special decoration for the occasion, 2 81 mm M34 Heavy Mortars (8 cm schw.Granatwerfer 34) had been placed on the turfed area in front of it. The ceremony began with the procession of the different participating units towards the place reserved for the ceremony. The order of the procession was as follows:

1. The Spielmannszug of the SA-Standarte *Feldherrnhalle*, ten fifes and drums with the Spielmannszugführer at its head.

2. The Musikzug of the SA-Standarte *Feldherrnhalle* with its musical director, Heuberger.

3. The Standard of the SA-Standarte *Feldherrnhalle* escorted by two of its officers, a Sturmführer and an Obersturmführer, both in SA uniform.

4. The Colour Flag (Fahne) of Inf.Rgt.271 (from 9.8.42 *Feldherrnhalle*), to which the Feldbataillon *Feldherrnhalle* belonged (III *FHH*/Inf.Rgt.271) escorted by two of its officers.

5. An honour guard belonging to Inf.Ers.Btl.*FHH*, consisting of 40-50 men armed with rifles and led by an officer.

6. The Recruit Company, armed only with bayonets. It may have been the case that these men were already waiting at the parade ground.

Photograph 4. Taking the oath

The units were placed with their backs to the eagle in the same order, aligned along a path about 2m wide, which cut across the grass parallel to the stone wall. The recruits were situated on their left perpendicular to them 3 or 4 m away from the other side of the path. There they awaited the arrival of *Oberstleutnant* Ritter von Eberlein[128], commander of the Inf.Ers.Btl.*FHH*. While they

---

[128] ***Oberstleutnant* August Ritter von Eberlein**
A veteran of World War I where he won the Iron Cross 1st and 2nd Class. In the Wehrmacht he was once again decorated with the same decorations. Had been in command of II/Inf.Ers.Rgt.612, a unit which had been acted as a security force for the Gouvernement-General (Poland), transferred to the Ukraine at the end of 1941, where it was integrated into Feldersatz Division B, later serving with Army Group South.
On 1st July 1942, von Eberlein received the German Cross in Gold, two months later taking charge of the Inf.Ers.Btl.*FHH*, which had been established don 11th September 1942. His tunic displayed, amongst other decoration (one of which seems to be Romanian) the Infantry Assault Badge and the Silver Wound Badge. His name ceases to appear in the officers list of 1944 on account of which one assumes that he must have retired.

Photograph 5. The newly sworn-in recruits take their leave of the Flag

were waiting, *Oberleutnant* Schumacher, followed by *Feldwebel* Bleichert approached in order to speak with Heuberger (It was at this moment that Photograph 2 was taken). Present at the ceremony were five officers who happened to be off-duty and a civilian, who were situated on the podium.

Von Eberlein then arrived accompanied by his Adjutant, *Leutnant* Mangels[129], and a guest of honour, *Leutnant der Reserve* Walter Evers, an officer who had won the Knight's Cross on the 4th December 1943 whilst leading the 11th Company of the Feldbataillon *Feldherrnhalle* on the Eastern Front. Evers was the first recipient that the *Feldherrnhalle* had and arrived wearing the uniform of an *SA-Sturmbannführer* of the SA-Standarte *Feldherrnhalle*.

Certainly von Eberlein and his party began the ceremony by reviewing the troops, then taking a position facing the Standard of the SA-Standarte *Feldherrnhalle*. A few seconds later, the regimental Colour Flag and its escort advanced 2 or 3 m, positioning themselves some way in the front of the main body. A group of four recruits came forwards from the main formation about 25-30 m, made a right turn and closed up to the spot to which the Colour Flag had been brought forward, positioning themselves facing the two escorting officers. Then they made another turn in order to face each other,

Photograph 6. The Final Parade. The colours march past

between them having been left a space into which the Colour Flag was lowered by the standard-bearer. With the left hand on the flagstaff and the right hand raised they uttered the current Wehrmacht oath. In the meantime the honour company presented arms and the officers saluted, von Eberlein in the military fashion and Evers raising his right arm in the SA manner. The oath over, the flag was raised up again, the four recruits made a turn marched back to their original places in the main formation.

The oath swearing over, the units arranged themselves to parade before von Eberlein, for which had been chosen as asphalt road which ran alongside the barracks.

---

[129] *Leutnant* **Mangels**
Adjutant to the commander of the Inf.Ers.Btl.*FHH*. Infantry Assault Badge, Iron Cross 1st Class and the ribbons of the Iron Cross 2nd Class and the Eastern Campaign Medal.

Photograph 7. Von Eberlein takes the salute of the newly sworn-in recruits

The order of the procession was the same as before: Spielmannszug - Musikzug - SA-Standarte *Feldherrnhalle* Standard - Colour Flag - Honour Company - Recruits Company.

They arranged themselves at the roadside, von Eberlein well to the front, with his adjutant behind him, a few yards to his right stood Evers and the five officers, with the civilian amongst them.

The band units, originally at the head of the procession, then located themselves facing the group of spectators. Behind them the rest of the parade marched past, some twenty metres away the Standard of the SA-Standarte *Feldherrnhalle*, ten metres behind this the Colour Flag, thirty metres behind this the Honour Company, all using the parade marching pace[130]. The Recruit Company brought up the rear at standard marching pace.

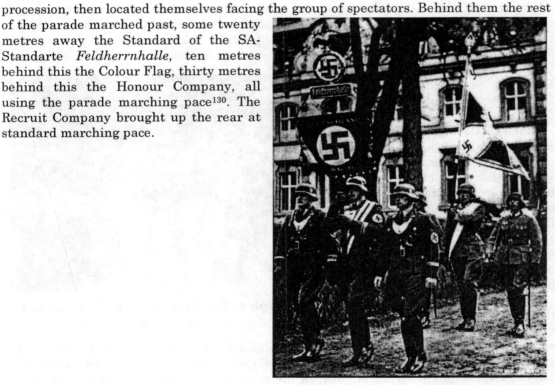

Photograph 8. The Standard of the SA-Standarte *Feldherrnhalle* and the Colour Flag of Inf.Rgt.271

---

[130] This "parade marching pace" presumably refers to the `goose-step'.

APPENDIX L

German Army Ranks and Appointments

The German Army of World War II consisted of seven classes of rank:

1.	Generäle	General Officers	Generalfeldmarschall-Generalmajor
2.	Stabsoffiziere	Field Officers	Oberst-Major
3.	Hauptleute	Captains	*Hauptmann*
4.	Leutnante	Lieutenants	Oberleutnant-Leutnant
5.	Unteroffiziere mit Portepee	Senior NCOs	Stabsfeldwebel-Feldwebel
6.	Unteroffiziere ohne Portepee	Junior NCOs	Unterfeldwebel-Unteroffizier
7.	Mannschaften	Men	Stabsgefreiter-Grenadier

Variations in the title of rank existed within different branches of the Service, for example, an Infantry Captain was referred to as a *Hauptmann* and a Captain in the Cavalry was a *Rittmeister*. Variations in title also existed where the holder had a special appointment, for example, a Cavalry saddler with the rank of Wachtmeister was known as a *Schirrmeister*. A basic comparison of ranks between the German Army, Waffen-SS, Sturmabteilung (SA) and the British Army is given below:

German Infantry	Waffen-SS	Sturmabteilung	British Infantry
Generalfeldmarschall			Field Marshal
Generaloberst	SS-Oberstgruppenführer		General
General	SS-Obergruppenführer	SA-Obergruppenführer	Lieutenant-General
Generalleutnant	SS-Gruppenführer	SA-Gruppenführer	Major-General
Generalmajor	SS-Brigadeführer	SA-Brigadeführer	Brigadier
	SS-Oberführer	SA-Oberführer	
Oberst	SS-Standartenführer	SA-Standartenführer	Colonel
Oberstleutnant	SS-Obersturmbannführer	SA-Obersturmbannführer	Lieutenant-Colonel
Major	SS-Sturmbannführer	SA-Sturmbannführer	Major
Hauptmann	SS-Hauptsturmführer	SA-Sturmhauptführer	Captain
Oberleutnant	SS-Obersturmführer	SA-Obersturmführer	Lieutenant
Leutnant	SS-Untersturmführer	SA-Sturmführer	2nd Lieutenant
Stabsfeldwebel[131]	SS-Sturmscharführer		
Oberfeldwebel[132]	SS-Hauptscharführer	SA-Haupttruppführer	Warrant Officer Class I
Feldwebel	SS-Oberscharführer	SA-Obertruppführer	Warrant Officer Class II
		SA-Truppführer	Colour-Sergeant
Unterfeldwebel	SS-Scharführer	SA-Oberscharführer	Sergeant
Unteroffizier	SS-Unterscharführer	SA-Scharführer	Lance-Sergeant
Stabsgefreiter			
Obergefreiter	SS-Rottenführer	SA-Rottenführer	Corporal
Gefreiter	SS-Sturmmann	SA-Obersturmmann	Lance-Corporal
Obergrenadier	SS-Obermann		
Grenadier[133]	SS-Mann	SA-Sturmmann	Private

[131] Comparison between German *Unteroffiziere mit Portepee* and British Infantry *Sergeants-Major* is difficult due to the fact that the German Army fielded Regiments with Battalions as sub-divisions and the British Army only Battalions. A British Infantry Warrant Officer Class I is referred to as *Regimental Sergeant-Major* although is in reality the senior Battalion NCO and corresponds to Oberfeldwebel (Battalion Sergeant-Major).

[132] A further rank *Hauptfeldwebel* exists above *Oberfeldwebel*. This was the name given to the senior NCO within a Regiment and is literally *Regimental Sergeant-Major* and commonly known as '*Der Spiess*'.

[133] Note that a German Private was referred to as a Grenadier. This was due to a special order of November 1942 when the previous designations; Schütze, Füsilier, Musketier were replaced by the title Grenadier throughout the German Army. Gebirgsjäger and Jäger troops were not affected by this order.

Variations amongst the branches of the Service are given below:

Officers

Infantry	Rifle/Mountain	Cavalry	Armoured
Generalfeldmarschall	Generalfeldmarschall	Generalfeldmarschall	Generalfeldmarschall
Generaloberst	Generaloberst	Generaloberst	Generaloberst
General der Infanterie	General der Gebirgs/Jägertruppen	General der Kavallerie	General der Panzertruppen
Generalleutnant	Generalleutnant	Generalleutnant	Generalleutnant
Generalmajor	Generalmajor	Generalmajor	Generalmajor
Oberst	Oberst	Oberst	Oberst
Oberstleutnant	Oberstleutnant	Oberstleutnant	Oberstleutnant
Major	Major	Major	Major
Hauptmann	*Hauptmann*	Rittmeister	*Hauptmann*
Oberleutnant	Oberleutnant	Oberleutnant	Oberleutnant
Leutnant	Leutnant	Leutnant	Leutnant

Artillery	Armoured Infantry	Medical
Generalfeldmarschall	Generalfeldmarschall	
Generaloberst	Generaloberst	
General der Artillerie	General der Panzergrenadiere	Generaloberstabsarzt
Generalleutnant	Generalleutnant	Generalstabsarzt
Generalmajor	Generalmajor	Generalarzt
Oberst	Oberst	Oberstarzt
Oberstleutnant	Oberstleutnant	Oberfeldarzt
Major	Major	Oberstabsarzt
Hauptmann	*Hauptmann*	Stabsarzt
Oberleutnant	Oberleutnant	Oberarzt
Leutnant	Leutnant	Assistenzarzt

Other Ranks

Infantry	Rifle/Mountain	Cavalry	Artillery	Armoured
Stabsfeldwebel	Stabsfeldwebel	Stabswachtmeister	Stabswachtmeister	Stabsfeldwebel
Oberfeldwebel	Oberfeldwebel	Oberwachtmeister	Oberwachtmeister	Oberfeldwebel
Feldwebel	Feldwebel	Wachtmeister	Wachtmeister	Feldwebel
Unterfeldwebel	Unterfeldwebel	Unterwachtmeister	Unterwachtmeister	Unterfeldwebel
Unteroffizier	Oberjäger	Unteroffizier	Unteroffizier	Unteroffizier
Stabsgefreiter	Stabsgefreiter	Stabsgefreiter	Stabsgefreiter	Stabsgefreiter
Obergefreiter	Obergefreiter	Obergefreiter	Obergefreiter	Obergefreiter
Gefreiter	Gefreiter	Gefreiter	Gefreiter	Gefreiter
Obergrenadier	Obergrenadier	Oberreiter	Oberkanonier	Panzer-Obergrenadier
Grenadier	Jäger	Reiter	Kanonier	Panzergrenadier

Armoured Infantry	Engineers	Signals
Stabsfeldwebel	Stabsfeldwebel	Stabsfunkmeister
Oberfeldwebel	Oberfeldwebel	Oberfunkmeister
Feldwebel	Feldwebel	Funkmeister
Unterfeldwebel	Unterfeldwebel	Unterfunkmeister
Unteroffizier	Unteroffizier	Unteroffizier
Stabsgefreiter	Stabsgefreiter	Stabsgefreiter
Obergefreiter	Obergefreiter	Obergefreiter
Gefreiter	Gefreiter	Gefreiter
Oberpanzergrenadier	Oberpionier	Oberfunker
Panzergrenadier	Pionier	Funker

Horse Transport	Mech. Transport	Medical	Officer Cadets
Stabswachtmeister	Stabsfeldwebel	Sanitätstabsfeldwebel	
Oberwachtmeister	Oberfeldwebel	Sanitätsoberfeldwebel	Oberfahnrich
Wachtmeister	Feldwebel	Sanitätsfeldwebel	
Unterwachtmeister	Unterfeldwebel	Sanitätsunterfeldwebel	Fahnrich
Unteroffizier	Unteroffizier	Sanitätsunteroffizier	Fahnenjunker-Unteroffizier
Stabsgefreiter	Stabsgefreiter		
Obergefreiter	Obergefreiter	Sanitätsobergefreiter	
Gefreiter	Gefreiter	Sanitätsgefreiter	Fahnenjunker-Gefreiter
Oberfahrer	Oberkraftsfahrer	Sanitätsobersoldat	
Fahrer	Kraftsfahrer	Sanitätssoldat	

Appointments

A range of special appointments within the German Army is given below with the resulting rank title:

Mannschaften

Appointment	Grenadier	Obergrenadier	Gefreiter
Bandsman	Musikergrenadier	Musikerobergrenadier	
Cavalry Farrier	Beschlagschmiedreiter	Beschlagschmiedoberreiter	Beschlagschmiedgefreiter
Cavalry Trumpeter	Trompeterreiter	Trompereroberreiter	
Farrier	Beschlagschmiedgrenadier	Beschlagschmiedobergrenadier	Beschlagschmiedgefreiter

Unteroffiziere ohne Portepee

Appointment	Unteroffizier	Unterfeldwebel
Cavalry Farrier	Beschlagschmiedunteroffizier	Beschlagschmiedunterwachtmeister
Farrier	Beschlagschmiedunteroffizier	

Unteroffiziere mit Portepee

Appointment	Feldwebel	Oberfeldwebel	Stabsfeldwebel
Carrier Pigeon NCO	Brieftaubenmeister	Oberbrieftaubenmeister	Stabsbrieftaubenmeister
Farrier	Beschlagmeister	Oberbeschlagmeister	Stabsbeschlagmeister
Farrier Instructor			Hufbeschlaglehrmeister
Fortifications NCO	Wallfeldwebel	Walloberfeldwebel	Wallstabsfeldwebel
Fortress Construction Master			Festungswerkmeister
Fortress Engineer NCO	Festungspionierfeldwebel	Festungspionieroberfeldwebel	Festungspionierstabsfeldwebel
Ordnance NCO	Feuerwerker	Oberfeuerwerker	Stabsfeuerwerker
Saddler NCO	Schirrmeister	Oberschirrmeister	Stabschirrmeister
Senior Farrier Instructor			Oberhufbeschlaglehrmeister
Senior Fortress Construction Master			Festungsoberwerkmeister

Other appointments existed, especially in the Administrative (Wehrmachtbeamten) Services for Officers and Other Ranks, ranging from *Feldbischof* (Chaplain-General) to *Futtermeister* (Fodder NCO) and *Lagerwarte* (Storeman).

APPENDIX M

Shelf Books' General Translation Policy

The Treatment of Eastern European Placenames

Insofar as German-language primary sources bearing on the activities of the armed forces of the Third Reich have begun to appear in translation in recent years (mainly published in Canada and the USA) they have been flawed in their treatment of Eastern European placenames: these have been left exactly as found in the German text, with the result that the English eye encounters the unpronounceable "Wassiljewschtschina", or the unfamiliar "Charkow", hindering attempts to trace the course of the war on contemporary English-language atlases. SHELF policy is to attempt to get the English rendition as close to the original native-language version as possible, with exceptions given below.

Prior to 1945, extensive German settlement in the Eastern European lands and trade with their peoples resulted in the adoption of German names for local places which are distinctively different from those of the native languages. In some cases, these are simply Germanicisations of the local placenames which can readily be recognised therein. In others, particularly where the German is a translation of a Slavic, Baltic, Romanian or Magyar (Hungarian) locality, no similarity at all will be evident to the English reader. In still other cases, German settlers imported radically new names. These terms, therefore, occur in the primary sources: SHELF policy is to replace them with the native term, except in documents where such a transformation would be inauthentic, in which case, the native term is given in brackets following. Examples of such problems are:

Slovak: Bratislava	German: Preßburg
Polish: Rzeszów	German: Reichshof
Magyar: Pécs	German: Fünfkirchen
Magyar: Székesfehérvár	German: Stuhlweißenburg
Latvian Jelgava	German: Mitau
Estonian Tallinn	German: Reval
Russian: Pskov	German: Pleskau

In some particularly awkward cases the German text term is taken over from a third language, given the vicissitudes of history and the complexity of inter-ethnic penetration, thus:

Lithuanian 'Kaunas' may be taken over into the German as 'Kowno' from the Russian-Polish in preference to the strictly-German 'Kauen'.
The West Ukrainian (Galician) city of 'Lviv' is 'Lwów' to a Pole, 'Lvov' to a Russian, and 'Lemberg' to a German.
The Latvian city of 'Daugavpils' (on the 'Daugava' river) is 'Dvinsk' (on the 'Western Dvina') to a Russian, 'Dünaburg' (on the 'Düna') to a German.
'Oradea Mare' (Romania) is 'Nagyvarad' to a Hungarian, 'Großwardein' to a German.

In such cases, Shelf policy is to choose the term used by the local ethnic group insofar as this enjoys the status of a 'Nation State' within the frontiers established around 1945, reinforced by the more recent break-up of the Soviet Empire (USSR), that is, the consolidation of the non-Russian identities of the Baltic, Ukrainian, Georgian, etc. nations.

As a result of the treaties of Versailles and St. Germain, many German-populated localities were lost to the German Reich or to the Habsburg successor state of Austria, soon after World War I. Since 1945, the whole of the historic German provinces of East Prussia, Pomerania and Silesia have been simply amputated from the main body of Germany and given by the victorious Allies to the Poles in compensation for the loss of correspondingly large swathes of their eastern marchlands (Kresy) to Stalin. The 1945 settlement confirmed the loss of the Sudetenland to Czechoslovakia (as it then was) and of West Prussia and *Danzig* to Poland. These displacements of frontiers were accompanied by the mass expulsion, and on occasion extermination of the German inhabitants of these regions. A similar fate befell the Volksdeutsche (ethnic Germans) of Romania (Banat and Transylvania (German 'Siebenbürgen')) of Yugoslavia, of Hungary (principally the Bácska) and *a fortiori* of the lands further east.

Naturally, German language texts utilise the placenames familiar to Germans for centuries, even though these will not now be found in contemporary atlases. However, to imply that German troops were fighting for their homes and families in Wroclaw, Kostrzyn, Kolobrzeg or Gdansk hardly seems appropriate: at the time these were *Breslau*, Küstrin, Kolberg and *Danzig* respectively. To indicate to the reader that such placenames have subsequently been transformed, they will be signalled in the text in italics, and given their post-1945 terms in a special gazetteer at the end, except in rare cases when the whole book concerns a lost city or province, whereby such usage would be come unbearable. In such cases, the German forms would be left unitalicised, and reference made at the beginning of the book to the gazetteer at the end.

The SHELF rule is therefore: places which were part of Germany before 1939, together with *Danzig* and West Prussia will be given in the German form; places never part of Germany in the local form consolidated since 1945 (1990) but placed in the gazetteer where helpful. A few hard cases - places incorporated into the Reich during the war years - for example Poznan (*Posen*), Lódz (Litzmannstadt) or Maribor (Marburg) will be dealt with in context.

Subsequent to this elimination of the German element in the Eastern European landscape, the collapse of Communism in the 1990s resulted in the redesignation of some historic cities purely for political reasons: thus, Leningrad reverted to being St. Petersburg, Gorkii to Nizhnyi Novgorod, Ordzhonikidze to Vladikavkaz, whereas Stalingrad had already become Volgograd (not the historic Tsaritsyn) somewhat earlier. However, for most people the siege of Leningrad and the Battle of Stalingrad are such familiar terms that to update them would seem to tear history up by its roots. In any case, since the 1939-45 war was very largely perceived by a majority of Europeans (not only National-Socialist Germany) as the confrontation with Communism (as the strength of the European volunteer movement showed), such a change in nomenclature would at a stroke wipe from sight the very reasons for which these battles took place.

To the English or American reader this preoccupation may seem pointless: it is no coincidence that neither country has suffered the humiliating loss of territory or subjection to alien rule which has been such a feature of twentieth century Eastern Europe. It is impossible to understand the bitterness of the 1939-45 conflict without empathising with the participants, for whom such namings and re-namings reflected the very essence of their struggle for national self-assertion, an ethnic identity, even existence itself. Whether we are living through a period after the 'end of history' or merely an interlude in the cycle remains to be seen.

APPENDIX N

Russian Pronunciation Guide

For the purposes of the transliteration of Russian throughout this book, SHELF BOOKS uses its own system which is consistent and as simplified as possible. Considerable accuracy of pronunciation has also been taken into account.

The Cyrillic alphabet

Cyrillic	English
А	a
Б	b
В	v
Г	g
Д	d
Е	ye
Ё	yo
Ж	zh
З	z
И	i
Й	i
К	k
Л	l
М	m
Н	n
О	o
П	p
Р	r
С	s
Т	t
У	u
Ф	f
Х	kh
Ц	ts
Ч	ch
Ш	sh
Щ	shch
Ъ	-
Ы	y
Ь	-
Э	e
Ю	yu
Я	ya

Notes on the Pronunciation of Russian

Only sounds and letters that are ambiguous, or that differ greatly from English have been selected here. Otherwise the reader can assume that the normal English pronunciation will suffice.

Consonants

A first point to note is that Russian pronunciation is very foreign. Consonants may appear unpronounceable to an English speaker. Do not be deterred by this; pronounce the consonants separately giving each its full value. For example DNYEPR, GDYE, GNYEV.

"CH" as in "cheque".

"G" always pronounced hard, as in "Get".

"KH" has no English equivalent. It is similar to the "ch" sound in the German word "ich" or in the Scottish word "loch".

"R" always rolled as in Scottish.

"SH" as in "shore".

"SHCH" stands for one letter in Russian! It can be created by isolating the "shch" between the words "fresh cheese" and pronounced together as one sound. This is the traditional Russian text-book pronunciation. In spoken Russian it is also pronounced as a long "SH", which is simpler and more acceptable.

"TS" pronounced as the "ts" in "bits".

"ZH" similar to the "s" in "measure" or "j" in the French word "je", however it is pronounced to a greater degree.

Double Consonants

When the following combinations occur: SCH, ZCH, ZHCH, they are pronounced "SHCH" (see note above).

Voicing and devoicing of consonants

A voiced consonant is one that is accompanied by vibration of the vocal chords during production. The reader should be aware that, in certain circumstances, voiced consonants take on the sound of their unvoiced counterparts. The voiced consonants referred to are: B, D, G, V, Z, ZH and are pronounced P, T, K, F, C, SH respectively in unvoiced positions.

When a voiced consonant occurs at the end of a word it is devoiced. For instance the final "v" in the word "Kirov" will be pronounced as "f". (It is especially useful to note that certain other transliteration systems, especially those from German sources, would take this into account and write it as "Kiroff").

In any position in a word, where a voiced consonant comes before an unvoiced consonant, then the voiced consonant will become de-voiced. For example in the word "Yubka", the voiced "b" will be pronounced "p" as it appears before the unvoiced "k".

The reverse happens when an unvoiced consonant comes before a voiced consonant. Therefore in "Takzhye", for example, the unvoiced "k" will be pronounced "g" as it occurs before the voiced consonant "zh" .

Vowels

"YE"   normally pronounced like "ye" in "yet".

"Yo"   pronounced like "yo" at the beginning of "Yorkshire" but with the lips not quite so rounded.

"I"   always pronounced as the "ee" sound in "teeth".

"U"   always pronounced like "oo" as in "coot".

"Y"   represents a vowel sound that does not exist in English so it can only be approximated. It is a bit like the "i" sound in "ill", but pronounced with the lips stretched downwards. The sound tends very slightly towards the "oy" sound in "boy".

"YU"   pronounced like the English word "you".

"YA"   like the "Ya" in "yard".

It should be noted that "ye", "yo", "yu" and "ya" are separate vowels in their own right. Where Y occurs other than in these combinations it is to be pronounced as the separate vowel sound indicated above.

Combinations of letters

The pronunciation of certain combinations of letters that arise using this transliteration system, usually standing for adjectival endings, may seem awkward. The following should particularly be noted:

II is pronounced "i".

"IYE" is pronounced as "i" and then "ye".

"YI" is pronounced simply as "y".

"YYE" is pronounced as "y" and then "ye".

It is also worthy of note that where the same two consonants appear side by side, they take on a protracted pronunciation of the one sound. Contrary to the rule mentioned above, they are not pronounced separately, e.g. RUKI VVYERKH! = Hands up!

The same thing occurs when similar vowels appear together. In the following example the "OO" is pronounced as a longer "O": OBORONITYELNYYE SOORUZHYENIYA = defences. (also note that in the above examples, none of the "O" sounds are stressed.)

"OVO" and "YEVO" are transliterated in this way only to simplify pronunciation. These combinations are the only two spelling irregularities in Russian, they should be strictly written as "ogo" and "yego" but are not pronounced in this way. Where they occur, a footnote will be included stating deviation from the standard transliteration. The common word "mnógo", meaning "much", "many" or "a lot" is an exception to this rule, as it is pronounced with a "g" sound.

Extra Points to note:

1. Diacritical marks and soft and hard signs are omitted for the sake of convenience (with the only exception of the stressed "o", see note 3).

2. Where the name of a person, place, organisation, policy, etc. has already acquired an accepted, widely known transliteration deviating from that of our own system, the accepted transliteration will be used and a footnote included. For example, "Leningrad" instead of "Lyeningrad" and "Orel" instead of "Oryol".

3. Stressed "o" will only be indicated where actual Russian conversation occurs in the text for authenticity. Elsewhere the "o" will carry no stress marks whether it is stressed or not.

4. See "ovo" and "yevo" above.

APPENDIX O

Byelorussian Pronunciation Guide

The Byelorussian Alphabet

Cyrillic Form	Latin Form (obsolete)	*SHELF* Transliteration
А	A	A
Б	B	B
В	V / W	V
Г	H	H
Г'	G	G
Д	D	D
ДЖ	DŽ	DZH
ДЗ	DZ	DZ
Е	JE / IE	YE
Ё	JO / IO	YO
Ж	Ž / Ż	ZH
З	Z	Z
I	I	I
Й	J	I
К	K	K
Л	Ł	L
	L	L
М	M	M
Н	N	N
О	O	O
П	P	P
Р	R	R
С	S	S
Т	T	T
У	U	U
ў	Ŭ	W
Ф	F	F
Х	CH	KH
Ц	C	TS
Ч	Č / CZ	CH
Ш	Š / SZ	SH
Ы	Y	Y
Ь	-	-
Э	E	E
Ю	YU / IU	YU
Я	YA / IA	YA

Byelorussian, which is also known as "White Russian", is an East Slavonic language closely related to Polish, Russian and Ukrainian. The Byelorussian language, as well as the country which is only recently becoming known globally as the "Belarus", had always been overshadowed by Russian. Byelorussian, as a written language, dates from the 14th century when, under the Grand Duchy of Lithuania, Byelorussian was permitted to be used as a language of commerce. The earliest printed work is generally recognised as the translation by Skarýna of "The Book of Psalms", printed in Prague. Tsarist policy tended to regard Byelorussia simply as a province of Russia, and Byelorussian as a mere dialect of Russian, reflected in its policy of Russification. The publishing of Byelorussian inside Byelorussia was illegal until the beginning of the 20th century, after the revolution of 1905.

Byelorussian appears both in Latin and Cyrillic script. By 1914 the alphabet had been officially established in its Cyrillic form, however, even up to WWII the Latin script still endured in Western Byelorussia which was under Polish rule. Even today, the Latin alphabet can still be found within émigré communities scattered as far as Australia.

The original Byelorussian Latin script, (which is based on Polish), is included here for reference purposes only. The following guide to pronunciation refers to the *SHELF* transliterated Latin script used wherever Byelorussian occurs in *SHELF* texts. This transliteration system has been brought as far into line as possible with the *SHELF Russian Transliteration Policy*. In the following explanations the sound closest to the English equivalent is underlined, and in capitals, unless otherwise stated.

Vowels

a	cAlm		ya	Yard
e	gEt		ye	Yet
y	approximately the vowel in sIn		i	grEEt
o	gOt		yo	Yoghurt
u	cOOt		yu	Yule

Dipthongs

Dipthongs may occur when "i" (representing й), and "w" (representing ў) follow any vowels.

Consonants

h	aspirated as in Hotel
dzh	Jean
dz	wooDS
g	Get
zh	meaSure
r	rolled, as in Scottish pronunciation
w	as in Wood
kh	as in Scottish loCH, or German ICH
ts	eaTS
ch	Chew
sh	Sheep

Consonantal clusters in Slavonic languages often seem impossible to pronounce for the English speaker. Such consonants should be pronounced, one immediately after the other. For instance: "zginuts". Double consonants are not to be separated, but to be pronounced as the first consonant of the two, but longer. For example: "zbozhzha".

Voiced and Unvoiced Consonants

A voiced consonant is one that is accompanied by vibration of the vocal chords during production. The Byelorussian voiced consonants are as follows: B V D Z DZ ZH DZH G X.

The consonants listed above have the respective unvoiced counterparts, (which, contrary to voiced consonants are pronounced without vibration of the vocal cords): P F T S TS SH CH K H.

The distinction between voiced and unvoiced consonants is important as a voiced consonant takes on the pronunciation of its unvoiced counterpart in certain circumstances:

When a voiced consonant occurs at the end of a word, it takes on the pronunciation of its unvoiced counterpart. For instance in "Mahilyov" the "-v" at the end of the word is devoiced and pronounced as "-f".

Devoicing also occurs within a word where the voiced consonant comes directly before an unvoiced consonant. For example, in the word "kazka" the "-z-" is pronounced as "-s-", as it occurs directly before the unvoiced "-k-".

The opposite happens when an unvoiced consonant occurs before a voiced consonant; this has the effect of making the unvoiced consonant voiced, for instance, in the word "prosba" the "-s-" is pronounced as "-z-".

APPENDIX P

Hungarian Pronunciation Guide

The Hungarian language, which is also known as *Magyar*, is a Finno-Ugric language, related to Estonian and Finnish. It is the official language of Hungary's ten million or so inhabitants.

Hungarian uses the Roman alphabet, and many of the vowels carrying diacritical marks will be familiar to those with a sound knowledge of German pronunciation. Care must be taken, however, over the consonants, some of which will come as a surprise to the English speaker. Stress falls on the first syllable (without exception) which can make the language sound staccato at times.

The Hungarian Alphabet

a á b c cs d dzs e é f g gy h i í j k l ly m n ny o ó ö ő p r s sz t ty u ú ü ű v (w) wc z zs

In the following explanations the English sound, or approximate English equivalent is underlined and in capitals, except where another explanation is provided. Only letters representing sounds that are unfamiliar to the English speaker, or that represent different sound values are treated here. Otherwise the reader can assume that the usual English pronunciation for the letter will suffice.

Vowels

a	a neutral vowel sound in between (English) "o" and "a".
á	like the vowel sound in <u>Ai</u>r without the diphthong, but much more open.
dzs	<u>J</u>am
e	y<u>E</u>t
é	s<u>A</u>me
i	b<u>I</u>t
í	gr<u>EE</u>t
o	h<u>O</u>t
ó	w<u>A</u>r
ö	like the short German "ö".
ő	like the long German "ö".
r	A Scottish r pronounced with the tip of the tongue
u	h<u>U</u>t
ú	f<u>OO</u>l
ü	like the short German "ü".
ű	like the long German "ü".

It is worthy of note that there are no diphthongs in Hungarian.

Also note that where vowels are marked with an acute accent, this does not necessarily mean that the syllable is stressed. These marks modify the letters in such a way as to change their sound quality, which is evident from the above explanation.

Consonants

c	bi<u>TS</u>
cs	<u>Ch</u>ant
gy	The textbook form is <u>D</u>ew; <u>J</u>ury is the modern colloquial
j	<u>Y</u>et
ly	see "j" above.
ny	as in Spanish ma<u>Ñ</u>ana
s	<u>Sh</u>ip
sz	<u>S</u>it
ty	<u>T</u>ulip
zs	mea<u>S</u>ure

Note especially the pronunciation of "s" and "sz" above. Also note that "g" in Hungarian has a hard pronunciation, as in <u>G</u>et.

Where a double consonant (i.e. the same two letters side by side) occurs in a word, it is not pronounced as one (as in English) but lengthened such that the two letters are almost pronounced. As regards those consonants that are represented by two letters when found singly such as "gy", only the first letter is repeated to create the "double consonant", for example "ggy".

Agglutination

Hungarian, like the other Finno-Ugric languages, relies on agglutination rather than inflection, i.e., number, person case etc. are indicated by distinct syllables which are strung one after another rather than by a single syllable. Thus;

ház (house), házak (houses), házam (my house), házaím (my houses), házamban (in my house), házaímban (in my houses), házambol (from my house), házaímbol (from my houses).

Vowel Harmony

For the sake of euphony, the vowel in the first syllable determines the vowels in successive syllables, within a number of series: thus a, o and u (back vowels) are followed by a; e, i, ö and ü (front vowels) by e - but there are always exceptions depending on circumstances. Examples are:

If ház represents the a series, then taking Térem (hall) as an example of the e series we get Téremek, Térem, Téremem, Téremeím (with elision) Térmembe, Térmeímbe etc.

Again, if the abstract suffix ság is to be added to a concrete noun this has to be modified if the latter contains a front vowel.

Szabad (free) + ság = Szabadság (freedom); but Ember (man) + ság = Emberiség (humanity) - with an I infix for the sake of euphony!

APPENDIX Q

Czech and Slovak Pronunciation Guide

Both Czech and Slovak are West Slavonic languages, very close in form and vocabulary. Both are also written in the Roman alphabet, although some letters have been modified to encompass the Slavonic sounds, and many of the letters represent similar sound values in both languages. In fact, Czechs and Slovaks have very little difficulty in understanding each other. For this reason, both languages have been presented in parallel, where possible.

The following guide will give the reader a sufficient knowledge of the pronunciation of both languages; however some of the intricacies have been omitted for the sake of simplicity.

The Czech Alphabet

a á b c č d ď dz dž e ě é f g h ch i í j k l m n ň o ó p q r ř s š t ť u ú ů v w x y ý z ž

The Slovak Alphabet

a á ä b c č d ď dz dž é f g h ch i í j k l ĺ m n ň o ó ô p q r ŕ s š t ť u ú v w x y ý z ž

In the following examples the English sound equivalents are underlined and in capitals, except where an explanation is included in place of this.

Vowels

The following Czech and Slovak vowels have both a long and a short pronunciation: the long pronunciation being designated by a symbol above the letter. The symbol does make a difference to pronunciation, so they should be treated as separate letters. Note that "y/ý" are full vowels in Czech and Slovak, and carry the same sound values as "i/í" respectively.

a	t<u>A</u>p
e	g<u>E</u>t
i/y	s<u>I</u>t
o	g<u>O</u>t
u	r<u>OO</u>k
á	c<u>A</u>r
é	th<u>ERE</u> (but NOT as a diphthong)
í/ý	r<u>EE</u>d
ó	m<u>O</u>re
ú/ů	r<u>OO</u>m (note that "ů" does not occur in Slovak)

Vowels Peculiar to Czech

ě	<u>YE</u>t

Vowels Peculiar to Slovak

ä	as in <u>AI</u>r without the diphthong, but much more open
ô	<u>WA</u>r

Czech has three diphthongs: au, eu, ou
Slovak is more abundant in diphthongs: aj, áj, au, ej, eu, ia, ie, iu, oj, ój, ou, uj

Consonants

Only letters representing consonants that differ from their English counterparts are treated here, in addition to those that appear unfamiliar to the English speaker. Otherwise, the reader can assume that the normal English pronunciation will suffice.

c	bi<u>TS</u>
č	<u>Ch</u>ew
ď	<u>D</u>ew
dz	woo<u>DS</u>
dž	<u>J</u>ane
ch	as in Scottish: lo<u>CH</u>, or German i<u>CH</u>
j	<u>Y</u>ou, or German <u>J</u>a
ĺ	(Slovak only) long "l" sound
ľ	(Slovak only) soft "l" as in <u>L</u>eaf.
ň	As in Spanish Ma<u>N</u>ana
r	Rolled lightly
ř	(Czech only) This letter represents a sound that is, initially, very difficult to pronounce for English speakers. It really needs to be heard to be appreciated. It is pronounced as "ž" (see below) while simultaneously rolling an "r"! If this is difficult, simply pronounce it as "ž" (Most Slovaks do!)
š	<u>Sh</u>ock
ť	A sound in between "t" and "č".
ž	mea<u>S</u>ure

Analysis of Voiced and Unvoiced Consonants

Voiced consonants are those pronounced accompanied by vibration of the vocal cords. Such consonants are as follows: B D Ď DZ DŽ G H V Z Ž

Unvoiced consonants are pronounced without vibration of the vocal cords during pronunciation. The following are the respective unvoiced counterparts of the voiced consonants presented above: P T Ť C Č K CH F S Š

Where a voiced consonant occurs at the end of a word it takes on the pronunciation of its unvoiced counterpart, for instance, in the pronunciation of the town "Cheb", the "-b" at the end of the word is pronounced as "-p". Within a word, where a voiced consonant is followed by an unvoiced consonant , the voiced consonant becomes devoiced, e.g. in: "pražský", the "-ž-" will be pronounced as "-š-". The opposite occurs where an unvoiced consonant is followed by a voiced consonant within a word, e.g. in "svatba", the "t" will be pronounced as "d".

Stress

The stress in both Czech and Slovak falls on the first syllable of a word. This may cause a little confusion in such cases where a long vowel occurs after the first syllable in a word, as it may be tempting to pronounce a long vowel as a stressed vowel. In the name "Dvořák", for example, the pulse is on the first syllable but the long vowel is still drawn out.

Other Peculiarities of Czech and Slovak

Czech

The combination "mě" is pronounced as though it were written "mně"

Before "-i/-í" , "d", "t" and "n" are pronounced as "ď", "ť" and "ň".

Slovak

"Zs" is pronounced as "s".
"Zš" is pronounced as "š".

APPENDIX R

Gazetteer

Parts of Germany Now Forming Parts of Other Countries

Poland

Arnswalde	Choszczno
Arys	Orzysz
Breslau	Wrocław
Danzig	Gdańsk
Elbing	Elblag
Graudenz	Grudziądz
Hela	Hel
Küstrin	Kostrzyn
Marienburg	Malbork
River Vistula	River Wisła
Schneidemühl	Piła
Stettin	Szczecin
Thorn	Toruń
Warsaw	Warszawa

Russia

Ebenrode	Nyestyerov

Places with German Equivalents

Breclav	Lundenburg
České Budějovice	Büdweis
Esztergom	Gran
Mława	Mielau
Nitra	Neutra
Nové Zámky	Neuhäusel
Tallinn	Reval
Trnava	Thyrnau
Moravsky Beroun	Bärn

Common English Spellings of German Names

Munich	München
Nuremberg	Nürnberg

APPENDIX S

Glossary

AOK *Armee Oberkommando*. The High Command of a Field Army, not to be confused with the OKH, the High Command of the entire German Ground Forces.

Abteilung *Detachment* Unit between a Regiment and a Company in those German units which did not use the term Bataillon (Battalion). The difference between an Abteilung and a Bataillon being in their command responsibilities, although in simple terms both refer to a collection of Companies (Kompanien)

Ausbildung *Training*

Brigade Eberhardt According to Werner Haupt, this formation consisted of the *Danzig* State Police Command (Kommando der Landespolizei *Danzig*), the State Police organised into two infantry regiments (Danziger Landespolizei Regiment 1 and 2) and an artillery detachment from the same source. Later, both regiments were incorporated into the 60th Infantry Division (mot); Landespolizei Regiment 1 as Infanterie Regiment 243, Landespolizei Regiment 2 as Infanterie Regiment 244 and the artillery detachment as Artillerie Regiment 160. The Division was one of those lost at Stalingrad

Deutsch-Nationale Volkspartei (DNVP)

Ersatz Replacement

Feldersatz *Field Replacement*

Flak *Fliegerabwehrkanone* Anti-aircraft gun.

Gepanzerte *Armoured* Used in the sense of military units which would not be normally considered armoured units, for example, infantry with armoured vehicles at their disposal.

German Cross in Gold *Deutscheskreuz in Gold*

Höherer Küsten-Artillerie-Kommandeur West Supreme Head of Artillery on the Western Coast.

Roll of Honour Clasp *Ehrenblattspange* Decoration awarded for personnel "Mentioned in Dispatches", provided the recipient was already holder of both classes of the Iron Cross.

Hummel *Bumble-Bee* Self-propelled heavy field howitzer (150 mm) on a modified Pzkpfw IV chassis. Used by artillery units.

Infantry Assault Badge *Infanteriesturmabzeichen* Infantry version of the family of assault badges available in various grades awarded for participation in three or more assaults.

Jagdpanther Heavy fully armoured tank destroyer (88 mm L/71 gun) mounted on a Pzkpfw V Panther chassis. A type of Jagdpanzer (see below).

Jagdpanzer Final development of self-propelled anti-tank gun resembling the Artillery's assault gun, but with sloped armour (e.g. 75 mm on Pz. IV, Pz. 38t, 88mm on Pzkpfw V Panther chassis).

Kampfgruppe *Battle Group* A feature of the German Army: ad hoc combined-arm formations of sub-divisional size rapidly adapted to the tactical situation, very influential with regard to all later military thinking (adopted by British as Brigade Group etc., by US Army as Regimental Combat Teams, Combat Commands etc.). Later in the War, used for remnants of decimated formations.

Knight's Cross of the Iron Cross (*Ritterkreuz zum Eisernen Kreuz*). The version of the Iron Cross worn around the neck. Subsequent awards were denoted by the wearing of Oakleaves,

Oakleaves and Swords, Oakleaves, Sword and Diamond and finally, awarded only once, Golden Oakleaves, Swords and Diamonds.

Königstiger *King Tiger* Name given to the Pzkpfw VI Ausf B. Also known as the Tiger II.

Kradschützen Motorcycle-mounted infantry.

Panzerfaust Shaped-charge (hollow-charge) anti-tank grenade projector useful only at close range (progressively extended from 30 to 150 m).

Leichte Division A formation developed in the immediate pre-war years as a more mobile complement to the classic Panzer Division. These utilised tanks as well as more lightly armed carriers and half tracks. After the Polish Campaign these formations were found to have too little striking power and were upgraded to Panzer Divisions.

Close Combat Clasp *Nahkampfspange* Decoration awarded for participation in hand-to-hand combat of a specified number of days, graded into Bronze, Silver and Gold for successively greater endurance; the latter was regarded as highly as the Knight's Cross.

NSDAP *National-Sozialistische Deutsche Arbeiter-Partei* Nazi Party

OKW (Oberkommando der Wehrmacht) *High Command of the German Armed Forces* Command organisation set up by Hitler to oversee the notoriously independently-minded services - Heer (Army), Kriegsmarine (Navy) and Luftwaffe (Air Force) - respectively controlled by the OKH, OKM and OKL. - enabling Hitler, through Keitel and Jodl, to bypass the General Staff etc. Later, the OKH was left to run the Eastern Front whilst the OKW took responsibility for the other theatres

Pak *Panzerabwehrkanone* Anti-tank gun.

Panther *Panzerkampfwagen V*. Heavy tank with sloping armour, produced in response to the success of the Russian T-34 and reproducing some of its better features.

Panzer Group West Armoured reserve in northern France to defend against invasion.

Panzerjäger Anti-Tank

Reichsführer-SS *RF-SS* National Leader of the SS, Heinrich Himmler

Ritterkreuzträger *Holder of the Knight's Cross of the Iron Cross*: awarded for outstanding gallantry or successful leadership in combat, provided the recipient was already holder of both classes of the Iron Cross. The recipient could be further honoured by, successively, the Oak Leaves, Swords and Diamonds.

SA *Sturmabteilung* NSDAP 'order service' evolving into a private army capable of dealing with Communist street-fighters in the violent politics of the Weimar period. Less dedicated to Hitler than the SS, it's leader, Ernst Röhm, dreamed of turning the SA into a People's Army. This led to the bloody 'Night of the Long Knives' when he and many other senior SA leaders were killed, mainly in an attempt by Hitler to appease the understandably concerned German Army. Later an auxiliary to the Wehrmacht.

Sapper *Pionier* Does not correspond to British Army Pioneer Corps, rather the British Corps of Royal Engineers, dealing with bridge-building, mine laying and clearance, assault with explosives etc.

schwere Panzer-Abteilung Literally "Heavy Tank detachment", but used to denote the special units operating the *Tiger* and *Königstiger* vehicles

Siegrune The runic symbol for the letter 'S', also symbolising victory. Best known as the symbol of the SS.

sitzkrieg The early part of Word War II prior to the Battle of France 1940, notable for the non-activity of all combatants. Also known as the `Phoney War'.

Sperrverband A 'blocking' formation usually consisting of combat engineers, anti-tank artillery and some infantry.

SS-Verfügungstruppe Forerunner of the Waffen-SS arising out of the local squads organised to protect key speakers; Hamburg (*Germania*) and *München* (*Deutschland*) regiments formed the basis of SS-Verfügungs Division later joined by Austrians of *Der Führer*; SS-VD became (*Das*) *Reich*, probably the most effective Waffen-SS Division of all.

Stahlhelm Early post-World War I paramilitary formation, made up of Great War veterans.

State Police Landespolizei

StuG *Sturmgeschütze*

Sturmgeschütze *Assault gun.* Armoured self propelled 75 mm gun operated by the Artillery as an infantry support weapon - a turretless equivalent of the British Infantry Tank. During the Russian campaign, found to be one of the few weapons capable of knocking out heavy tanks (e.g. T-34); progressively incorporated in Infantry and Panzergrenadier Divisions and ultimately replacing tanks in Panzer Divisions; supplemented by heavier calibre (106-160 mm) howitzers in primary role.

Sturzkampfgeschwader Literally Dive Bomber group - associated with the Junkers Ju87 aircraft, the famous Stuka Bomber

Ulan Imperial German Army term for Lancer Regiments. Considered to be elite mounted troops.

VGAD (Verstärkter-Grenz-Aufsichts-Dienst) *Reinforced Border Surveillance Service.*

Volksdeutsche Ethnic German peoples living outside the Reich.

War Merit Cross *Kriegsverdienstkreuz* Decoration available for distinguished conduct behind the combat zone e.g. service echelons, available in various grades corresponding to classes of the Iron Cross.

Wehrkreis *Military District* The German Reich was split up into various districts which dealt with recruiting, training and, in time of war, replenishing military formations.

Wespe Wasp Self-propelled light field howitzer (105 mm) mounted on a Pzkpfw II chassis.

Acknowledgements

I should like to express my thanks to the Associations in which the survivors of the units which have been the subject of this work now congregate, without whose collaboration this would have been a great deal more difficult indeed. Firstly, the *Kameradschaft der Angehörigen der ehemaligen 60 Inf. Div. (mot) und deren Feldherrnhalle Nachfolgeverbande*, of Essen, several of whose members made themselves available to answer my long list of questions. I would particularly like to express thanks for the help given me by its President, the retired Bundeswehr Colonel and former Commander of the First Battalion of the Artillery Regiment *Feldherrnhalle*, Erich Klein, who very kindly placed at my disposal many extremely interesting reports regarding the constitution of the Division, as well as his unedited work on the 160th Artillery Regiment *Feldherrnhalle*.

I should also like to express my gratitude for the assistance afforded me by *Oberst* Klaus Voß, President of the Traditionsverband Panzerbrigade 106 *Feldherrnhalle* in Amorbach, whose suggestions and material permitted me to get the investigation into this work underway in earnest. In addition, there is the *Traditionsverband 13.Pz.Div./Div. Feldherrnhalle 2* in Hanover and the Veterans Association of the Schwere Panzer Abteilung 503/*Feldherrnhalle* in Göttingen.

Amongst the former combatants, I should like to highlight the collaboration of the following people: the former Commander of the *Feldherrnhalle* Armoured Formations, *Hauptmann* (a.D.) Erich Oberwöhrmann; *Major d.R.d.Bw.* and former Commander of the Alarmbataillon *Feldherrnhalle*, Kurt Bentin; Heinrich Wasmus of the 13.Pz.Div./*Feldherrnhalle*; Friedrich Bruns, former Panzer NCO with the 1.Pz.Div., one of the best specialists on the German Panzer arm whose works provided basic references for the current work.

I should also like to mention the invaluable assistance of Dr. Friedrich Hermann, from Bonn, who to a great extent, facilitated my work; Klaus Woche, of Berlin, an experienced investigator and great specialist in the men of the *Feldherrnhalle*, thanks to whom I was able to throw some light on some rather unclear areas of the subject, and Winfried Herrmann, through whom I was able to make some interesting contacts.

I should not like to overlook the help of my good friends Erik Norling and Alfonso R. Laporte, who gladly offered to re-read my manuscript and to whom I owe the accurate comment which eventually served as my title.

Lastly, I should like to mention Herr Verlande of the Bundesarchiv/Coblenz, and Herr Meyer, of the BA/Militärarchiv in Freiburg for their friendliness and efficiency.

Bibliography

Hans Bachmann, Hela, in <u>Wehrwissenschaftliche Rundschau</u>, 20 (1970)

Wolf Keilig, <u>Das Deutsche Heer 1939-1945</u> (1957) Podzun-Pallas, Bad Nauheim, Germany

K G Klietmann, <u>Die Waffen-SS</u>, (1980) [Biblio Verlag], Osnabrück, Germany

Rolf Michaelis, <u>Die Geschichte der SS-Heimwehr Danzig</u> (1990) Rodgau

Herbert Schindler, <u>Mosty und Dirschau 1939</u> (1971) Rombach, Freiburg

Bertil Stjernfelt and Klaus-Richard Böhme, <u>Westerplatte 1939</u> (1979) [Rombach] Freiburg

Georg Tesin, <u>Verbände und Truppen der deutschen Wehrmacht und Waffen-SS im 2. Weltkrieg</u> (1980) [Biblio Verlag], Osnabrück

Nikolaus von Vormann, <u>Der Feldzug 1939 in Polen</u> (1958) [Prinz Eugen] Weisenburg

Acknowledgements for the English Edition

Mr Philip Bond and the staff of Advance Reprographics, Bradford;

Mr Chris Byrnes of Uppermill, Saddleworth, nr Oldham, Lancs;

Ms Volga Galubovich of the Embassy of the Republic of Belarus in Great Britain, London;

Miss Kizzy Hanson of Shelf Books for last minute assistance;

Mr Károly Novák of Bradford, West Yorkshire for his generous and prompt assistance with all matters Hungarian.

Mr Andrew Sharp of Cassell plc, London

Mr Darren Shepherd and the staff of Jade Press, Leeds;

Piero, Michele and the staff of the Café Candia, 113 Legrams Lane, Bradford;

Mr Boris Wanzeck for his help with all things German;

Miss Cheryll Wood for her help with sorting out all the new photographs;

Above all, Mrs D A Lewthwaite of Westbury-on-Trym, Bristol, without whose financial generosity, Shelf Books, let alone this book, would not have been possible.

Additional Bibliography to the English Edition

This is the first full-length treatment of the *Feldherrnhalle* formations in English: all previous treatments are cursory, inaccurate or both. An example of the former is A J Barker Panzers at War (1978) Ian Allen, London, pp 138-9, 141-3; of the latter Bender and Odegarde cited in the existing Bibliography pp 35, 64-5, 97-8, which is full of contradictions. Of the reference sources available, the most accurate is R Stoves ...Großverbände... (1986), the second edition (1994) of which should be consulted as follows: 94-5 (13 Pz.Div.), 185-7 (60 Inf.Div.(mot)), 245-9 (Pz.Div.*FHH*1), 249-50, (Pz.Div.*FHH*2), 302-303 (Pz.Bde.109.*FHH*), 321-3 (Pz.Bde.106 *FHH*), 323-4 (Pz.Bde.110 *FHH*), 333-5 (Independent Pz Abt.).

The next best is German Order of Battle WW2 (no date) Vol 1 available from Military History Bookshop, Friern Barnet, London, specifically pp 17, 30-33,, 63, 64, 74, 78-9, 86, 88 of which 64 gives the complete order of battle for the Pz Div.*FHH*.

Finally W Haupt has produced a most useful book Das Buch der Panzertruppe 1916-1945 (1989) Podzun-Pallas-Verlag, Friedberg pp 108-10, 114-5, 127-33, 139, 141, 143-4 which is however marred by a serious error regarding 13 Pz.Div. and Pz.Div.*FHH*.

Battle of Budapest

J Desch, P McTaggert, P B Zwack Budapest `45 (1994) in Command Issue 31

R Landwehr Budapest. The Stalingrad of the Waffen-SS (1985) in Siegrunen Vol 7, No 1, Whole Number 37

J P Pallud Budapest (1983) in After the Battle

Battles in Hungary

Johannes Frießner Verratene Schlachten, Die Tragödie der deutschen Wehrmacht in Rumänien und Ungarn (1956) Holsten-Verlag, Hamburg, Germany

F Husemann Die guten Glaubens waren Band II Kampf und Untergang der 4. SS-Pol.Pz-Gren-Division (1986) Munin-Verlag (A 3rd edition is now in progress through Nation Europa)

H Kissel Die Pz.Schlachten in der Puzsta im Oktober 1944 (1960) Neckargemünd, Germany

Georg Maier Drama zwischen Budapest und Wien (1985) Munin Verlag, Osnabrück, Germany

E Rebentisch Zum Kaukasus und zu den Tauern. Die Geschichte der 23 Panzer-Division 1941-45, Angehöriger der 23 Panzer-Division Esslingen, Germany (Privately published)

The Russian Campaign

P Adair Hitler's Greatest Defeat Arms and Armour Press 1994

Paul Carell Hitler's War on Russia, Vol. II Scorched Earth (1970) Corgi Books, Transworld Publishers Ltd., London

Alan Clark Barbarossa. The Russian-German Conflict 1941-45 (1967) Orion, London

Peter Gosztony Endkampf an der Donau 1944/45 (1969) München, Germany

Werner Haupt Die Heeresgruppe Nord (1966) Podzun-Pallas Verlag, Friedberg, Germany

Werner Haupt Die Schlachten der Heeresgruppe Mitte 1941-1944 Aus der Sicht der Divisionen (1983) Podzun-Pallas-Verlag, Freidberg, Germany

Otto Heidkampe Witebsk. Kampf und Untergang der 3 Panzerarmee (1954) Kurt Vowinckel Verlag, Heidelberg, Germany

Richard Landwehr Narva 1944 Siegrunen, Glendale, Oregon.

Paul Reichelt The Battles of Armee Abteilung Narva, 2 February - 31 May 1944, pp 122-139, in S H Newton (ed) Retreat from Leningrad. Army Group North 1944-45, Schiffer Military History, Atglen, PA 1995

Wilhelm Tieke Tragödie um die Treue (1996) 4th Ed Nation Europa, Coburg pp 54-63

S Zaloga Bagration 1944 (1996) Osprey Campaign Series No 42, Reed International Books Ltd

General Unit Background

John R Angolia and Adolf Schlicht Uniforms and Traditions of the German Army James Bender Publishing, San José, California, USA

John R Angolia Cloth Insignia of the NSDAP and SA Roger James Bender Publishing, San Jose, California, USA

Arbeitsgruppe 13 Pz.Div. Der Schicksalsweg der 13 Panzerdivision 1939-1945 (1986) Podzun-Pallas-Verlag, Freidberg, Germany

Heinrich Bennecke Die Reichswehr und der Röhm Putsch (1964) Politische Studien, München

J. Bender & W. Odegard Uniforms, Organisation and History of the Panzertruppe (1980) R. James Bender Publishing, San José, California, USA

R.J. Bender and Hugh Page Taylor Uniforms, Organisations and History of the Waffen-SS Bender Publications, San José, California, USA

Friedrich Bruns Die Panzerbrigade 106 *Feldherrnhalle*. Eine dokumentation über den Einsatz im Westen vom Juli 1944-Mai 1945 (1983) Celle, Germany

Brian L Davis German Army Uniforms and Insignia of the Luftwaffe 1933-1945 (1971) Arms and Armour Press, London

Brian L Davis Uniforms and Insignia of the Luftwaffe. Volume 1: 1933-1940 (1991) Arms and Armour Press, London

Jill Halcomb The SA: A Historical Perspective (1985) Crown/Agincourt, Overland Park, Kansas, USA

Rudolf Kahl Uniforms and Badges of the III Reich Military Collectors Service, Holland, Vol. II

E. Klein and W. Kühn Tiger. The History of a Legendary Weapon 1942-1945 (1989) J J Federowicz, Manitoba, Canada

R Landwehr The SS Heimwehr Danzig (1982) in Siegrunen Vol V, No 4, Whole Number 28 pp 34-36

D Littlejohn and R Volstad The SA: Hitler's Stormtroopers (1990) Osprey Men-at-Arms 220, Osprey, London

R Michaelis SS-Heimwehr Danzig 1939 (1996) Shelf Books, Bradford, UK

R Nederling Die Reichsparteitage der NSDAP 1923-1939 (1981) Druffel Verlag, Landsberg am Lech, Germany 1981.

Wolfgang Paul Panzer General Walther K. Nehring (1986) Motorbuch-Verlag, Stuttgart, Germany

Albert Seaton German Army 1939-45 (1985) Meridian Book, New York

Horst Shreiber Panzergrenadier Division Großdeutschland (1986) Podzun-Pallas-Verlag, Friedberg, Germany

Helmut Spaeter Die Einsätze der Panzergrenadier Division Großdeutschland (1986) Podzun-Pallas-Verlag, Friedberg, Germany

Helmut Spaeter Panzercorps Großdeutschland. Berichte und Bilder über das Erleben, Einsätze, die Männer und Kampfräume (1988) Podzun-Pallas-Verlag, Friedberg, Germany

Helmut Spaeter Panzerkorps Großdeutschland. Bilddokumentation (1984) Podzun-Pallas-Verlag, Friedberg, Germany

Helmut Spaeter The History of the Panzerkorps Großdeutschland, Vol 1 (1992) and Vol 2 (1995) J J Federowicz, Manitoba, Canada

Rolf O G Stoves Die Gepanzerten und Motorisierten Deutschen Großverbände 1935-45 (1986) Podzun-Pallas-Verlag, Friedberg, Germany

Rolf O.G. Stoves Die Gepanzerten und Motorisierten Deutschen Großverbände 1935-45 (1986) Podzun-Pallas-Verlag, Freidberg, Germany

Rolf Stoves Die gepanzerten und motorisierten deutschen Grossverbände 1935-1945 (1986) Podzun-Pallas-Verlag, Bad-Nauheim, Germany

G Tessin Verbände und Truppen der deutschen Wehrmacht und Waffen-SS 1939-45 (1980) Biblio Verlag, Osnabrück, Germany

Gerhard von Seemen Die Ritterkreuzträger 1939-45 Podzun-Pallas-Verlag, Germany

INDEX